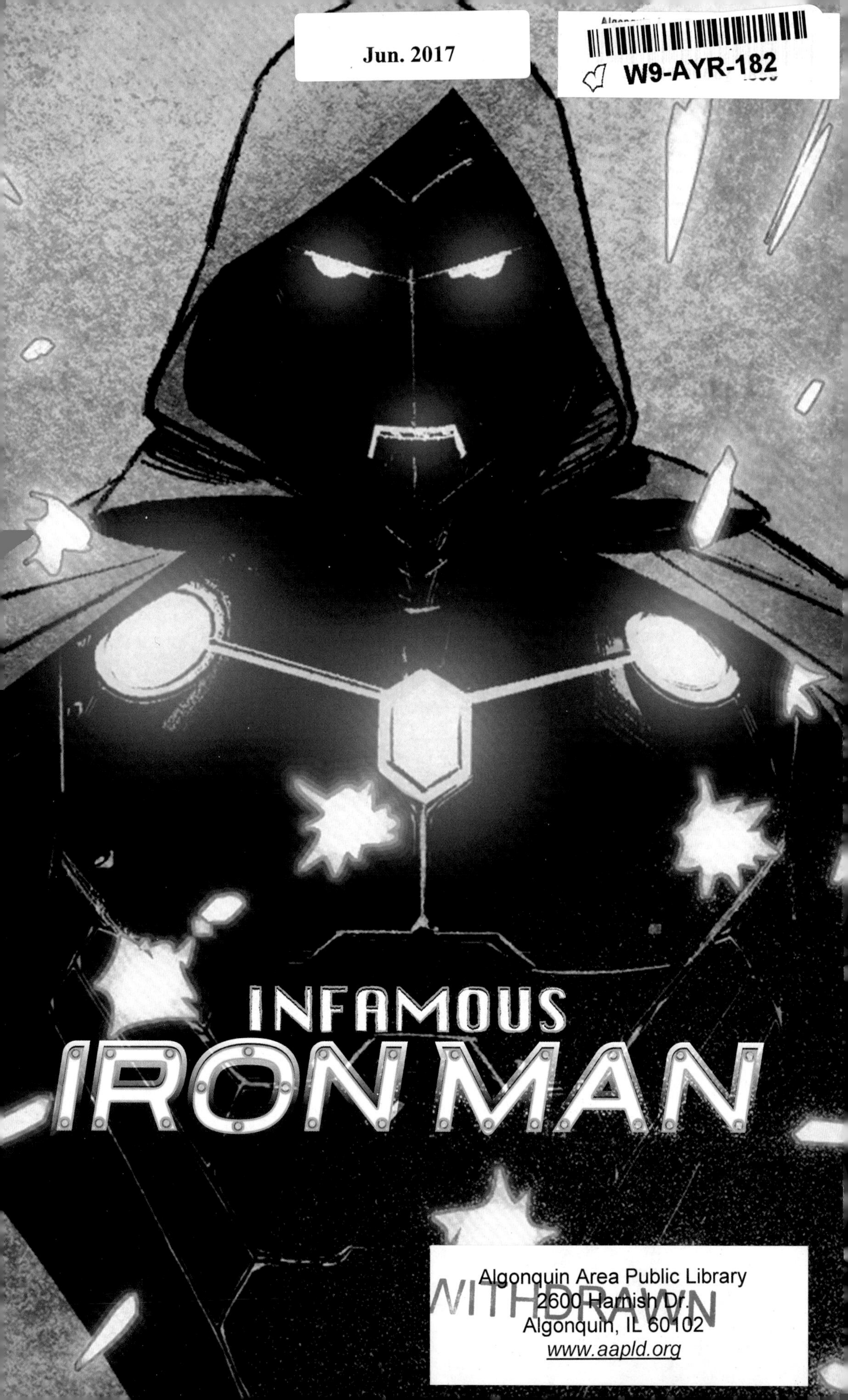
INFAMOUS
IRON MAN

Before the second super hero civil war, billionaire playboy and genius industrialist Tony Stark used a powerful suit of armor of his own invention to protect the world as the invincible Avenger Iron Man.

For reasons that remain his own, the powerful former super villain Doctor Doom assisted Iron Man in averting several world-ending catastrophes.

But Civil War II had dire consequences for Tony Stark, leaving Doom's mysterious mission unfinished...

INFAMOUS IRON MAN

INFAMOUS

BRIAN MICHAEL BENDIS
WRITER

ALEX MALEEV
ARTIST

MATT HOLLINGSWORTH
COLOR ARTIST

VC's CLAYTON COWLES
LETTERER

ALEX MALEEV
COVER ART

ALANNA SMITH
ASSISTANT EDITOR

TOM BREVOORT
EDITOR

COLLECTION EDITOR: **JENNIFER GRÜNWALD**
ASSISTANT EDITOR: **CAITLIN O'CONNELL**
ASSOCIATE MANAGING EDITOR: **KATERI WOODY**
EDITOR, SPECIAL PROJECTS: **MARK D. BEAZLEY**
VP PRODUCTION & SPECIAL PROJECTS: **JEFF YOUNGQUIST**
SVP PRINT, SALES & MARKETING: **DAVID GABRIEL**
BOOK DESIGNER: **ADAM DEL RE**

EDITOR IN CHIEF: **AXEL ALONSO**
CHIEF CREATIVE OFFICER: **JOE QUESADA**
PRESIDENT: **DAN BUCKLEY**
EXECUTIVE PRODUCER: **ALAN FINE**

IRON MAN CREATED BY STAN LEE, LARRY LIEBER, DON HECK & JACK KIRBY

INFAMOUS IRON MAN VOL. 1: INFAMOUS. Contains material originally published in magazine form as INFAMOUS IRON MAN #1-6. First printing 2017. ISBN# 978-1-302-90624-5. Published by MARVEL WORLDWIDE, INC., a subsidiary of MARVEL ENTERTAINMENT, LLC. OFFICE OF PUBLICATION: 135 West 50th Street, New York, NY 10020. Copyright © 2017 MARVEL No similarity between any of the names, characters, persons, and/or institutions in this magazine with those of any living or dead person or institution is intended, and any such similarity which may exist is purely coincidental. Printed in Canada. DAN BUCKLEY, President, Marvel Entertainment; JOE QUESADA, Chief Creative Officer; TOM BREVOORT, SVP of Publishing; DAVID BOGART, SVP of Business Affairs & Operations, Publishing & Partnership; C.B. CEBULSKI, VP of Brand Management & Development, Asia; DAVID GABRIEL, SVP of Sales & Marketing, Publishing; JEFF YOUNGQUIST, VP of Production & Special Projects; DAN CARR, Executive Director of Publishing Technology; ALEX MORALES, Director of Publishing Operations; SUSAN CRESPI, Production Manager; STAN LEE, Chairman Emeritus. For information regarding advertising in Marvel Comics or on Marvel.com, please contact Vit DeBellis, Integrated Sales Manager, at vdebellis@marvel.com. For Marvel subscription inquiries, please call 888-511-5480. Manufactured between 4/7/2017 and 5/9/2017 by SOLISCO PRINTERS, SCOTT, QC, CANADA.

10 9 8 7 6 5 4 3 2 1

1

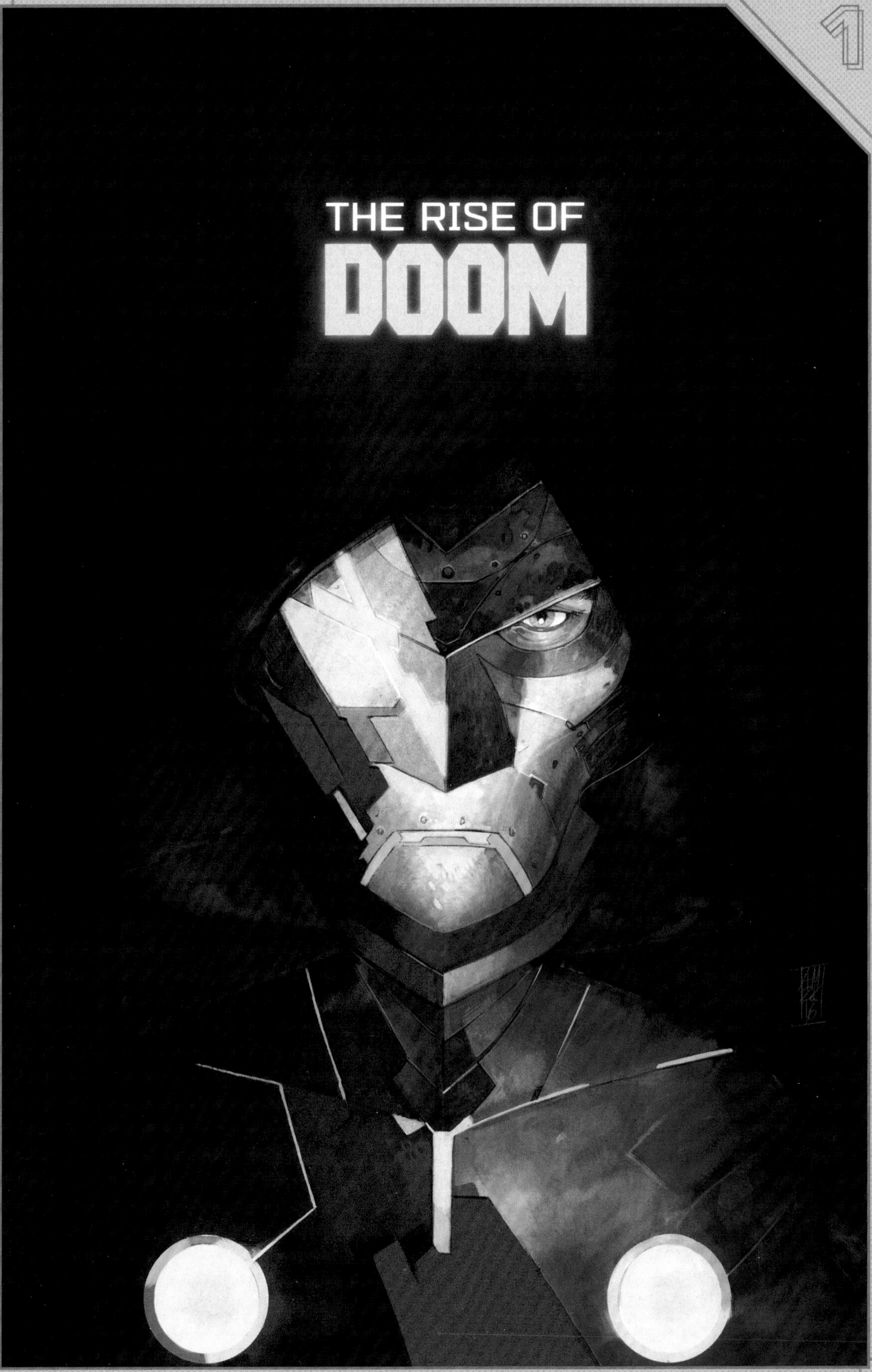
THE RISE OF
DOOM

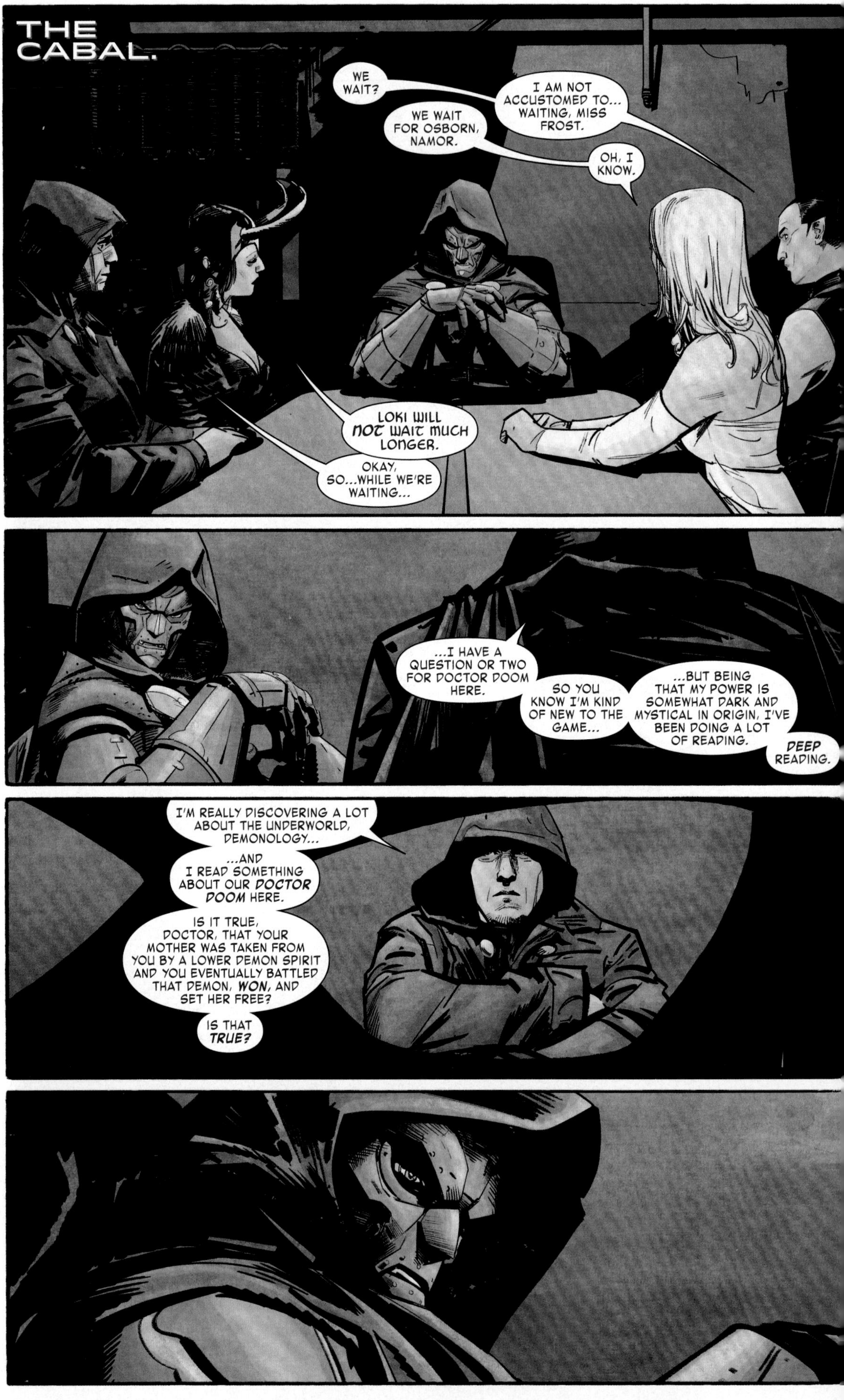
THE CABAL.
WE WAIT?
I AM NOT ACCUSTOMED TO... WAITING, MISS FROST.
WE WAIT FOR OSBORN, NAMOR.
OH, I KNOW.
LOKI WILL NOT WAIT MUCH LONGER.
OKAY, SO...WHILE WE'RE WAITING...
...I HAVE A QUESTION OR TWO FOR DOCTOR DOOM HERE.
SO YOU KNOW I'M KIND OF NEW TO THE GAME...
...BUT BEING THAT MY POWER IS SOMEWHAT DARK AND MYSTICAL IN ORIGIN, I'VE BEEN DOING A LOT OF READING.
DEEP READING.
I'M REALLY DISCOVERING A LOT ABOUT THE UNDERWORLD, DEMONOLOGY...
...AND I READ SOMETHING ABOUT OUR DOCTOR DOOM HERE.
IS IT TRUE, DOCTOR, THAT YOUR MOTHER WAS TAKEN FROM YOU BY A LOWER DEMON SPIRIT AND YOU EVENTUALLY BATTLED THAT DEMON, WON, AND SET HER FREE?
IS THAT TRUE?

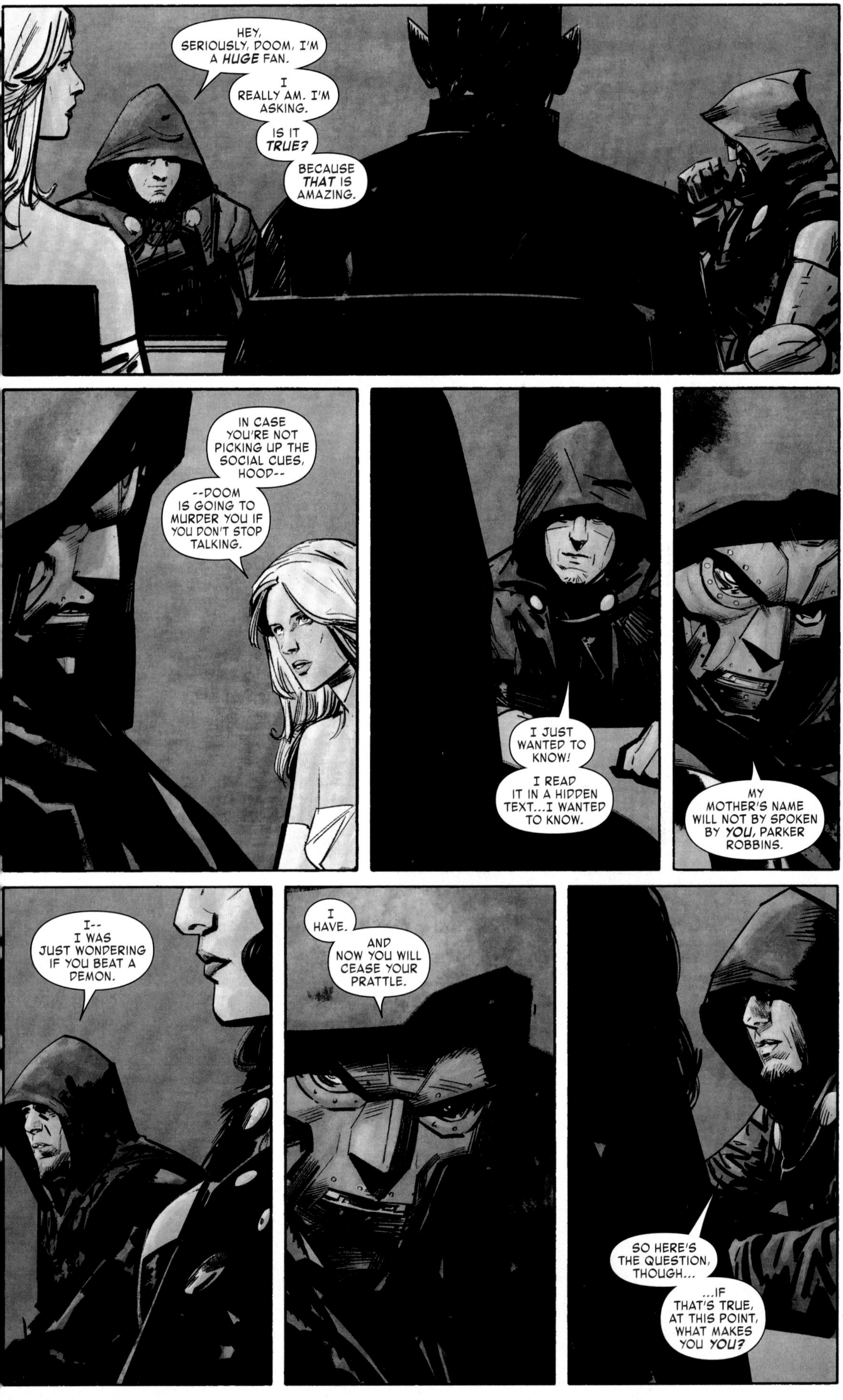
HEY, SERIOUSLY, DOOM, I'M A *HUGE* FAN.
I REALLY AM. I'M ASKING.
IS IT *TRUE?*
BECAUSE *THAT* IS AMAZING.
IN CASE YOU'RE NOT PICKING UP THE SOCIAL CUES, HOOD--
--DOOM IS GOING TO MURDER YOU IF YOU DON'T STOP TALKING.
I JUST WANTED TO KNOW!
I READ IT IN A HIDDEN TEXT...I WANTED TO KNOW.
MY MOTHER'S NAME WILL NOT BY SPOKEN BY *YOU*, PARKER ROBBINS.
I-- I WAS JUST WONDERING IF YOU BEAT A DEMON.
I HAVE.
AND NOW YOU WILL CEASE YOUR PRATTLE.
SO HERE'S THE QUESTION, THOUGH...
...IF THAT'S TRUE, AT THIS POINT, WHAT MAKES YOU *YOU?*

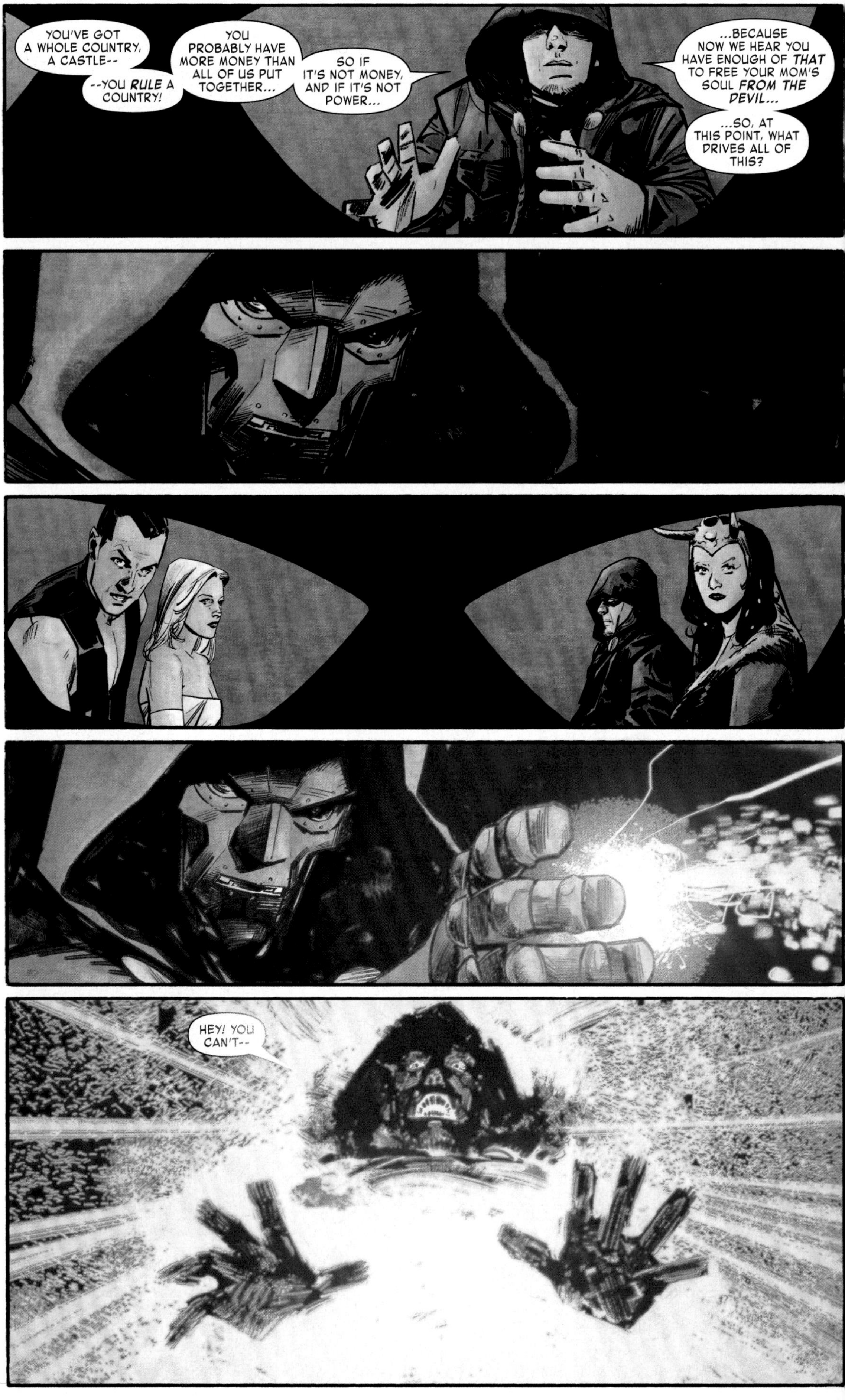
YOU'VE GOT A WHOLE COUNTRY, A CASTLE--
--YOU RULE A COUNTRY!
YOU PROBABLY HAVE MORE MONEY THAN ALL OF US PUT TOGETHER...
SO IF IT'S NOT MONEY, AND IF IT'S NOT POWER...
...BECAUSE NOW WE HEAR YOU HAVE ENOUGH OF THAT TO FREE YOUR MOM'S SOUL FROM THE DEVIL...
...SO, AT THIS POINT, WHAT DRIVES ALL OF THIS?
HEY! YOU CAN'T--

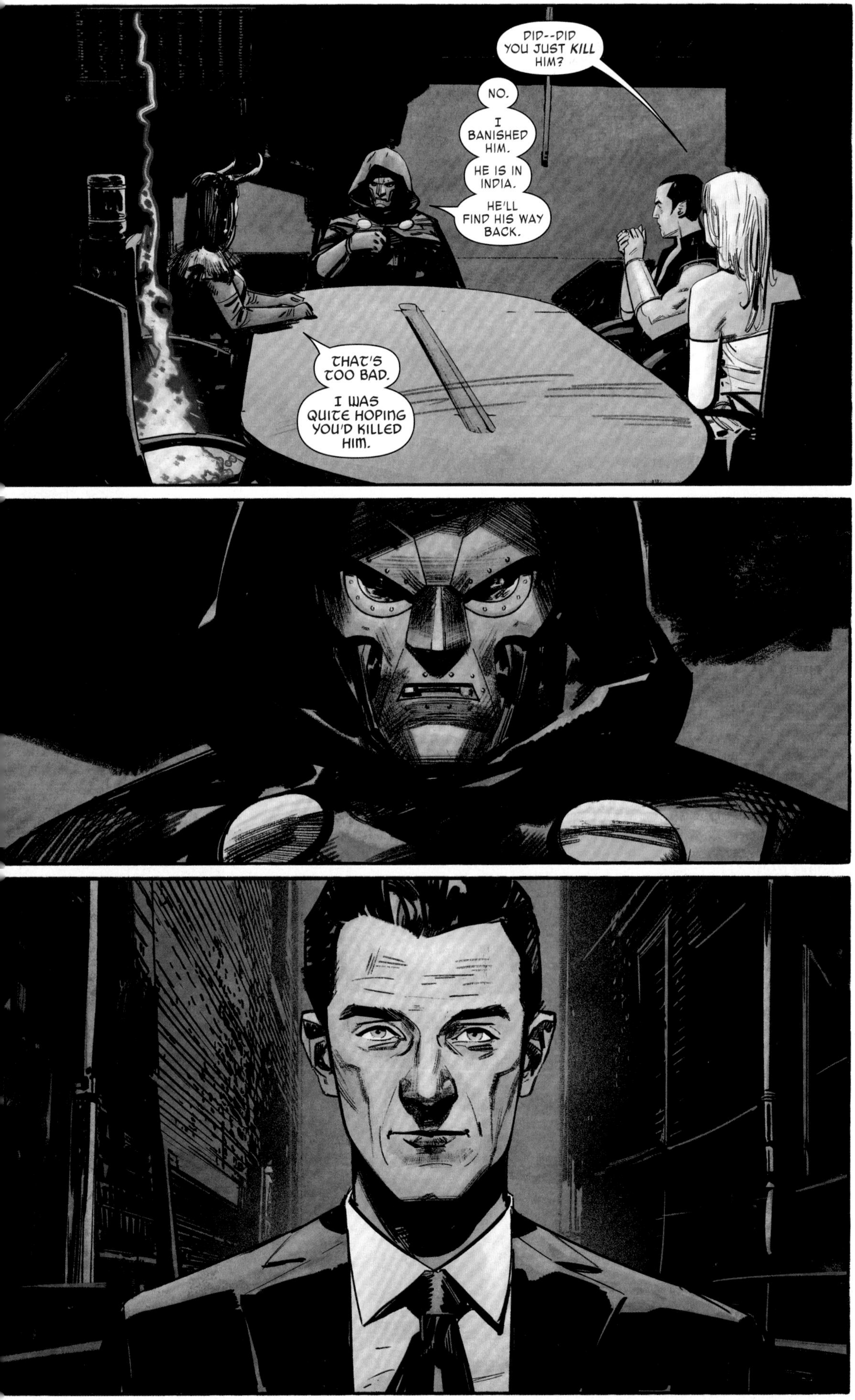
DID--DID YOU JUST KILL HIM?
NO.
I BANISHED HIM.
HE IS IN INDIA.
HE'LL FIND HIS WAY BACK.
THAT'S TOO BAD.
I WAS QUITE HOPING YOU'D KILLED HIM.

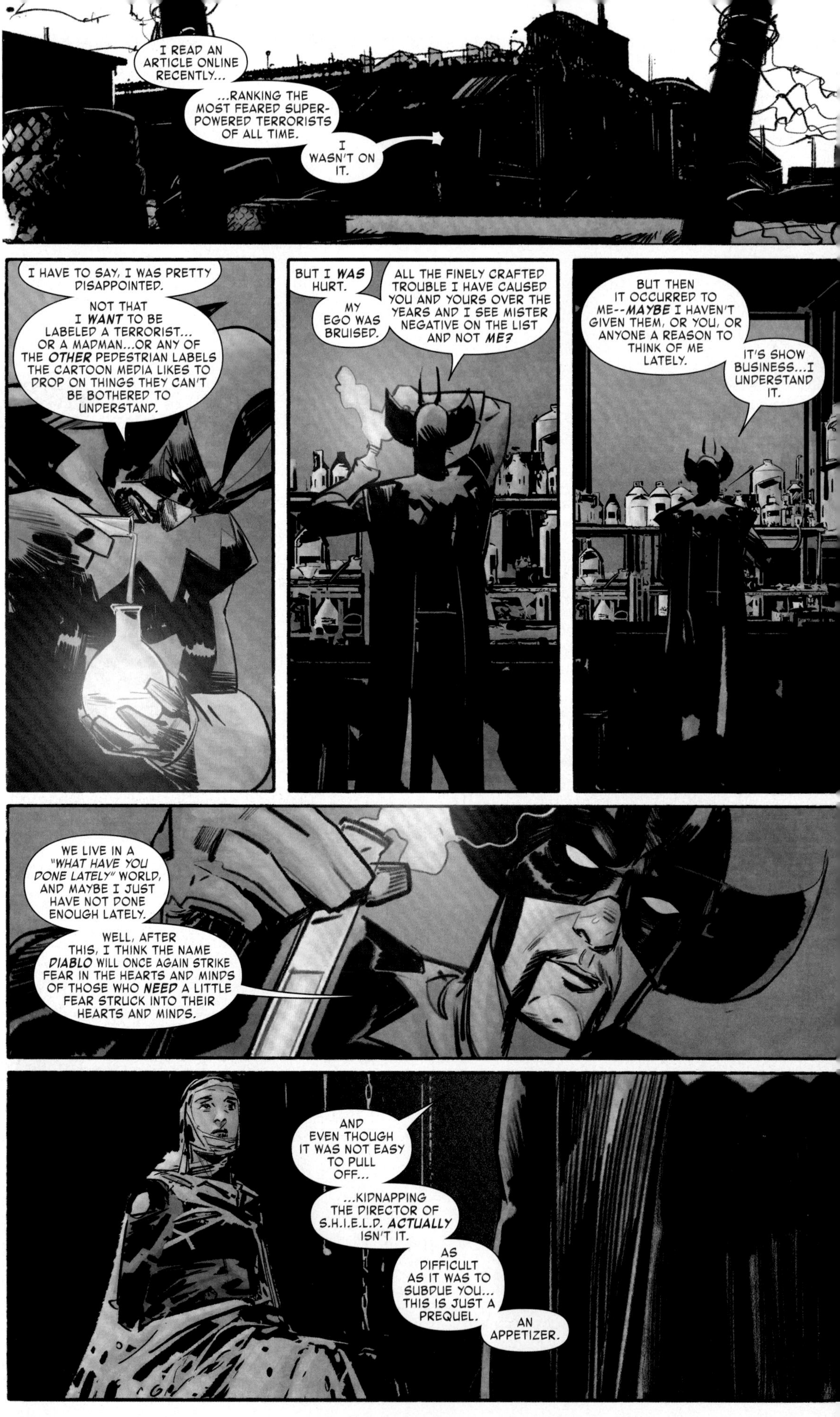

I READ AN ARTICLE ONLINE RECENTLY...
...RANKING THE MOST FEARED SUPER-POWERED TERRORISTS OF ALL TIME.
I WASN'T ON IT.
I HAVE TO SAY, I WAS PRETTY DISAPPOINTED.
NOT THAT I WANT TO BE LABELED A TERRORIST... OR A MADMAN...OR ANY OF THE OTHER PEDESTRIAN LABELS THE CARTOON MEDIA LIKES TO DROP ON THINGS THEY CAN'T BE BOTHERED TO UNDERSTAND.
BUT I WAS HURT.
MY EGO WAS BRUISED.
ALL THE FINELY CRAFTED TROUBLE I HAVE CAUSED YOU AND YOURS OVER THE YEARS AND I SEE MISTER NEGATIVE ON THE LIST AND NOT ME?
BUT THEN IT OCCURRED TO ME--MAYBE I HAVEN'T GIVEN THEM, OR YOU, OR ANYONE A REASON TO THINK OF ME LATELY.
IT'S SHOW BUSINESS...I UNDERSTAND IT.
WE LIVE IN A "WHAT HAVE YOU DONE LATELY" WORLD, AND MAYBE I JUST HAVE NOT DONE ENOUGH LATELY.
WELL, AFTER THIS, I THINK THE NAME DIABLO WILL ONCE AGAIN STRIKE FEAR IN THE HEARTS AND MINDS OF THOSE WHO NEED A LITTLE FEAR STRUCK INTO THEIR HEARTS AND MINDS.
AND EVEN THOUGH IT WAS NOT EASY TO PULL OFF...
...KIDNAPPING THE DIRECTOR OF S.H.I.E.L.D. ACTUALLY ISN'T IT.
AS DIFFICULT AS IT WAS TO SUBDUE YOU... THIS IS JUST A PREQUEL.
AN APPETIZER.

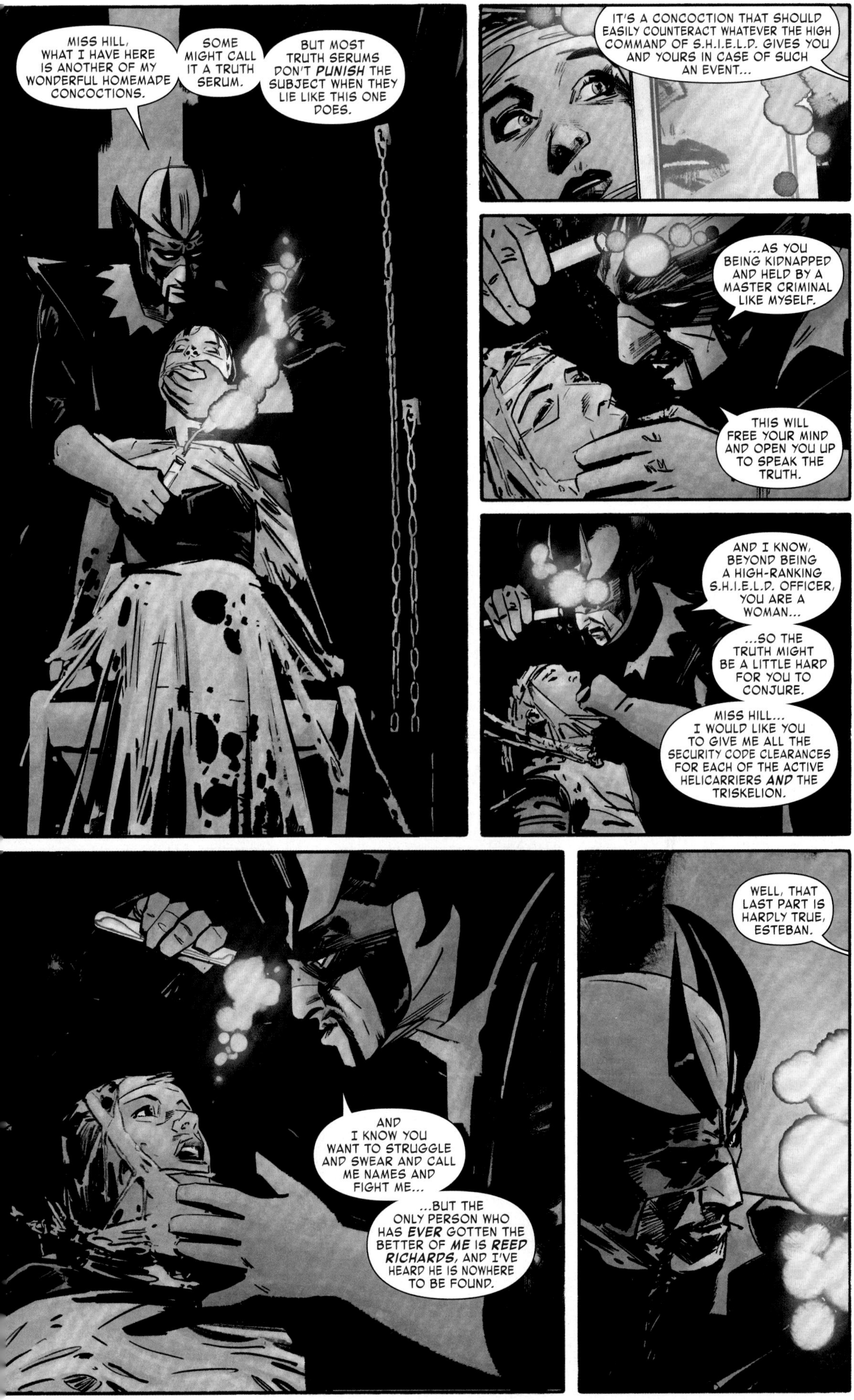
MISS HILL, WHAT I HAVE HERE IS ANOTHER OF MY WONDERFUL HOMEMADE CONCOCTIONS.
SOME MIGHT CALL IT A TRUTH SERUM.
BUT MOST TRUTH SERUMS DON'T PUNISH THE SUBJECT WHEN THEY LIE LIKE THIS ONE DOES.
IT'S A CONCOCTION THAT SHOULD EASILY COUNTERACT WHATEVER THE HIGH COMMAND OF S.H.I.E.L.D. GIVES YOU AND YOURS IN CASE OF SUCH AN EVENT...
...AS YOU BEING KIDNAPPED AND HELD BY A MASTER CRIMINAL LIKE MYSELF.
THIS WILL FREE YOUR MIND AND OPEN YOU UP TO SPEAK THE TRUTH.
AND I KNOW, BEYOND BEING A HIGH-RANKING S.H.I.E.L.D. OFFICER, YOU ARE A WOMAN...
...SO THE TRUTH MIGHT BE A LITTLE HARD FOR YOU TO CONJURE.
MISS HILL... I WOULD LIKE YOU TO GIVE ME ALL THE SECURITY CODE CLEARANCES FOR EACH OF THE ACTIVE HELICARRIERS AND THE TRISKELION.
AND I KNOW YOU WANT TO STRUGGLE AND SWEAR AND CALL ME NAMES AND FIGHT ME...
...BUT THE ONLY PERSON WHO HAS EVER GOTTEN THE BETTER OF ME IS REED RICHARDS, AND I'VE HEARD HE IS NOWHERE TO BE FOUND.
WELL, THAT LAST PART IS HARDLY TRUE, ESTEBAN.

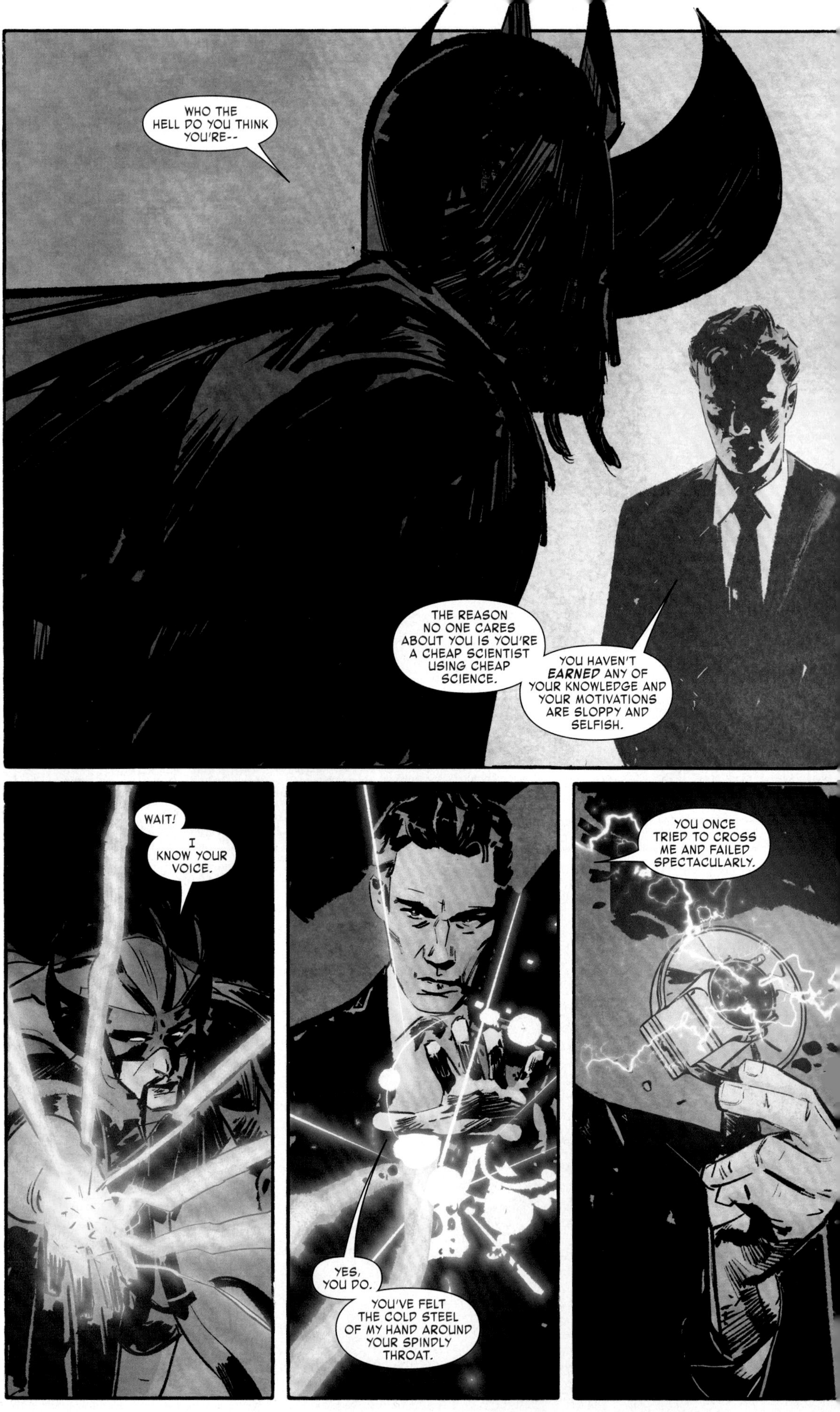

WHO THE HELL DO YOU THINK YOU'RE--
THE REASON NO ONE CARES ABOUT YOU IS YOU'RE A CHEAP SCIENTIST USING CHEAP SCIENCE.
YOU HAVEN'T EARNED ANY OF YOUR KNOWLEDGE AND YOUR MOTIVATIONS ARE SLOPPY AND SELFISH.
WAIT!
I KNOW YOUR VOICE.
YES, YOU DO.
YOU'VE FELT THE COLD STEEL OF MY HAND AROUND YOUR SPINDLY THROAT.
YOU ONCE TRIED TO CROSS ME AND FAILED SPECTACULARLY.

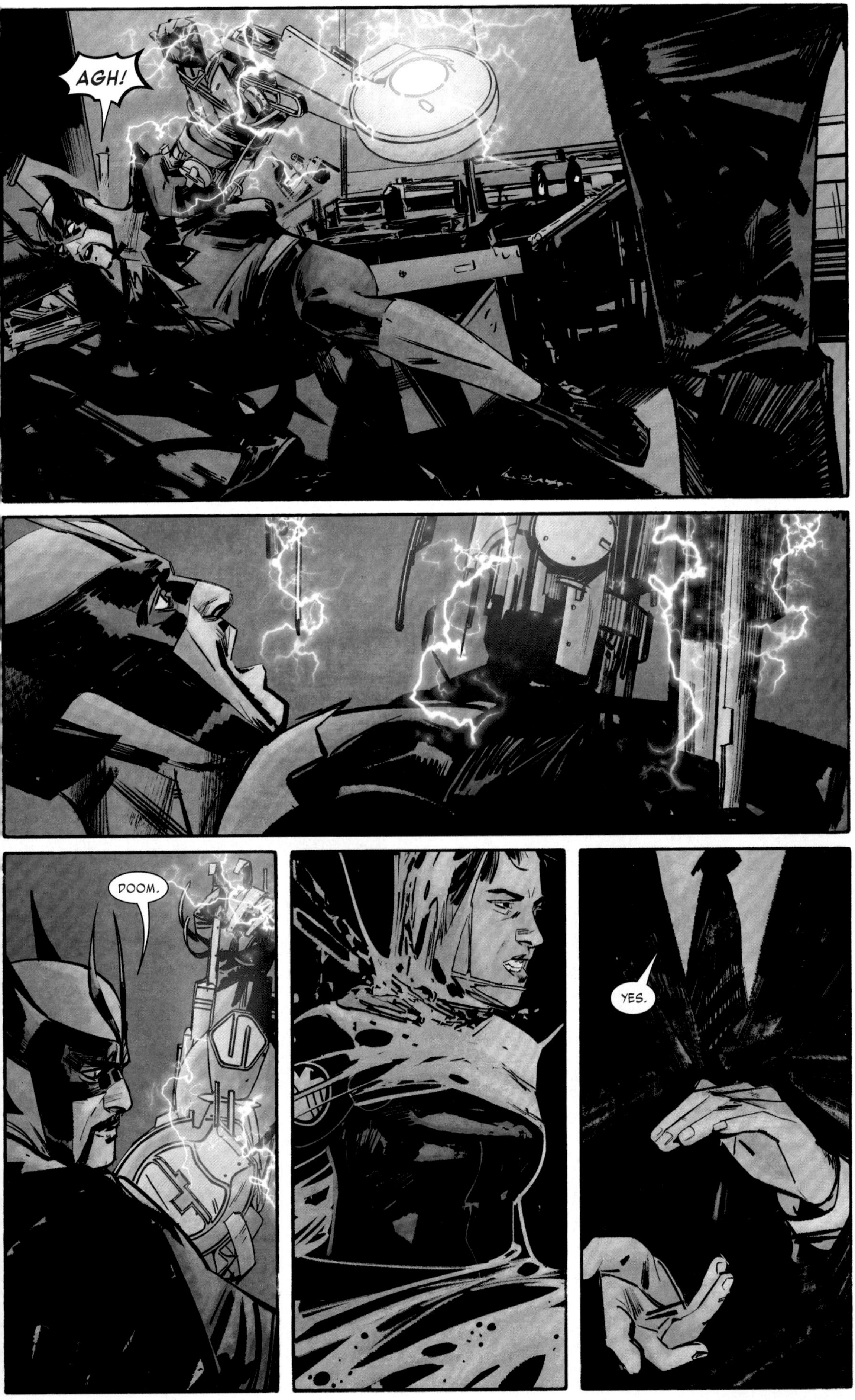
AGH!
DOOM.
YES.

AGH!

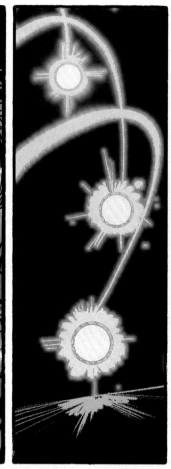

PSSSH

AGH!

COME ON,
COME ON...

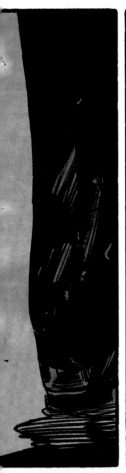

HUMOROUS.

MAYBE SOMEONE NEEDS TO SCAR THAT SMUG NEW FACE OF YOURS ALL OVER AGAIN.

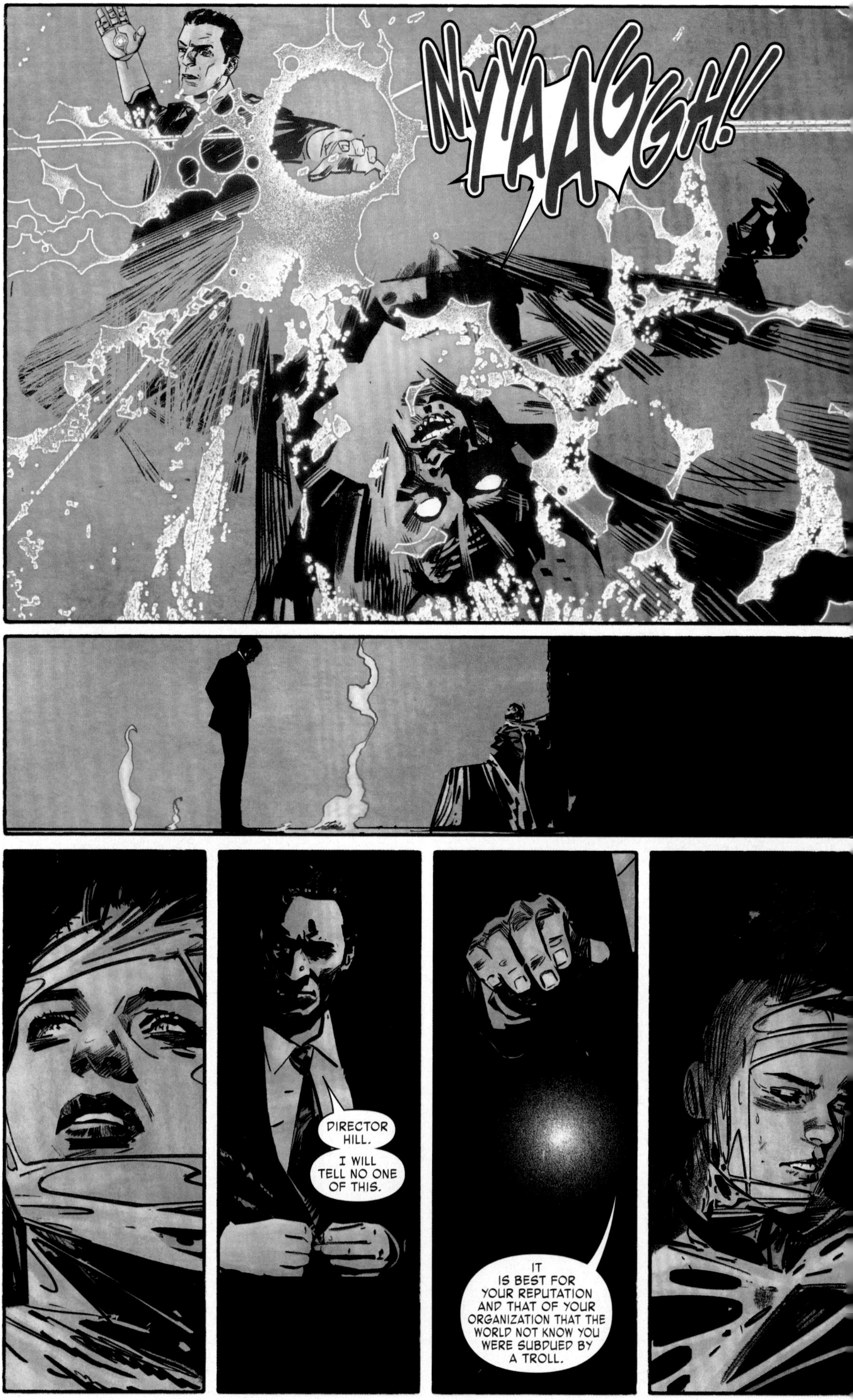
NYYAAGGH!
DIRECTOR HILL.
I WILL TELL NO ONE OF THIS.
IT IS BEST FOR YOUR REPUTATION AND THAT OF YOUR ORGANIZATION THAT THE WORLD NOT KNOW YOU WERE SUBDUED BY A TROLL.

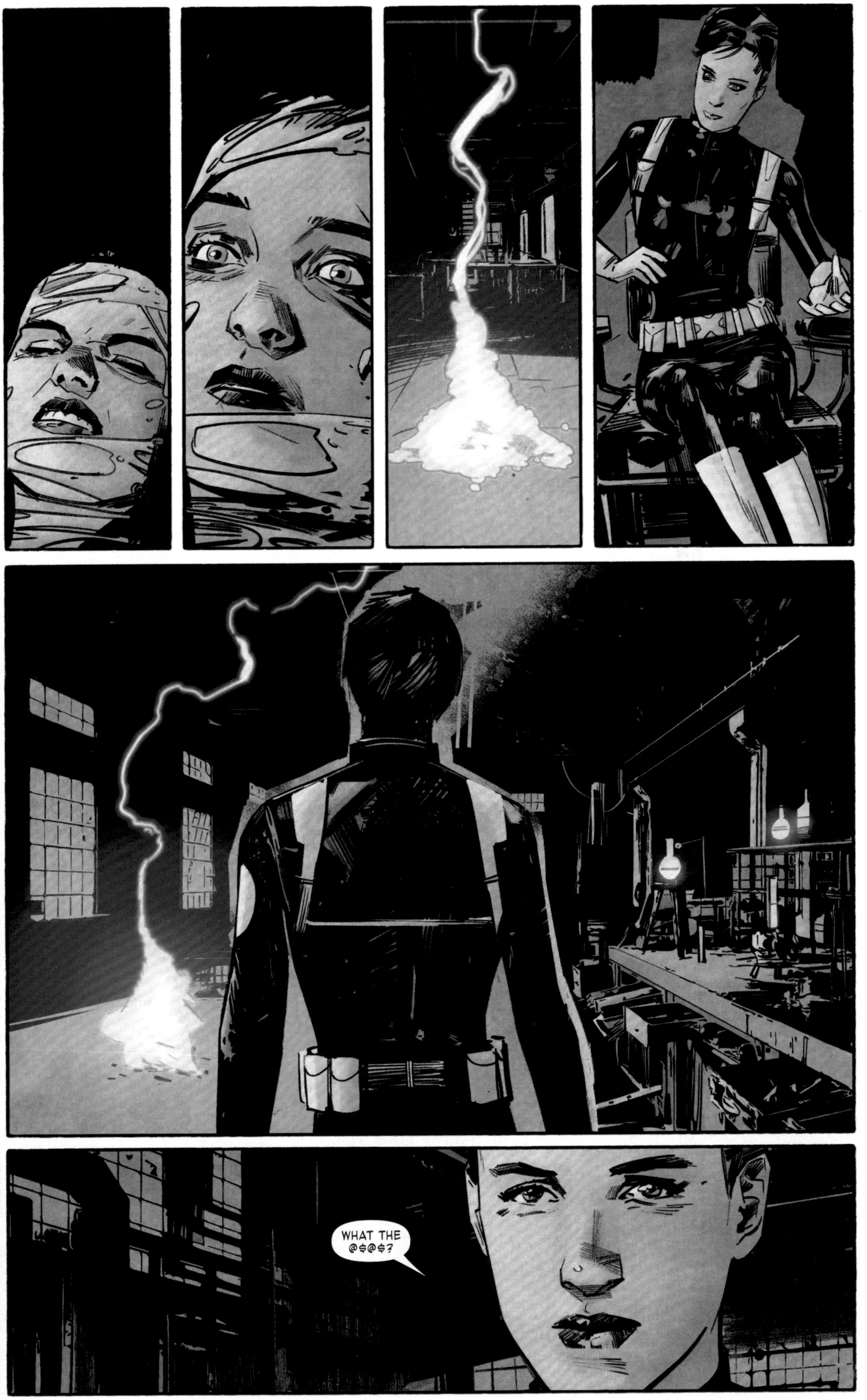
WHAT THE @$@$?

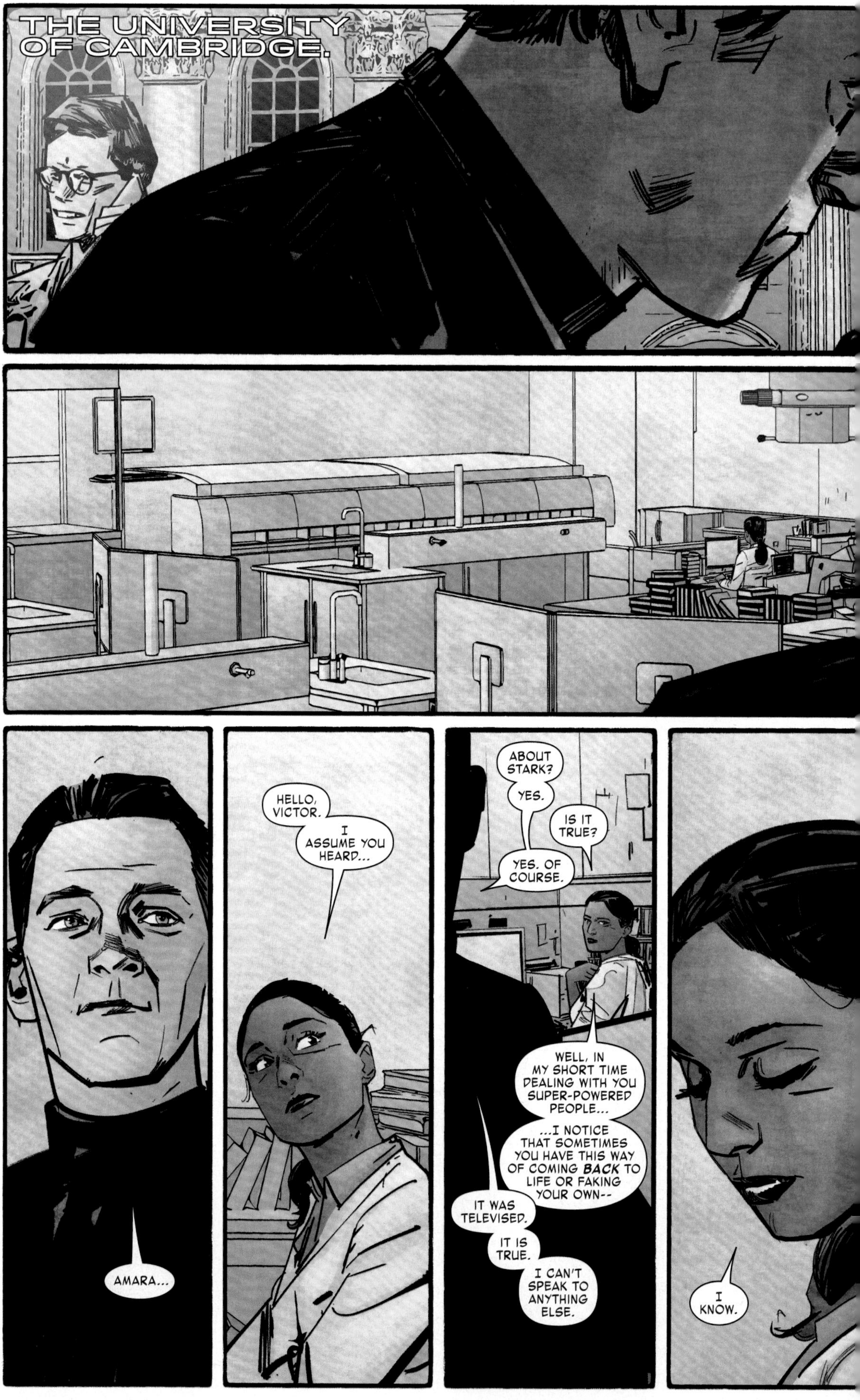
THE UNIVERSITY OF CAMBRIDGE.
AMARA...
HELLO, VICTOR.
I ASSUME YOU HEARD...
ABOUT STARK?
YES.
IS IT TRUE?
YES. OF COURSE.
WELL, IN MY SHORT TIME DEALING WITH YOU SUPER-POWERED PEOPLE...
...I NOTICE THAT SOMETIMES YOU HAVE THIS WAY OF COMING BACK TO LIFE OR FAKING YOUR OWN--
IT WAS TELEVISED.
IT IS TRUE.
I CAN'T SPEAK TO ANYTHING ELSE.
I KNOW.

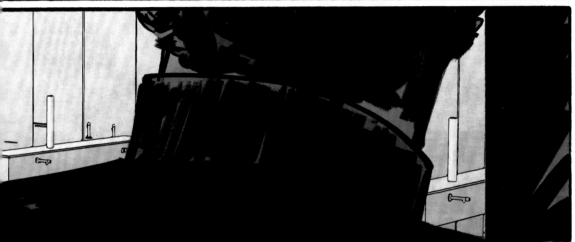

I'M SORRY.

I KNOW YOU HAVE CONFLICTED FEELINGS ABOUT HIM.

WHY DID YOU COME HERE, VICTOR?

TO SEE HOW YOUR WORK FIGHTING ALZHEIMER'S IS COMING ALONG.

YOU CAME HERE TO SEE HOW MY WORK IS COMING ALONG?

WHY ARE YOU HERE?

WHY DID YOU SET ME UP WITH A LAB HERE?

WHAT DO YOU WANT FROM ME?

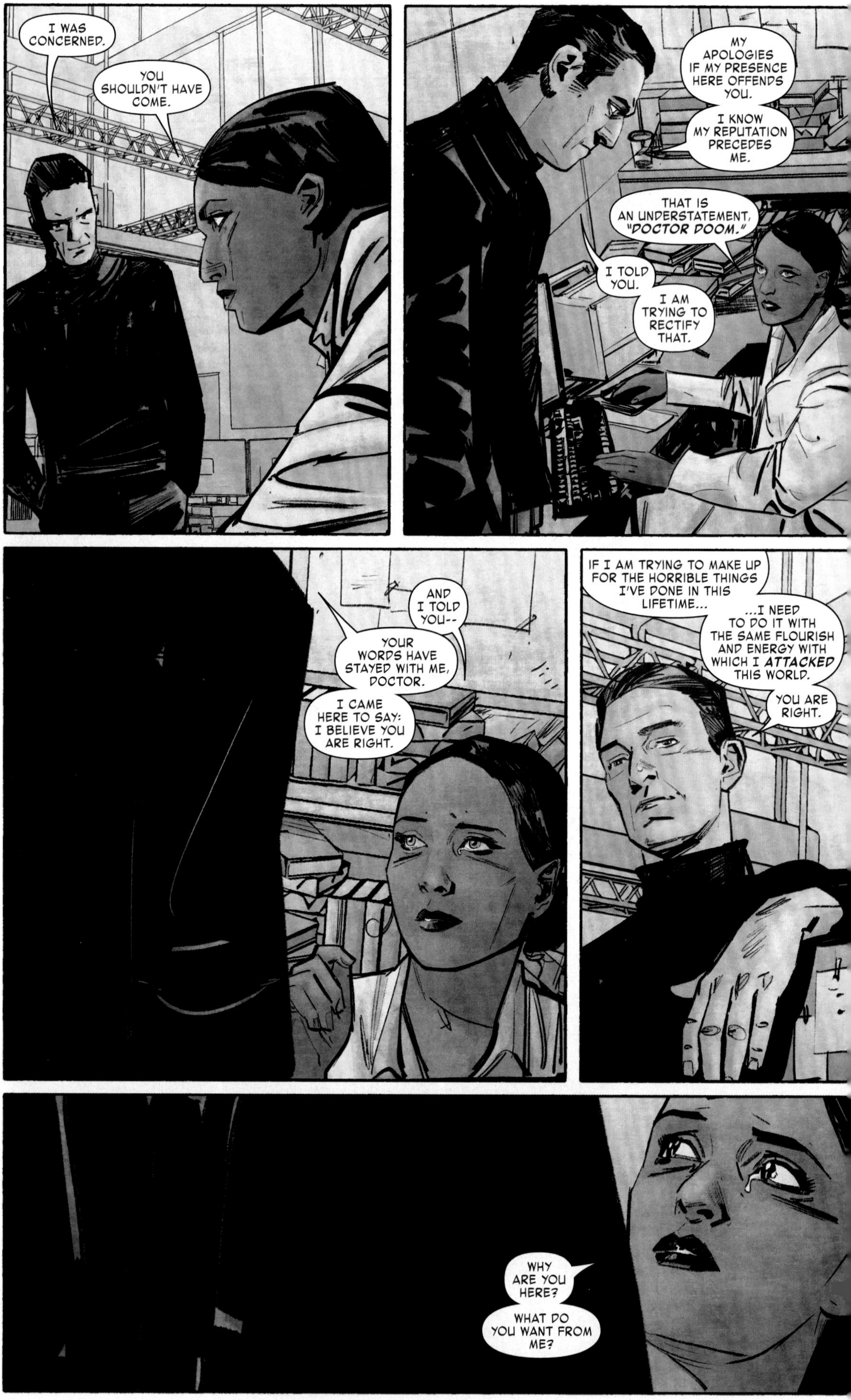
I WAS CONCERNED.
YOU SHOULDN'T HAVE COME.
MY APOLOGIES IF MY PRESENCE HERE OFFENDS YOU.
I KNOW MY REPUTATION PRECEDES ME.
THAT IS AN UNDERSTATEMENT, "DOCTOR DOOM."
I TOLD YOU.
I AM TRYING TO RECTIFY THAT.
AND I TOLD YOU--
YOUR WORDS HAVE STAYED WITH ME, DOCTOR.
I CAME HERE TO SAY: I BELIEVE YOU ARE RIGHT.
IF I AM TRYING TO MAKE UP FOR THE HORRIBLE THINGS I'VE DONE IN THIS LIFETIME...
...I NEED TO DO IT WITH THE SAME FLOURISH AND ENERGY WITH WHICH I ATTACKED THIS WORLD.
YOU ARE RIGHT.
WHY ARE YOU HERE?
WHAT DO YOU WANT FROM ME?

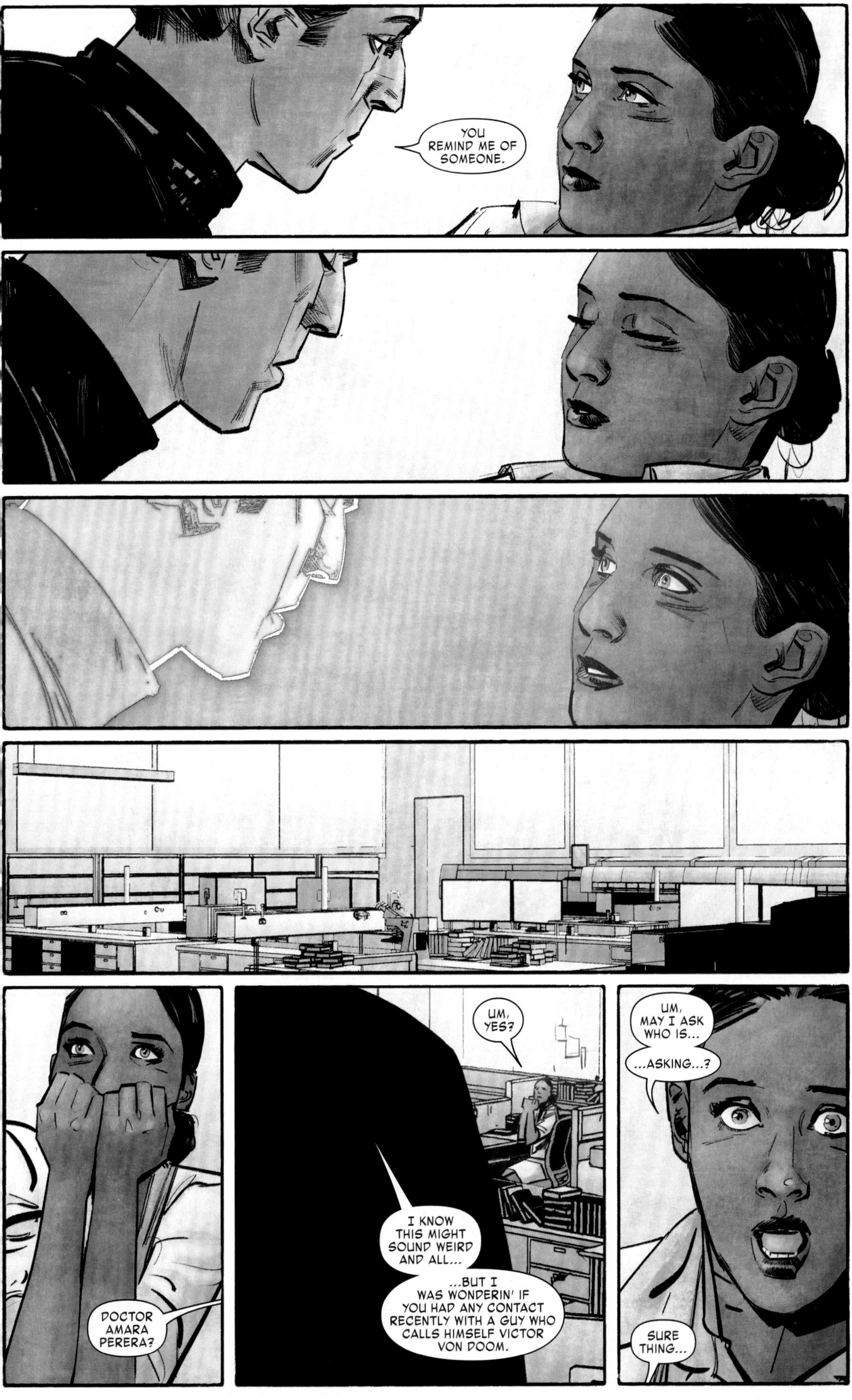
YOU REMIND ME OF SOMEONE.
DOCTOR AMARA PERERA?
UM, YES?
I KNOW THIS MIGHT SOUND WEIRD AND ALL...
...BUT I WAS WONDERIN' IF YOU HAD ANY CONTACT RECENTLY WITH A GUY WHO CALLS HIMSELF VICTOR VON DOOM.
UM, MAY I ASK WHO IS...
...ASKING...?
SURE THING...

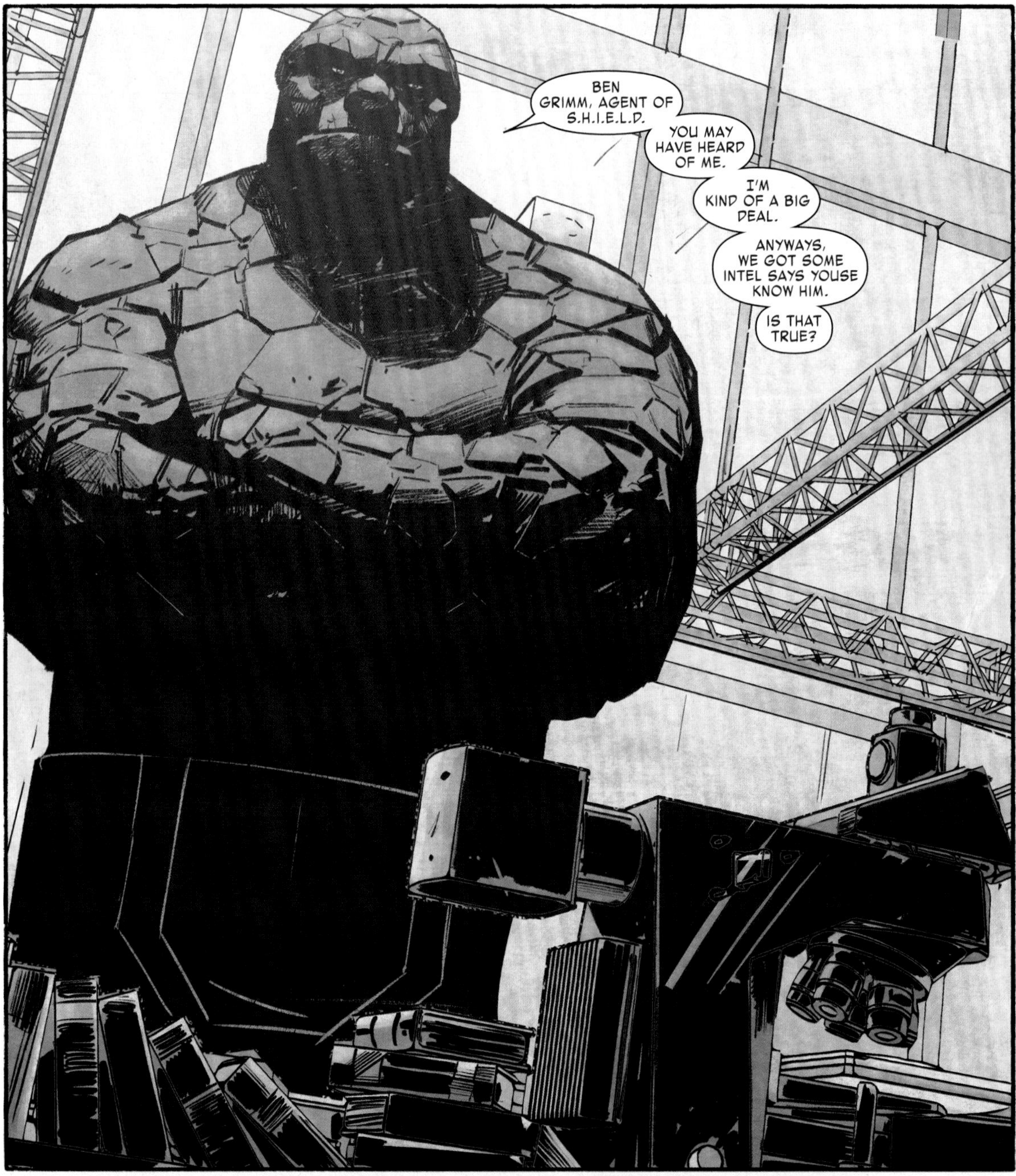
BEN GRIMM, AGENT OF S.H.I.E.L.D.
YOU MAY HAVE HEARD OF ME.
I'M KIND OF A BIG DEAL.
ANYWAYS, WE GOT SOME INTEL SAYS YOUSE KNOW HIM.
IS THAT TRUE?

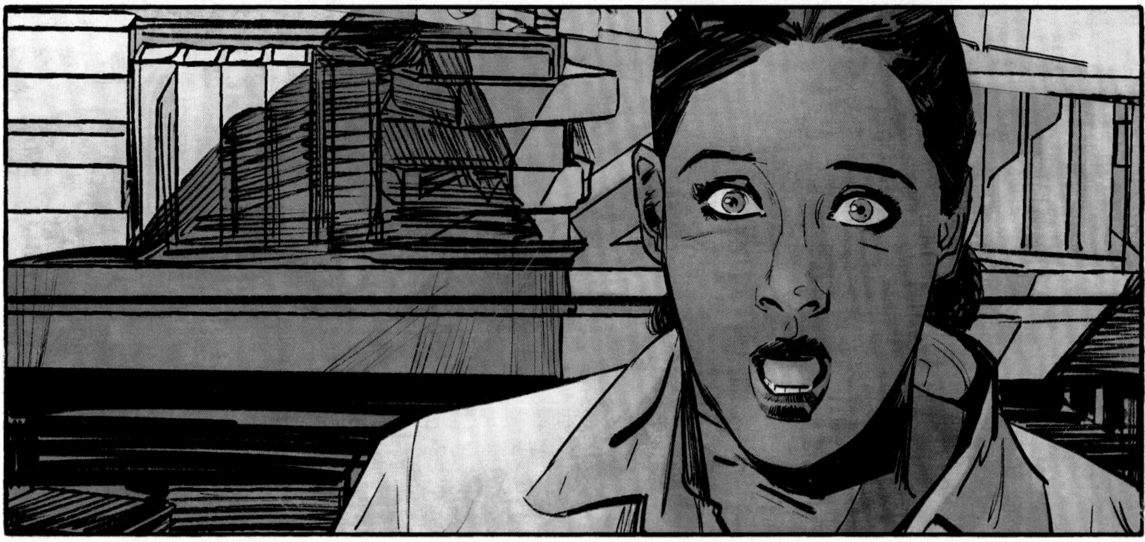

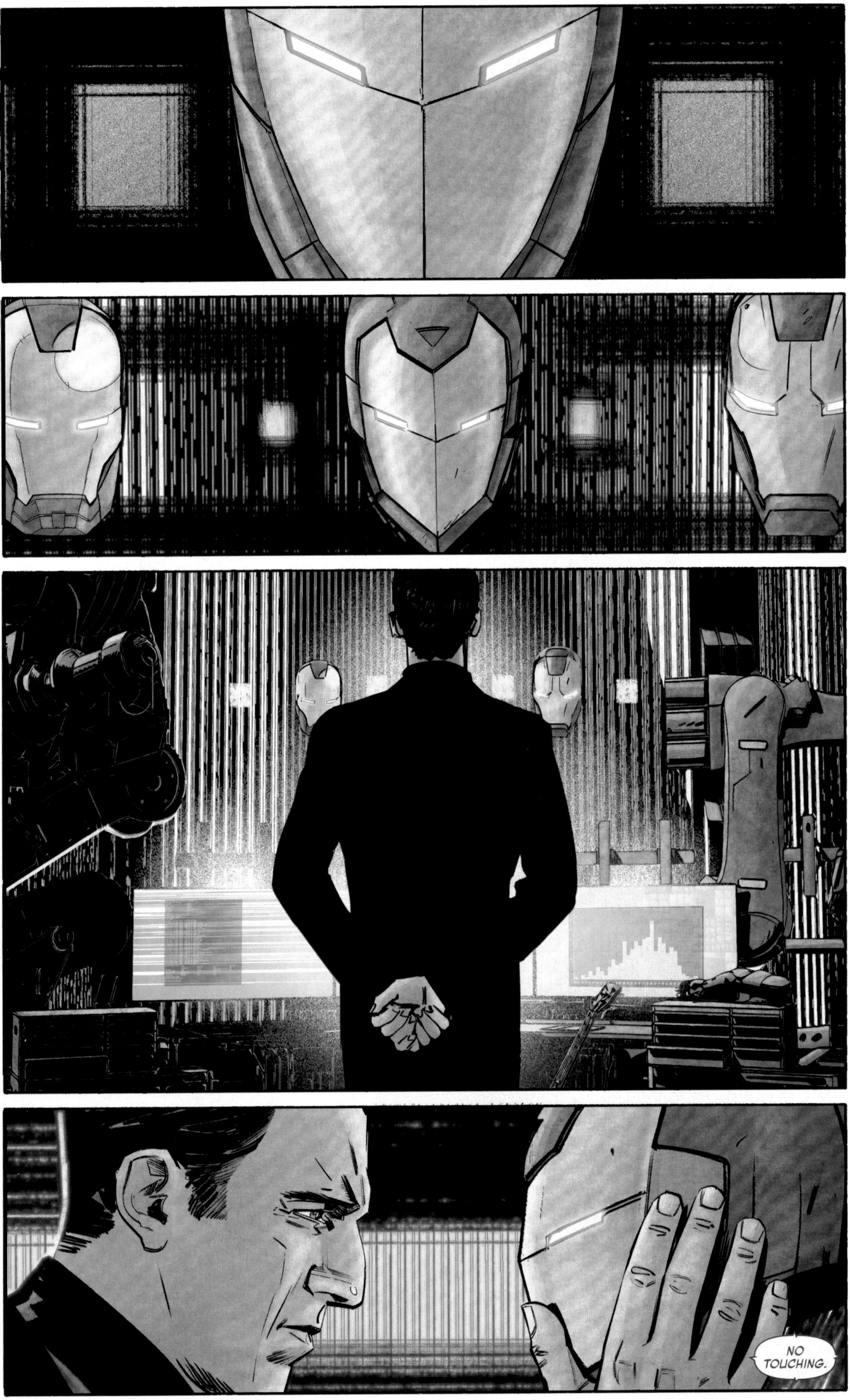
NO TOUCHING.

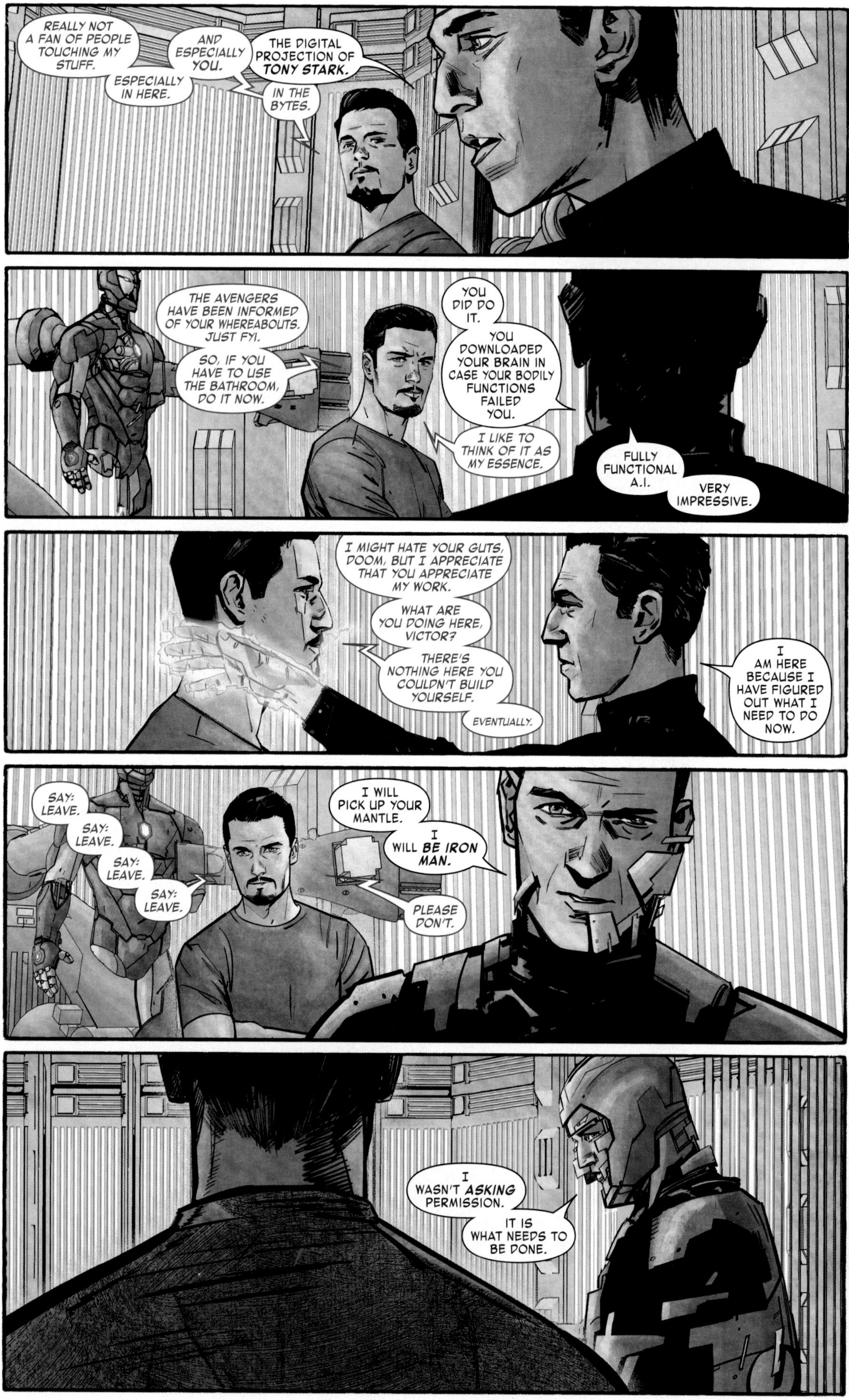
REALLY NOT A FAN OF PEOPLE TOUCHING MY STUFF.
ESPECIALLY IN HERE.
AND ESPECIALLY YOU.
THE DIGITAL PROJECTION OF TONY STARK.
IN THE BYTES.
THE AVENGERS HAVE BEEN INFORMED OF YOUR WHEREABOUTS. JUST FYI.
SO, IF YOU HAVE TO USE THE BATHROOM, DO IT NOW.
YOU DID DO IT.
YOU DOWNLOADED YOUR BRAIN IN CASE YOUR BODILY FUNCTIONS FAILED YOU.
I LIKE TO THINK OF IT AS MY ESSENCE.
FULLY FUNCTIONAL A.I.
VERY IMPRESSIVE.
I MIGHT HATE YOUR GUTS, DOOM, BUT I APPRECIATE THAT YOU APPRECIATE MY WORK.
WHAT ARE YOU DOING HERE, VICTOR?
THERE'S NOTHING HERE YOU COULDN'T BUILD YOURSELF.
EVENTUALLY.
I AM HERE BECAUSE I HAVE FIGURED OUT WHAT I NEED TO DO NOW.
I WILL PICK UP YOUR MANTLE.
I WILL BE IRON MAN.
SAY: LEAVE.
SAY: LEAVE.
SAY: LEAVE.
SAY: LEAVE.
PLEASE DON'T.
I WASN'T ASKING PERMISSION.
IT IS WHAT NEEDS TO BE DONE.

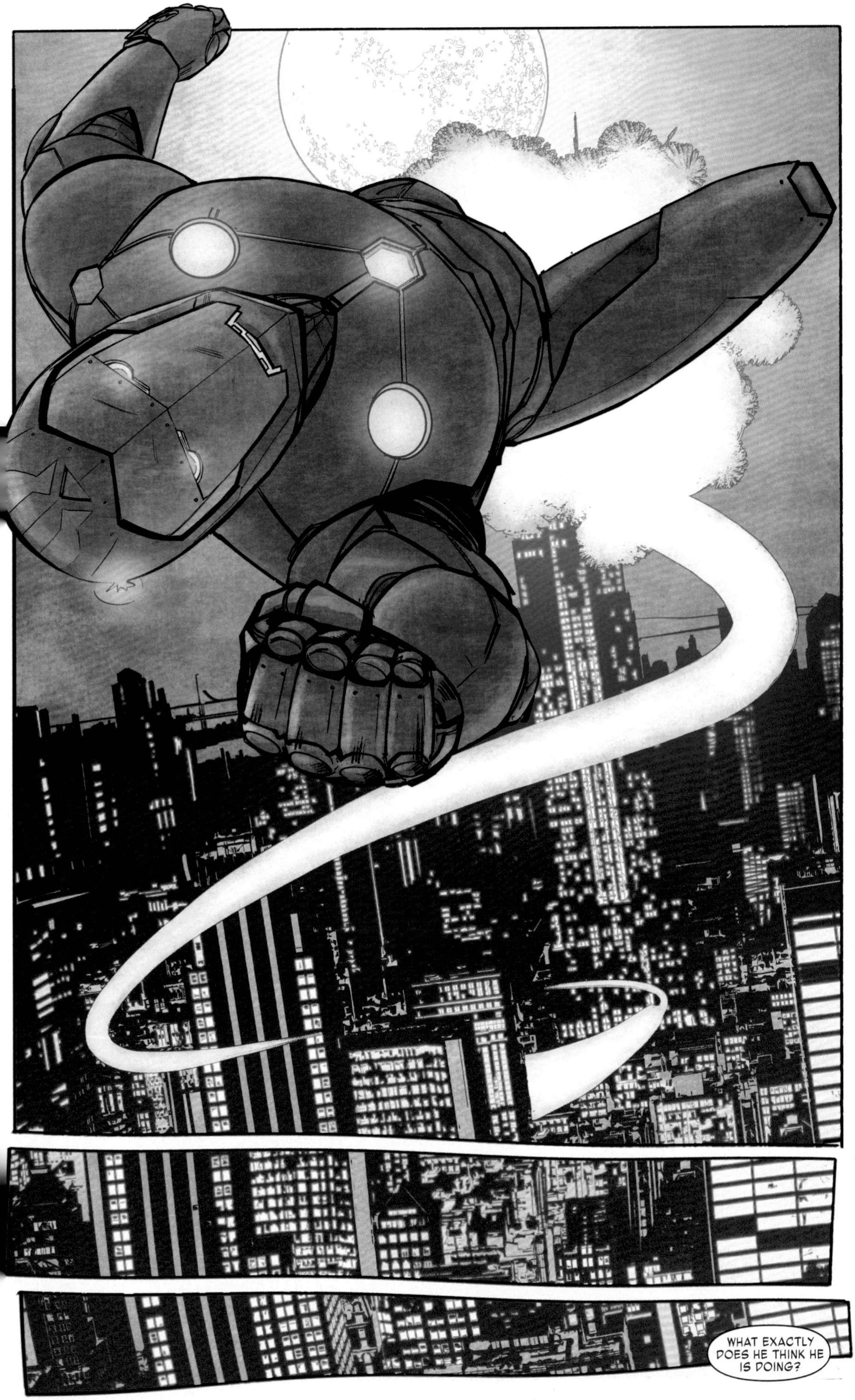
WHAT EXACTLY DOES HE THINK HE IS DOING?

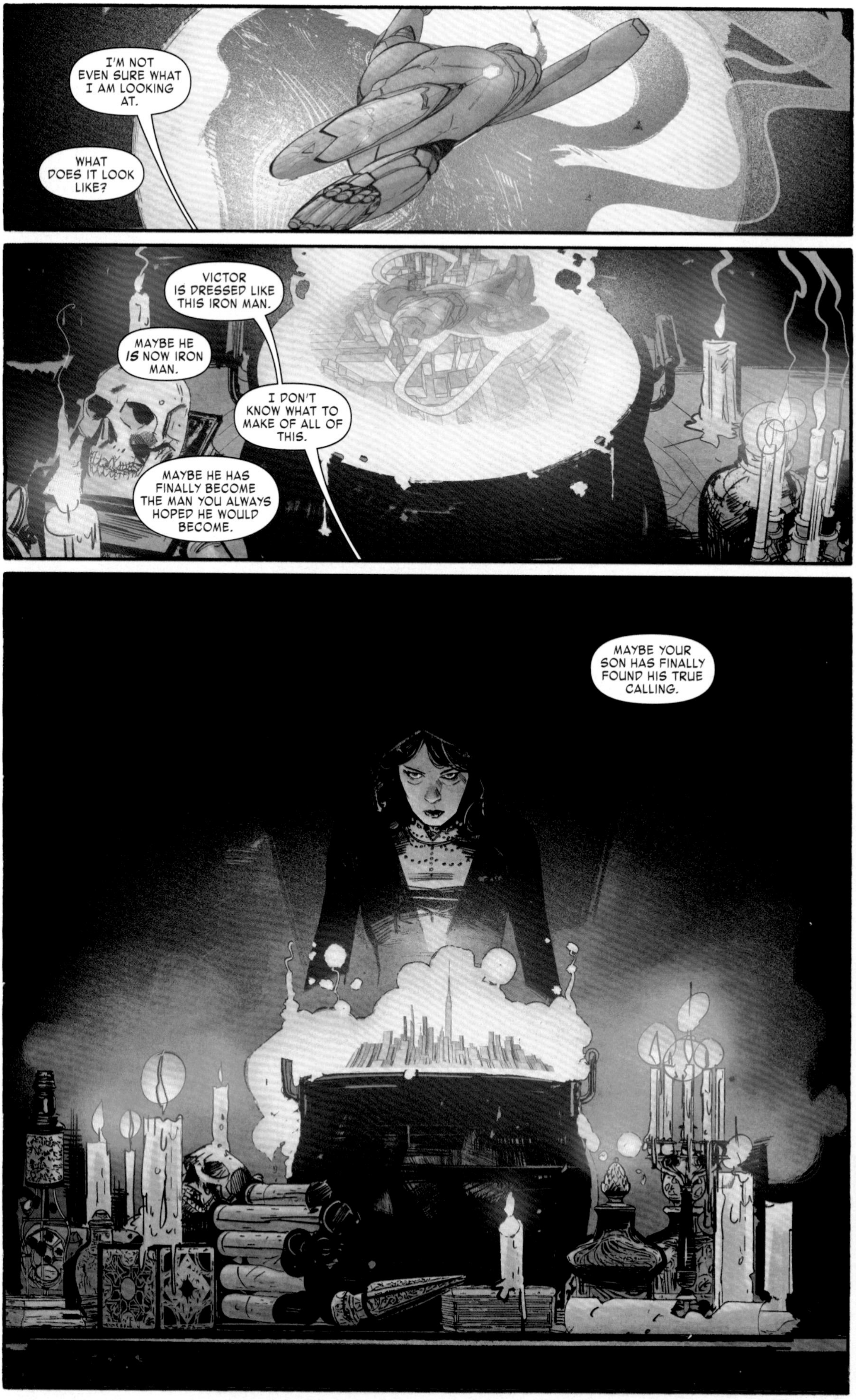
I'M NOT EVEN SURE WHAT I AM LOOKING AT.
WHAT DOES IT LOOK LIKE?
VICTOR IS DRESSED LIKE THIS IRON MAN.
MAYBE HE *IS* NOW IRON MAN.
I DON'T KNOW WHAT TO MAKE OF ALL OF THIS.
MAYBE HE HAS FINALLY BECOME THE MAN YOU ALWAYS HOPED HE WOULD BECOME.
MAYBE YOUR SON HAS FINALLY FOUND HIS TRUE CALLING.

2

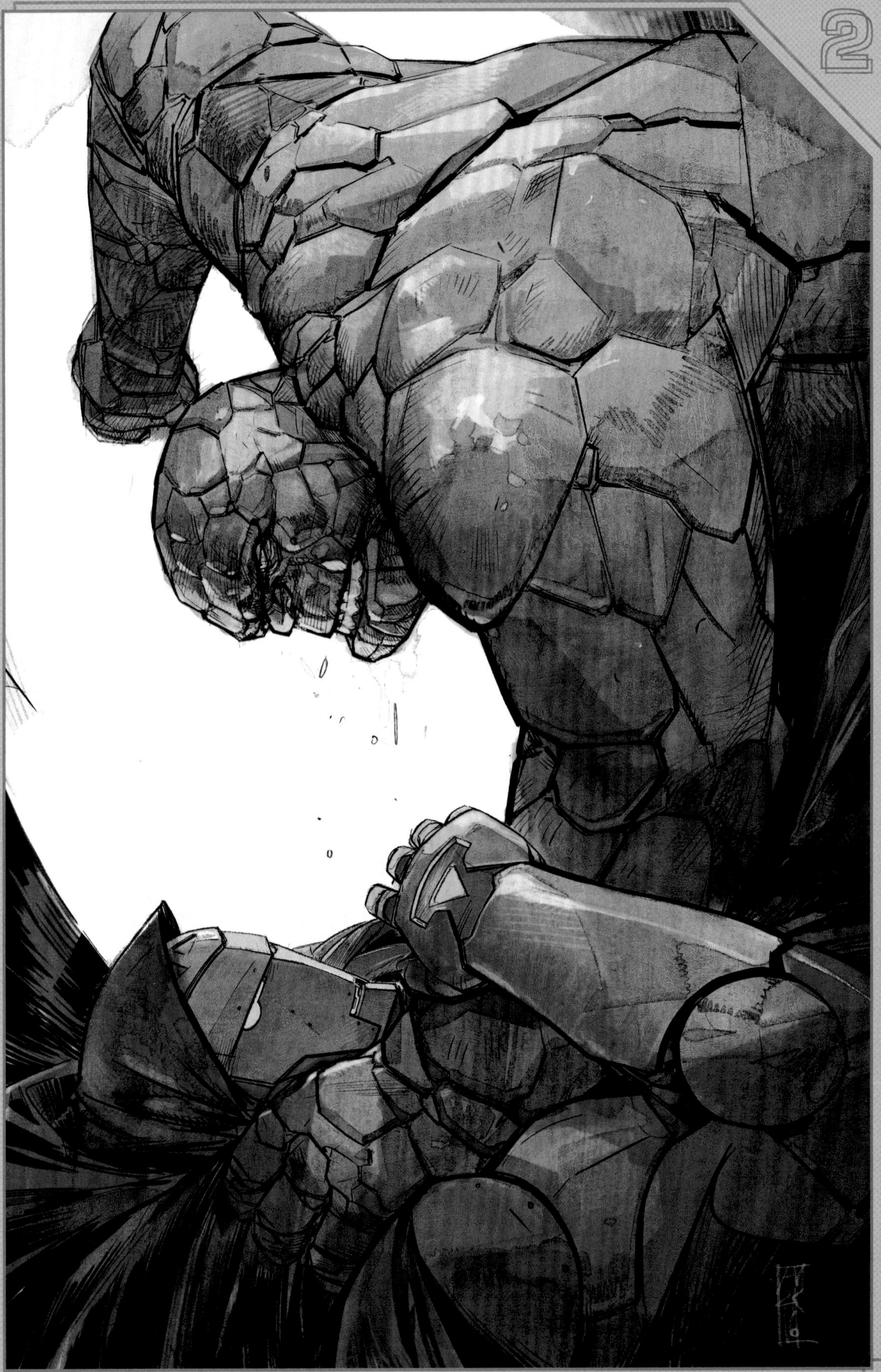

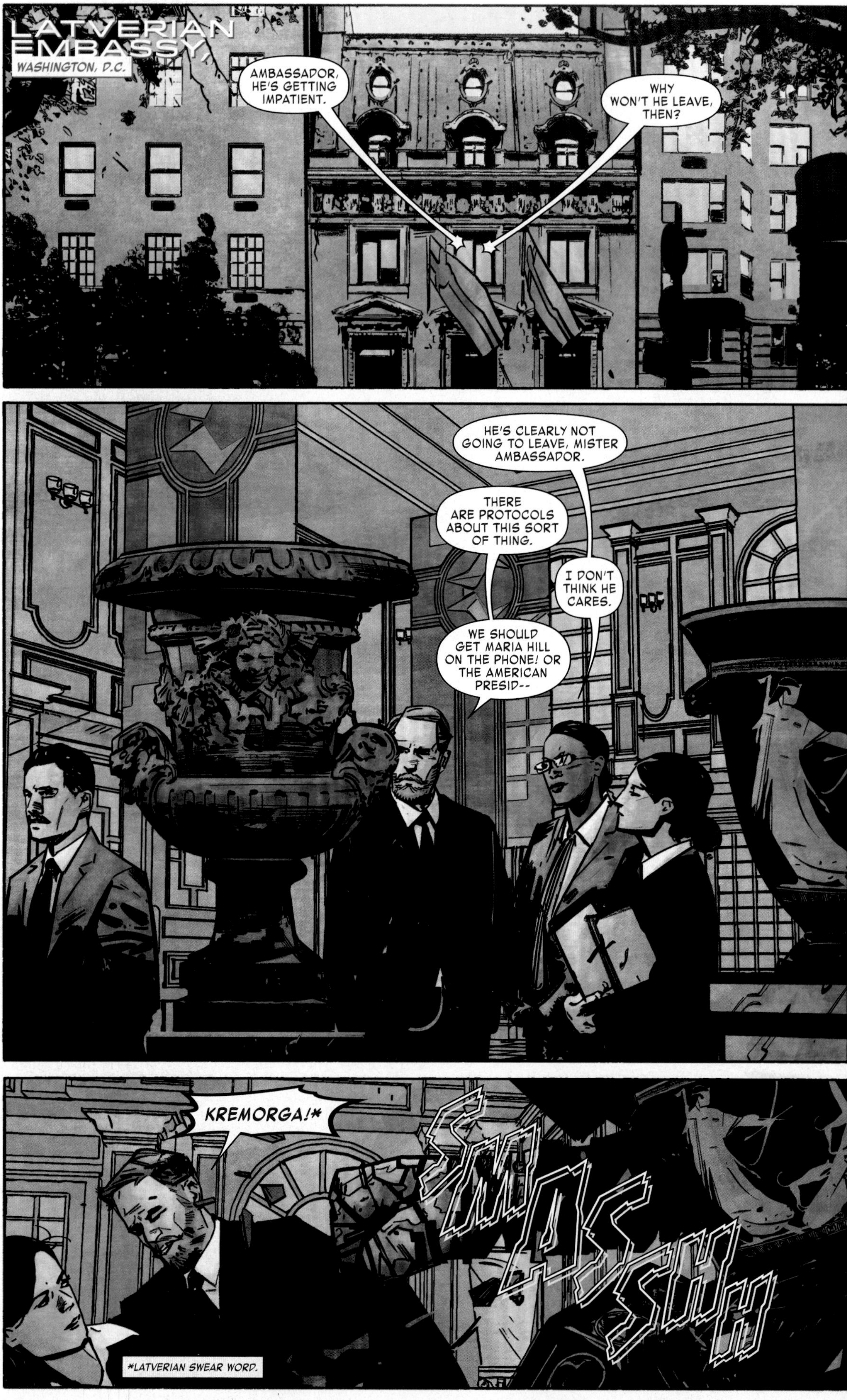
LATVERIAN EMBASSY,
WASHINGTON, D.C.
AMBASSADOR, HE'S GETTING IMPATIENT.
WHY WON'T HE LEAVE, THEN?
HE'S CLEARLY NOT GOING TO LEAVE, MISTER AMBASSADOR.
THERE ARE PROTOCOLS ABOUT THIS SORT OF THING.
I DON'T THINK HE CARES.
WE SHOULD GET MARIA HILL ON THE PHONE! OR THE AMERICAN PRESID--
KREMORGA!*
*LATVERIAN SWEAR WORD.

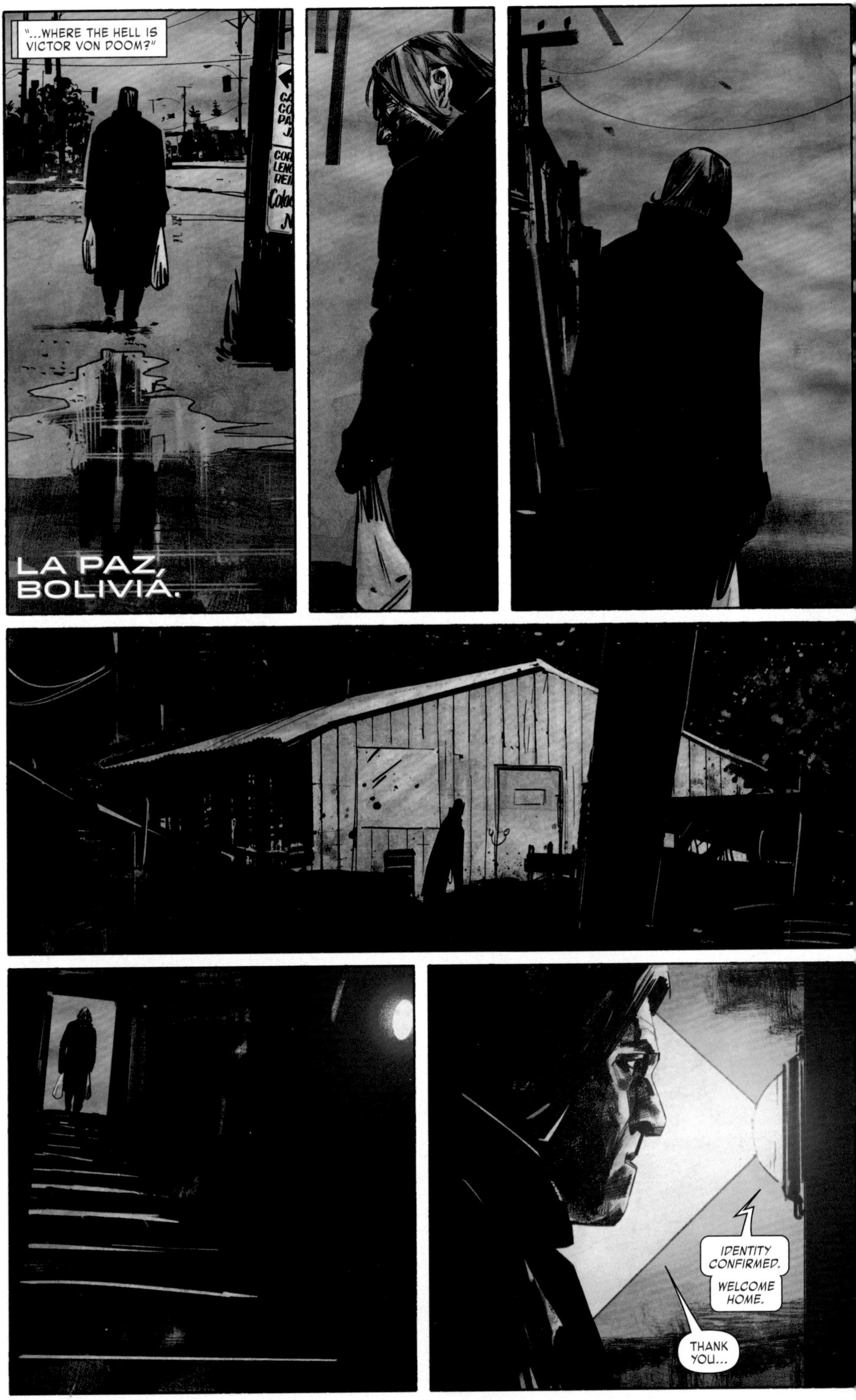
"...WHERE THE HELL IS VICTOR VON DOOM?"
LA PAZ, BOLIVIA.
IDENTITY CONFIRMED.
WELCOME HOME.
THANK YOU...

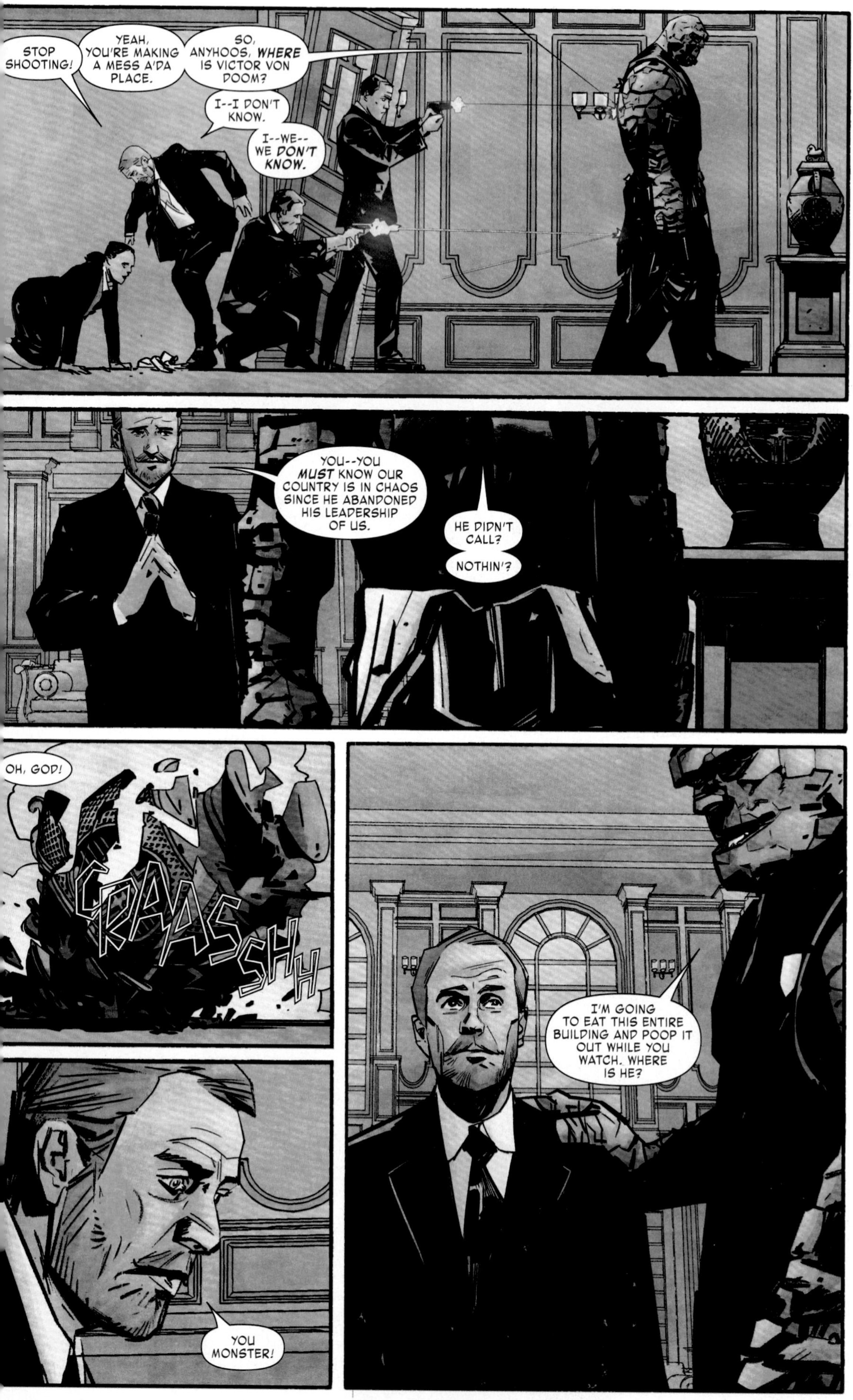
STOP SHOOTING!
YEAH, YOU'RE MAKING A MESS A'DA PLACE.
SO, ANYHOOS, WHERE IS VICTOR VON DOOM?
I--I DON'T KNOW.
I--WE-- WE DON'T KNOW.
YOU--YOU MUST KNOW OUR COUNTRY IS IN CHAOS SINCE HE ABANDONED HIS LEADERSHIP OF US.
HE DIDN'T CALL?
NOTHIN'?
OH, GOD!
CRAASSHH
YOU MONSTER!
I'M GOING TO EAT THIS ENTIRE BUILDING AND POOP IT OUT WHILE YOU WATCH. WHERE IS HE?

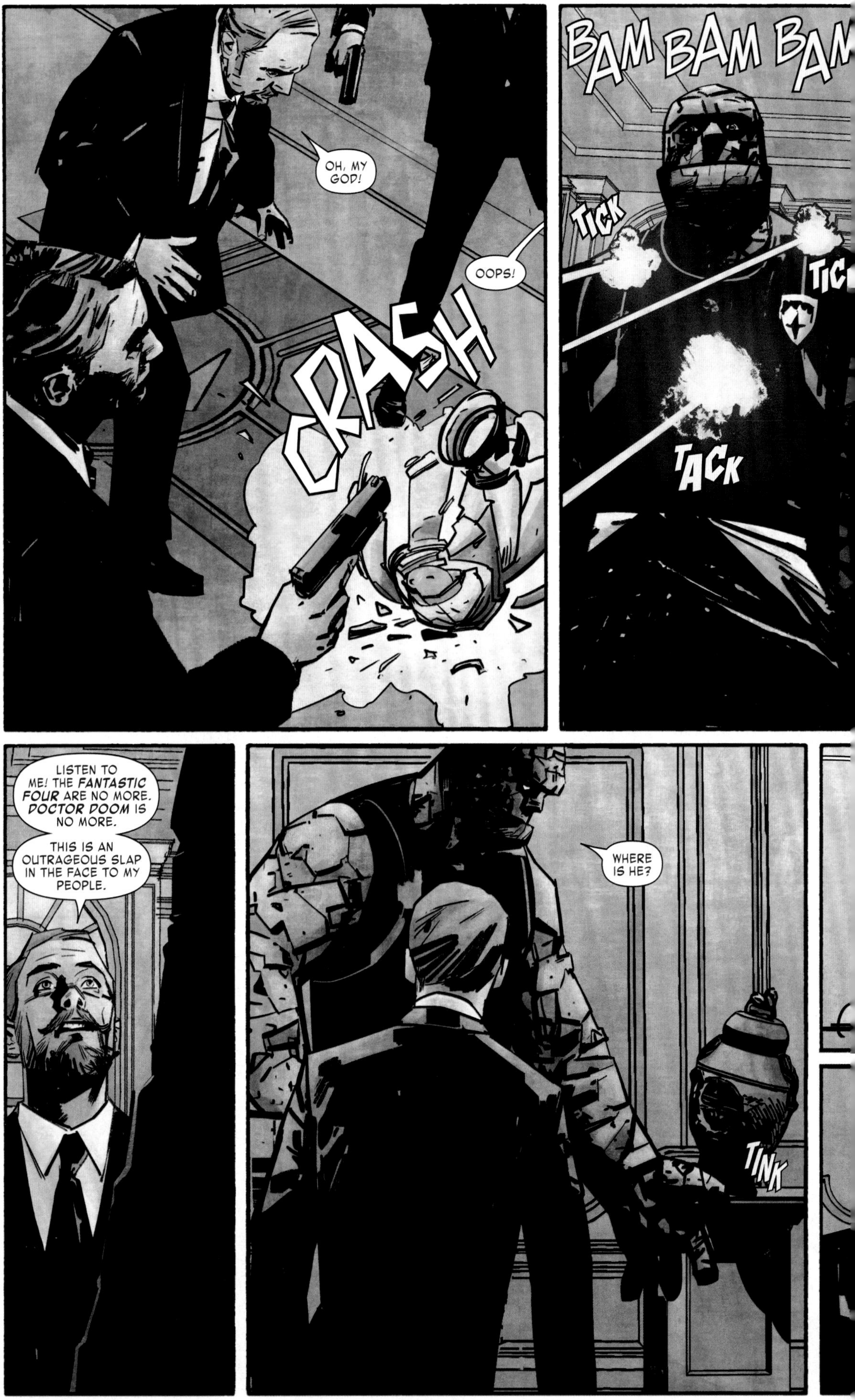
OH, MY GOD!
OOPS!
CRASH
BAM BAM BAM
TICK
TIC
TACK
LISTEN TO ME! THE FANTASTIC FOUR ARE NO MORE. DOCTOR DOOM IS NO MORE.
THIS IS AN OUTRAGEOUS SLAP IN THE FACE TO MY PEOPLE.
WHERE IS HE?
TINK

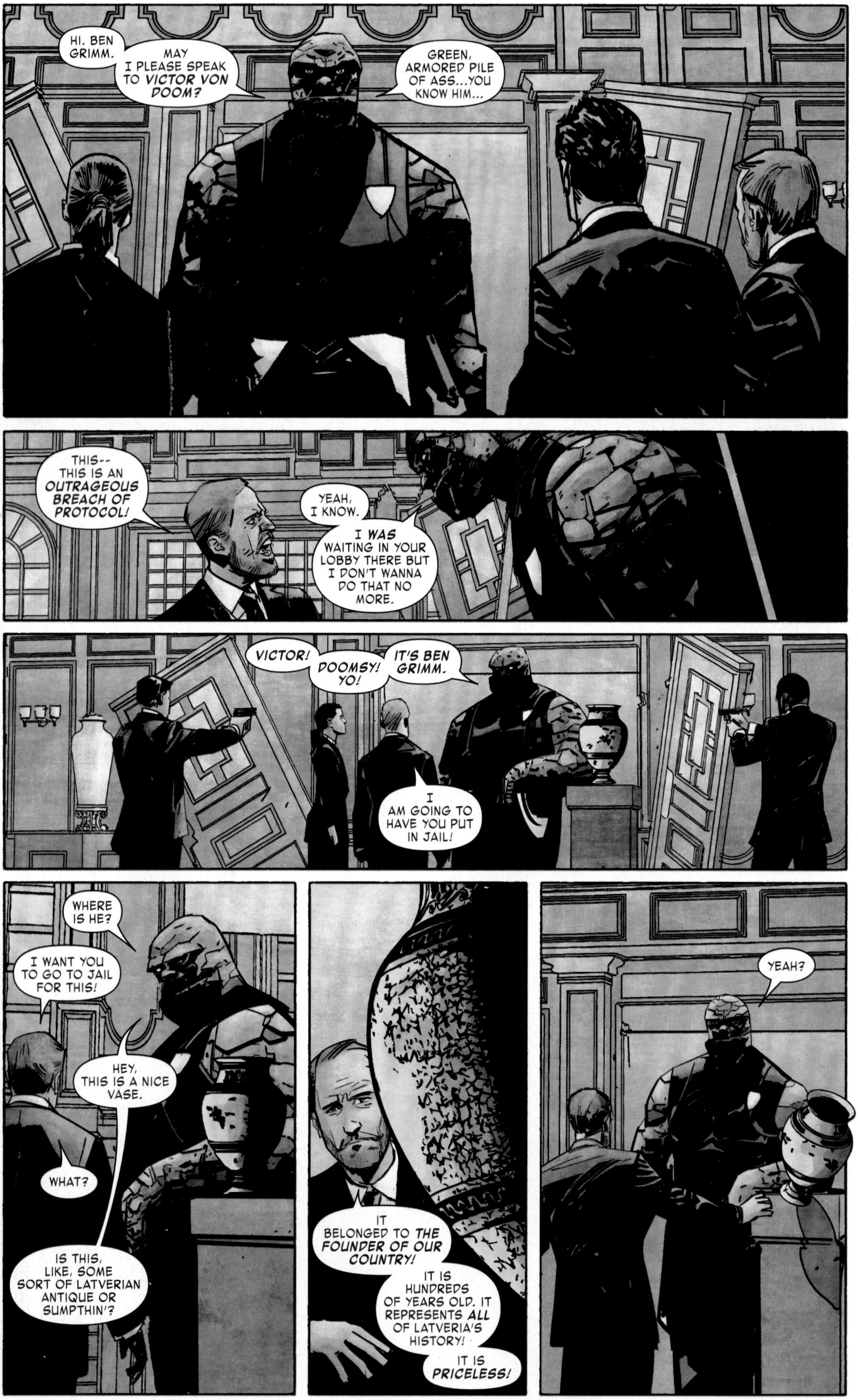
HI. BEN GRIMM.
MAY I PLEASE SPEAK TO VICTOR VON DOOM?
GREEN, ARMORED PILE OF ASS...YOU KNOW HIM...
THIS-- THIS IS AN OUTRAGEOUS BREACH OF PROTOCOL!
YEAH, I KNOW.
I WAS WAITING IN YOUR LOBBY THERE BUT I DON'T WANNA DO THAT NO MORE.
VICTOR!
DOOMSY! YO!
IT'S BEN GRIMM.
I AM GOING TO HAVE YOU PUT IN JAIL!
WHERE IS HE?
I WANT YOU TO GO TO JAIL FOR THIS!
HEY, THIS IS A NICE VASE.
WHAT?
IS THIS, LIKE, SOME SORT OF LATVERIAN ANTIQUE OR SUMPTHIN'?
IT BELONGED TO THE FOUNDER OF OUR COUNTRY!
IT IS HUNDREDS OF YEARS OLD. IT REPRESENTS ALL OF LATVERIA'S HISTORY!
IT IS PRICELESS!
YEAH?

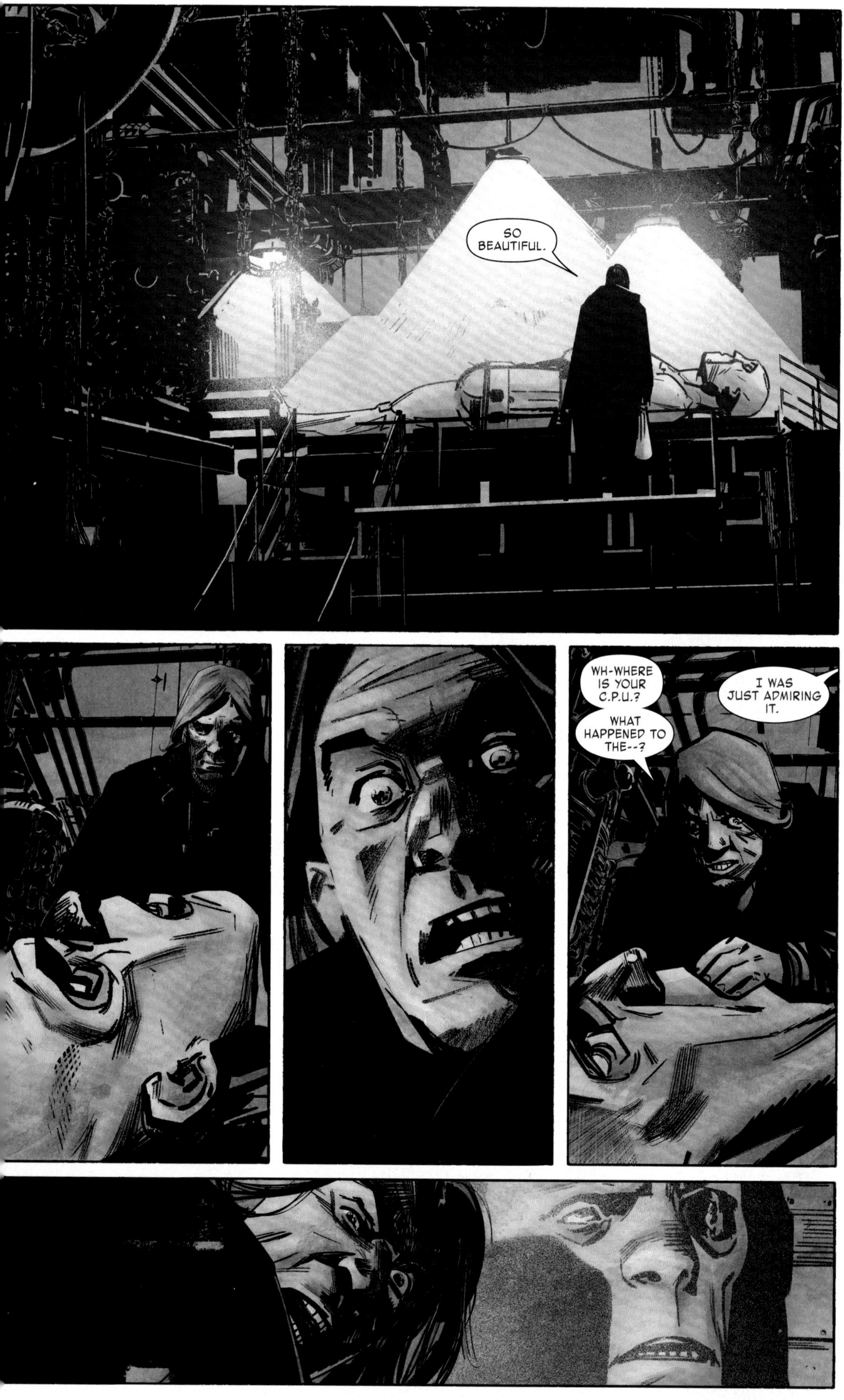

SO BEAUTIFUL.
WH-WHERE IS YOUR C.P.U.?
WHAT HAPPENED TO THE--?
I WAS JUST ADMIRING IT.

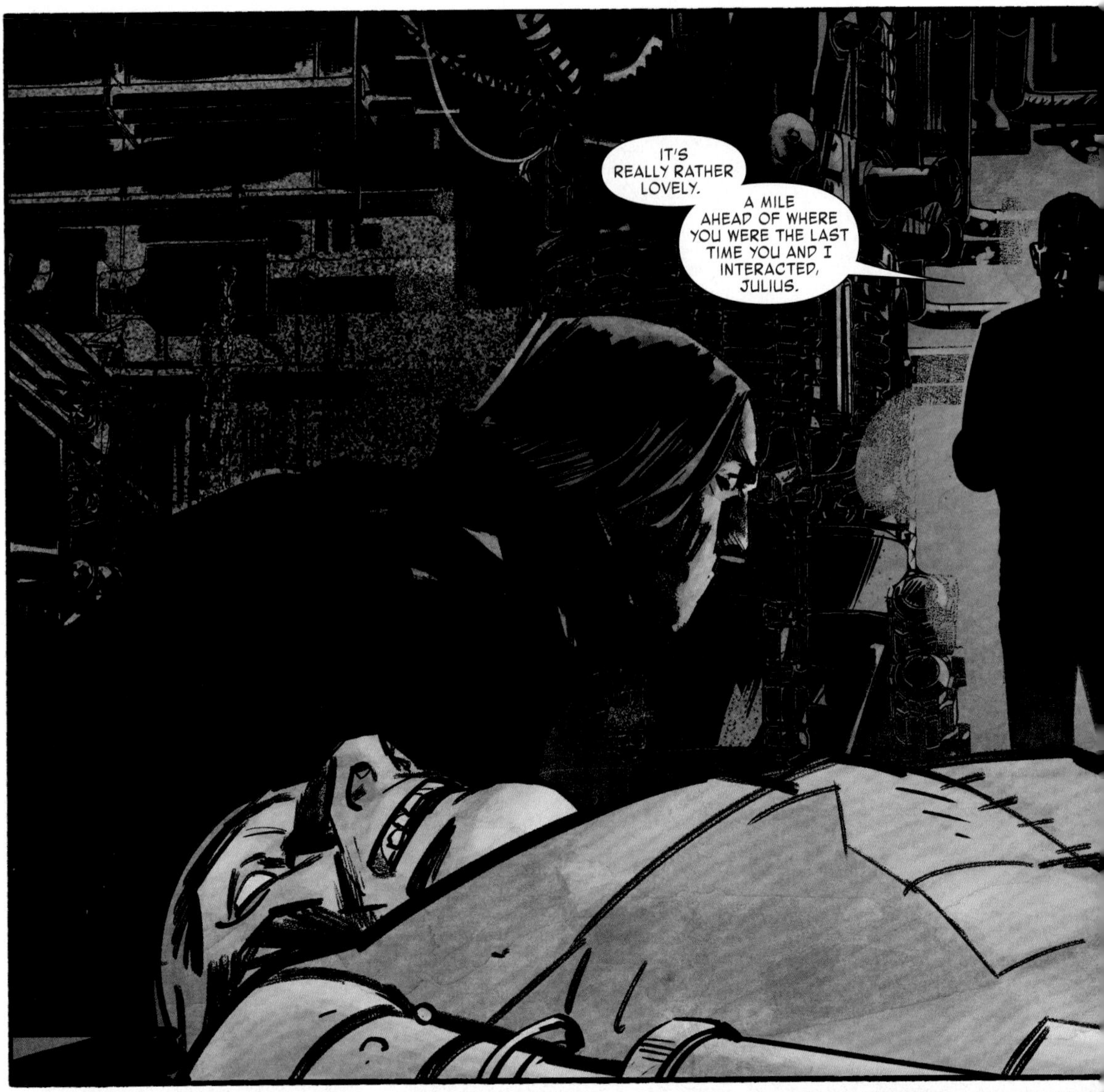
IT'S REALLY RATHER LOVELY.
A MILE AHEAD OF WHERE YOU WERE THE LAST TIME YOU AND I INTERACTED, JULIUS.

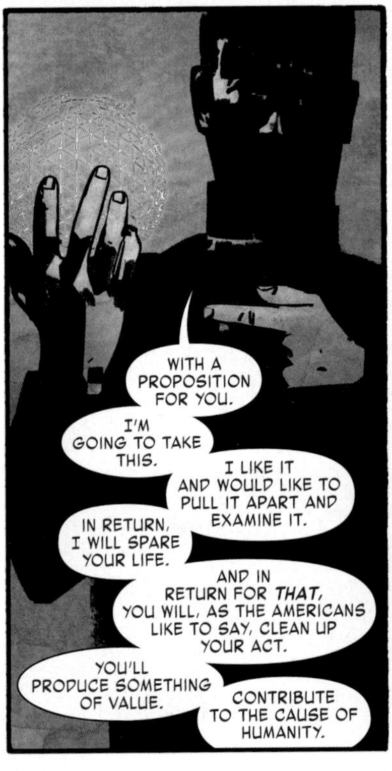
WITH A PROPOSITION FOR YOU.
I'M GOING TO TAKE THIS.
I LIKE IT AND WOULD LIKE TO PULL IT APART AND EXAMINE IT.
IN RETURN, I WILL SPARE YOUR LIFE.
AND IN RETURN FOR *THAT*, YOU WILL, AS THE AMERICANS LIKE TO SAY, CLEAN UP YOUR ACT.
YOU'LL PRODUCE SOMETHING OF VALUE.
CONTRIBUTE TO THE CAUSE OF HUMANITY.

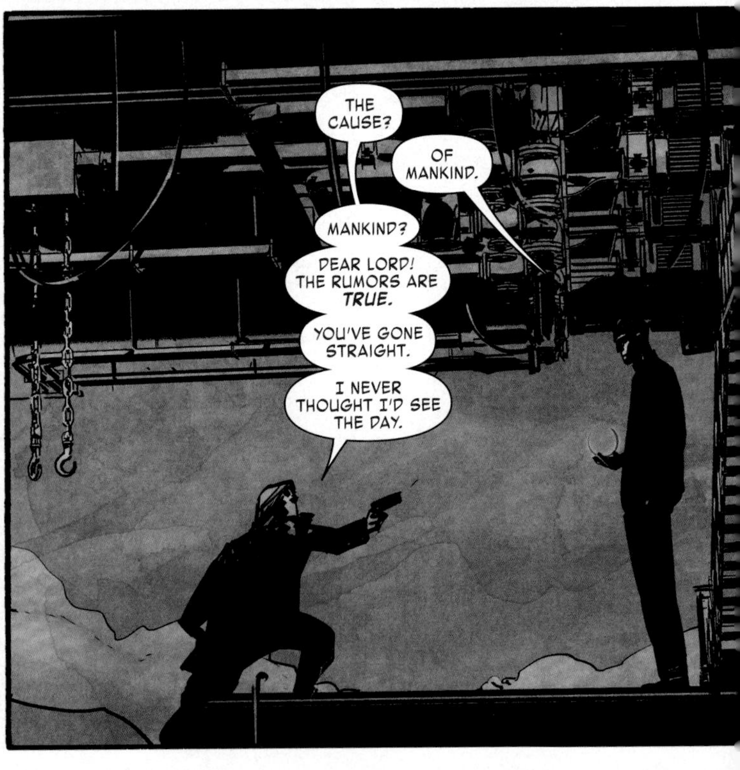
THE CAUSE?
OF MANKIND.
MANKIND?
DEAR LORD! THE RUMORS ARE *TRUE*.
YOU'VE GONE STRAIGHT.
I NEVER THOUGHT I'D SEE THE DAY.

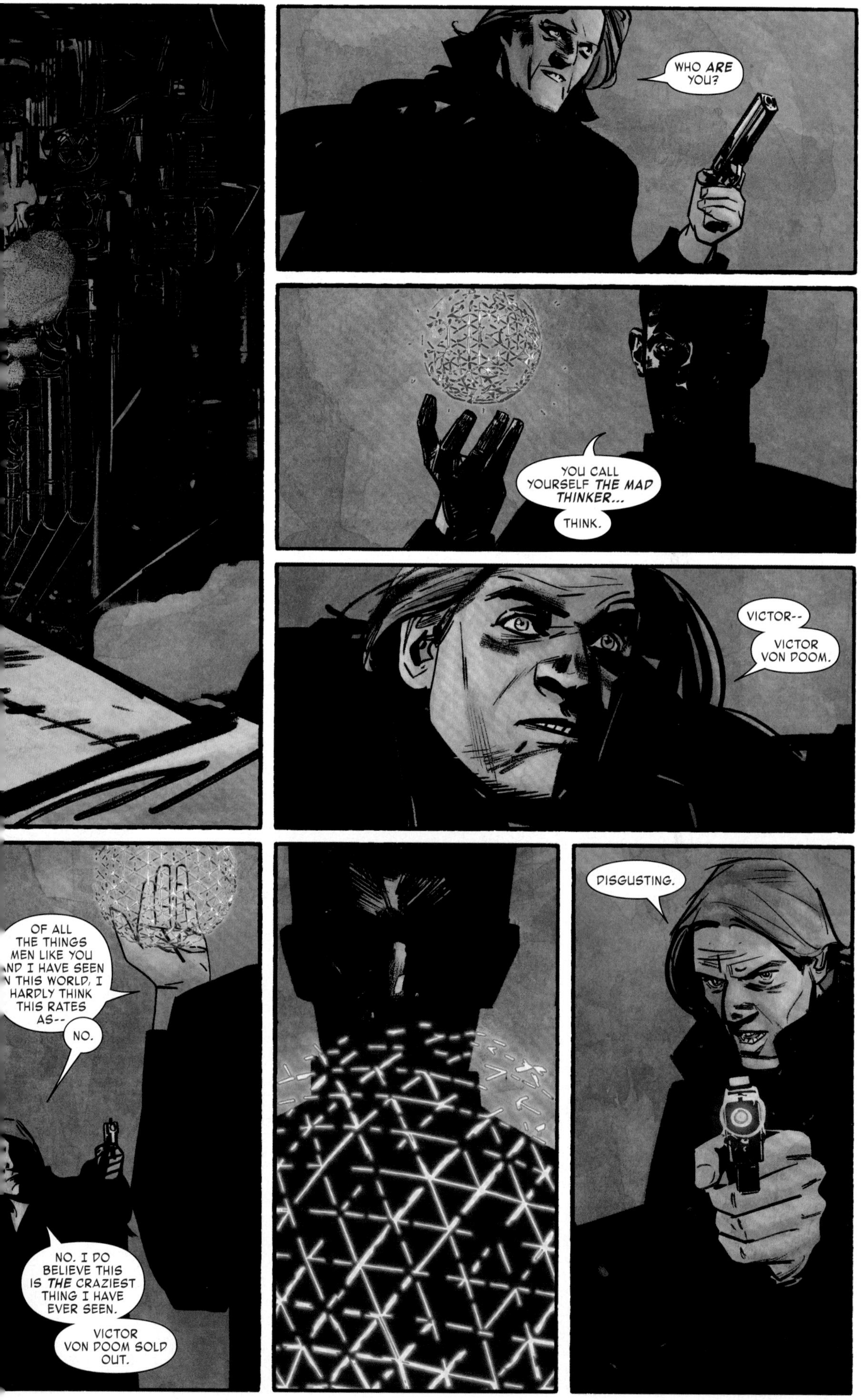
WHO *ARE* YOU?
YOU CALL YOURSELF *THE MAD THINKER...*
THINK.
VICTOR--
VICTOR VON DOOM.
OF ALL THE THINGS MEN LIKE YOU ND I HAVE SEEN N THIS WORLD, I HARDLY THINK THIS RATES AS--
NO.
NO. I DO BELIEVE THIS IS *THE* CRAZIEST THING I HAVE EVER SEEN.
VICTOR VON DOOM SOLD OUT.
DISGUSTING.

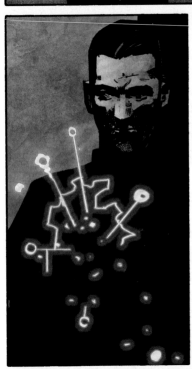

AGH!

HAVE YOU TAKEN THIS MOMENT TO RECONSIDER MY OFFER?

NAGH!

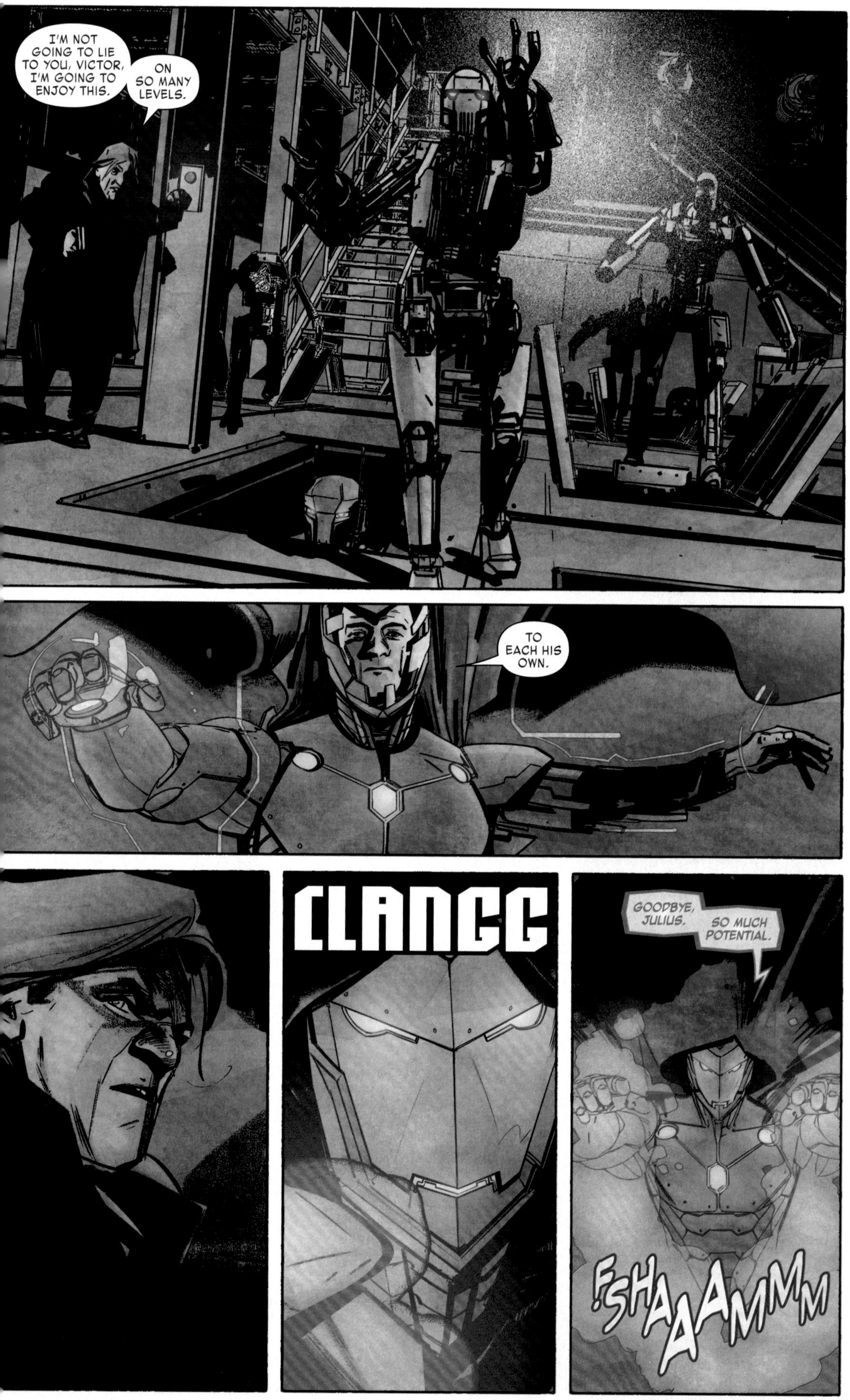
I'M NOT GOING TO LIE TO YOU, VICTOR, I'M GOING TO ENJOY THIS.
ON SO MANY LEVELS.
TO EACH HIS OWN.
CLANGG
GOODBYE, JULIUS.
SO MUCH POTENTIAL.
FSHAAAMMM

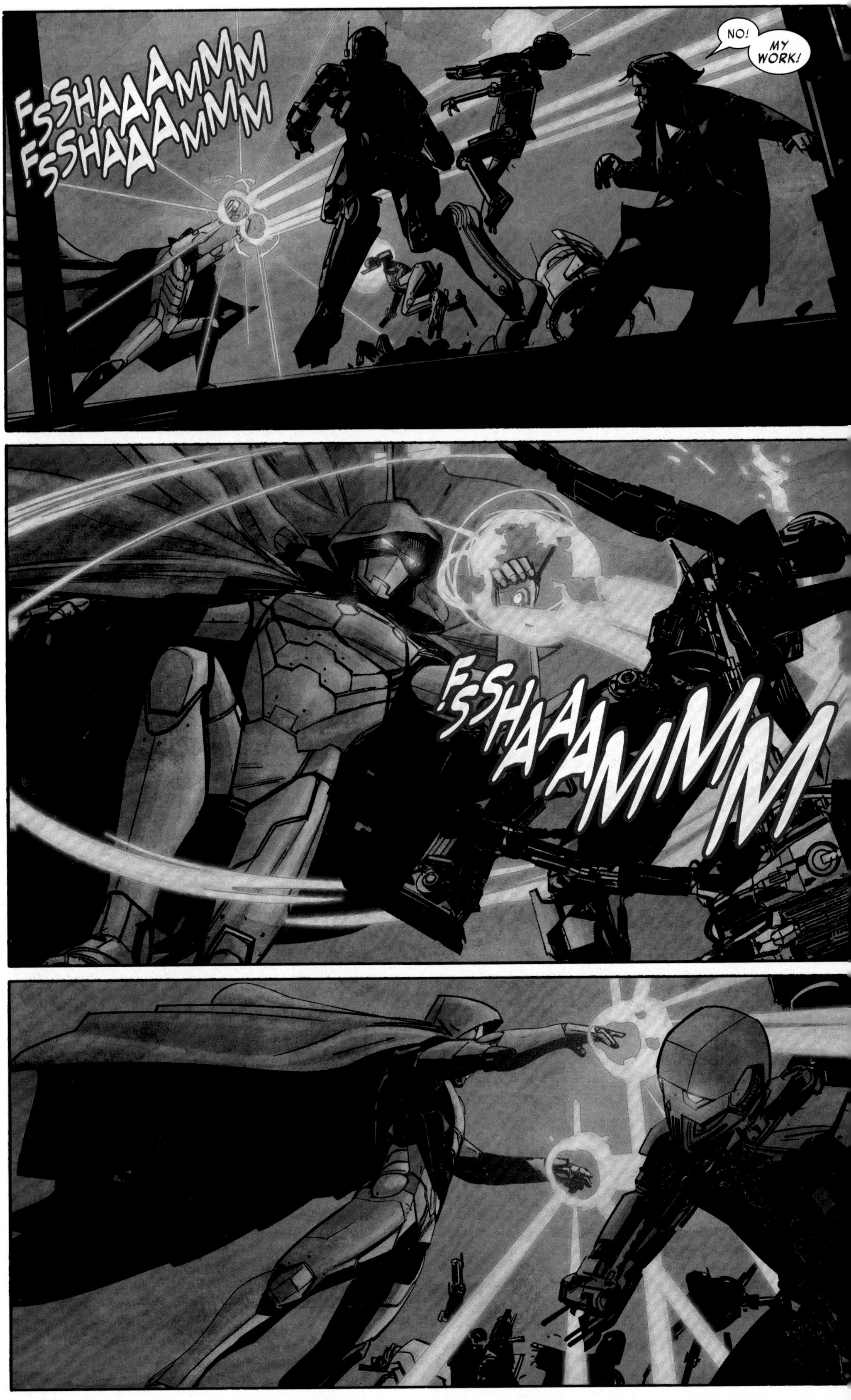
FSSHAAAMMMM
FSSHAAAMMMM
NO!
MY WORK!
FSSHAAAMMMM

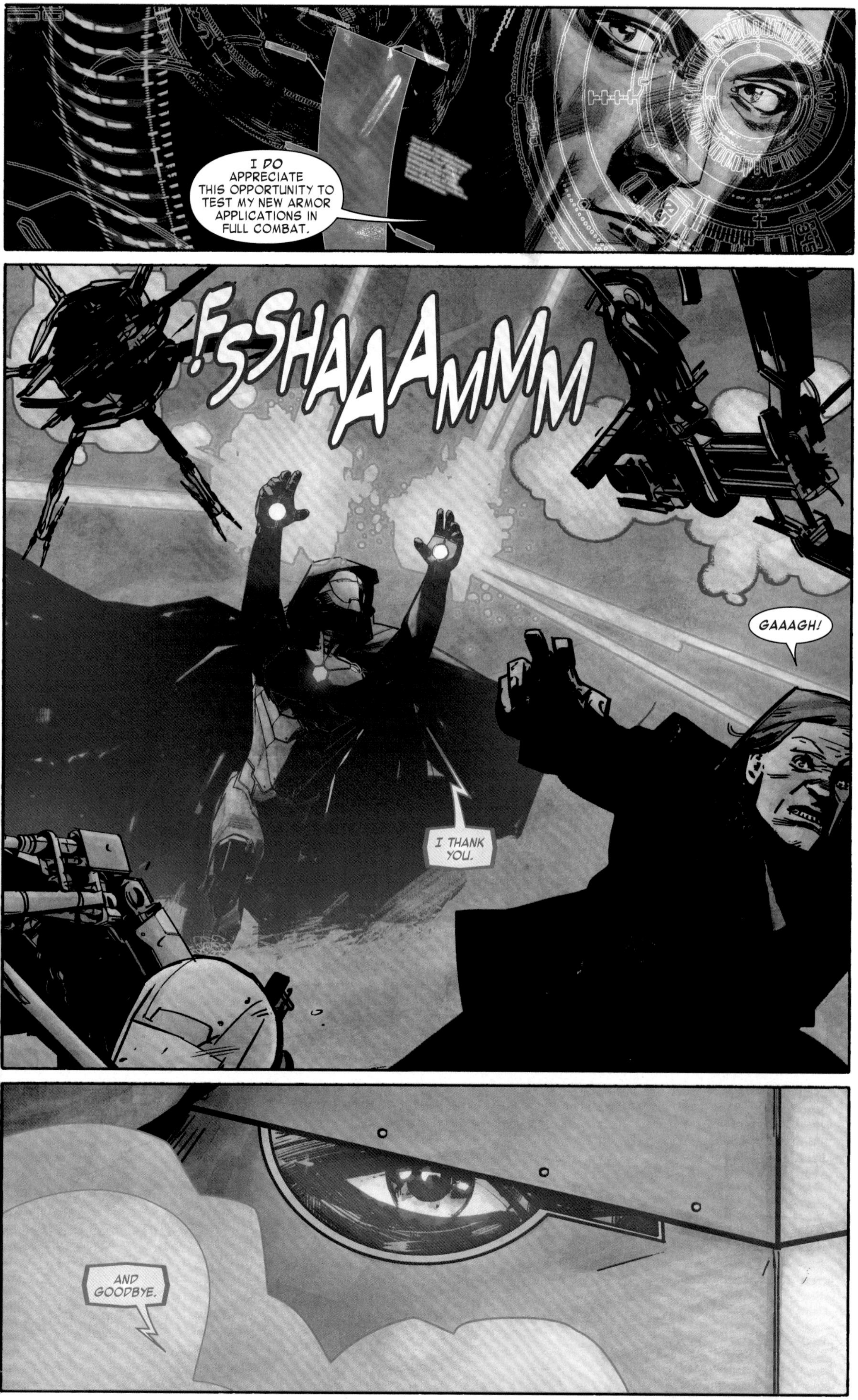
I DO APPRECIATE THIS OPPORTUNITY TO TEST MY NEW ARMOR APPLICATIONS IN FULL COMBAT.
FSSHAAAMMM
GAAAGH!
I THANK YOU.
AND GOODBYE.

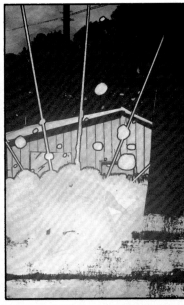

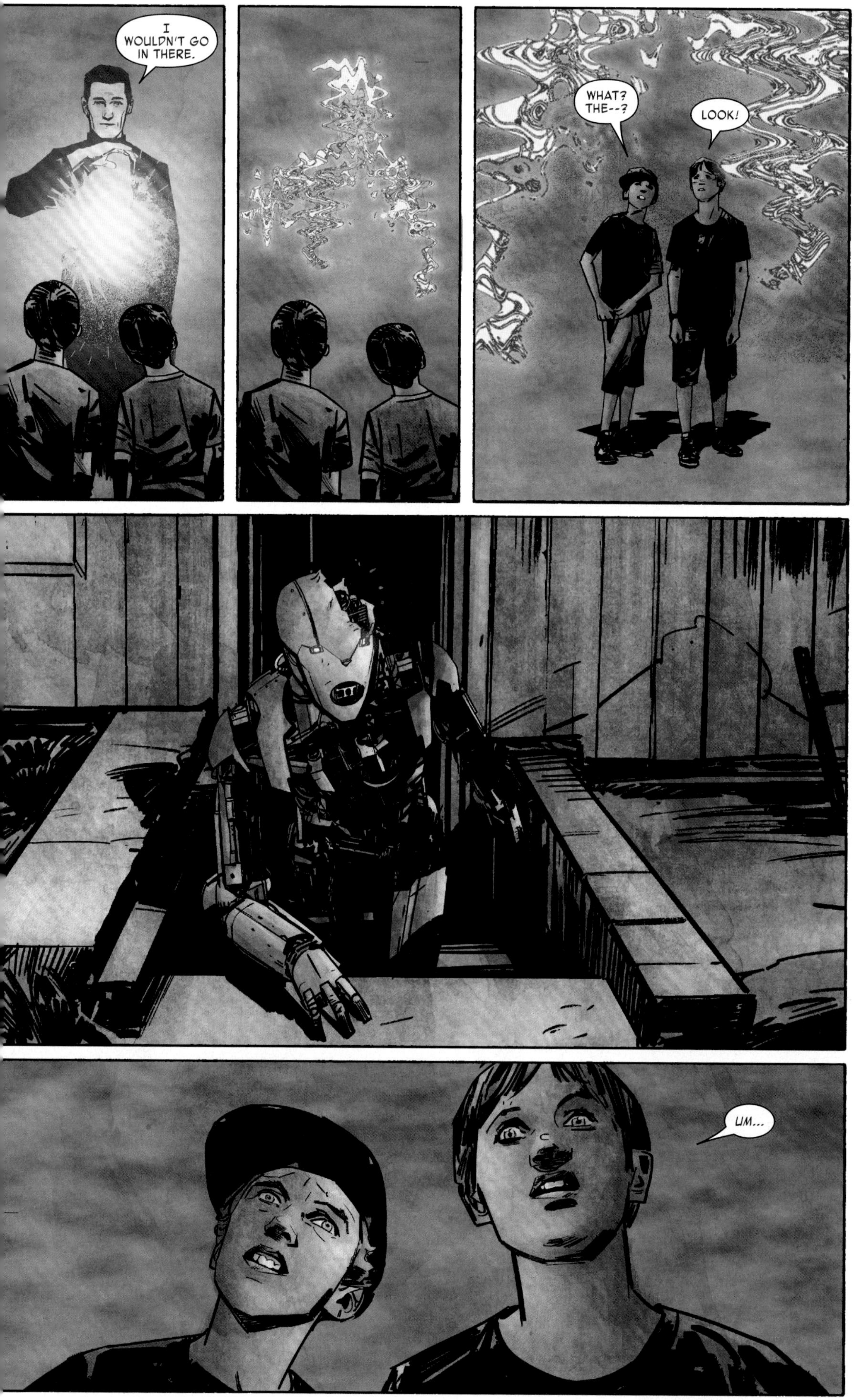
I WOULDN'T GO IN THERE.
WHAT? THE--?
LOOK!
UM...

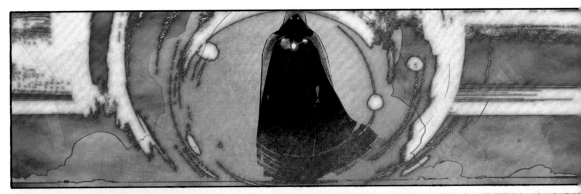

FSSHAAMM

BOOM

MY APOLOGIES.

MAKING SURE NO HARM WILL COME TO OTHERS IS RELATIVELY NEW TO ME.

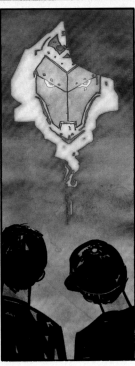

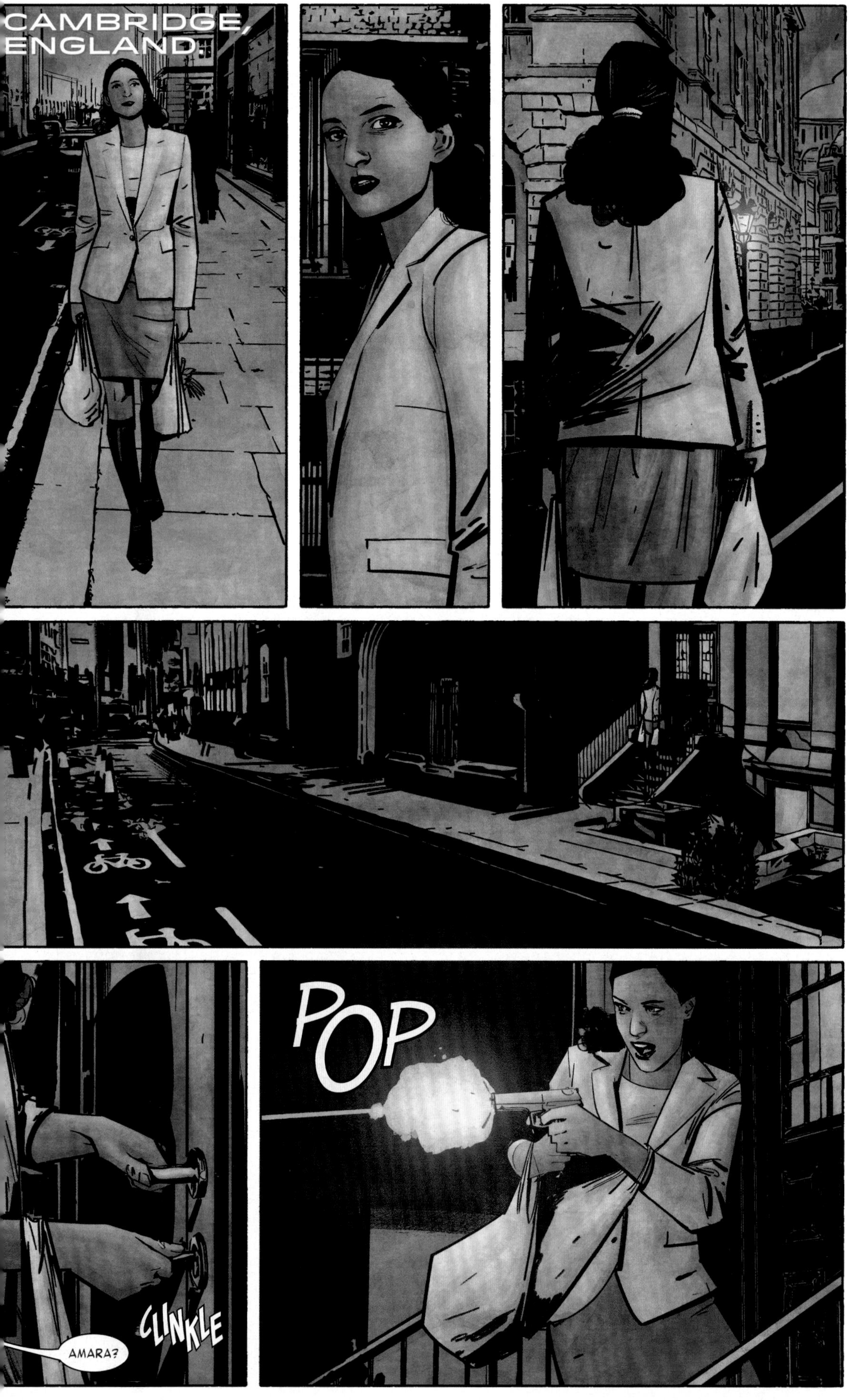
CAMBRIDGE, ENGLAND.
CLINKLE
AMARA?
POP

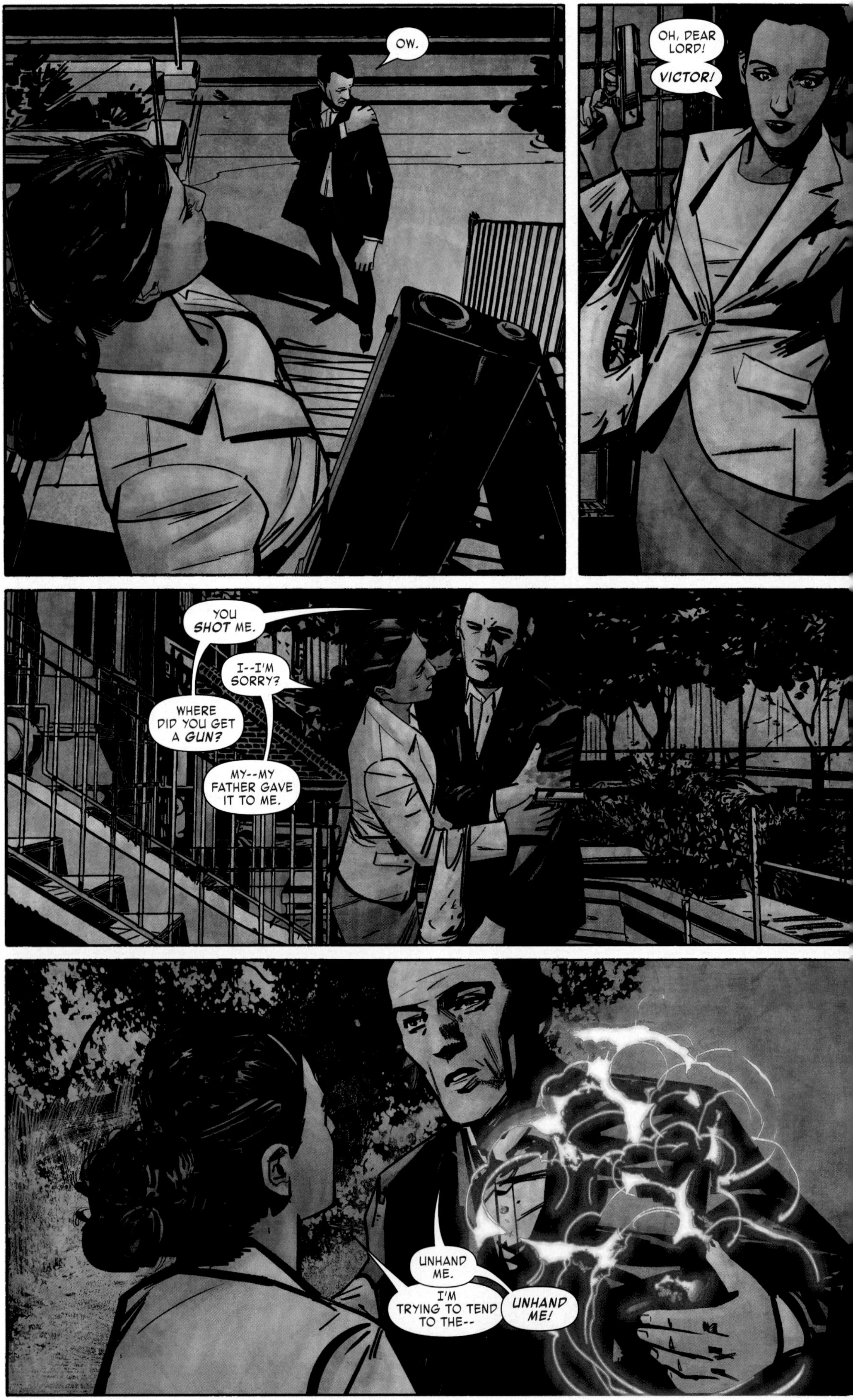
OW.
OH, DEAR LORD!
VICTOR!
YOU SHOT ME.
I--I'M SORRY?
WHERE DID YOU GET A GUN?
MY--MY FATHER GAVE IT TO ME.
UNHAND ME.
I'M TRYING TO TEND TO THE--
UNHAND ME!

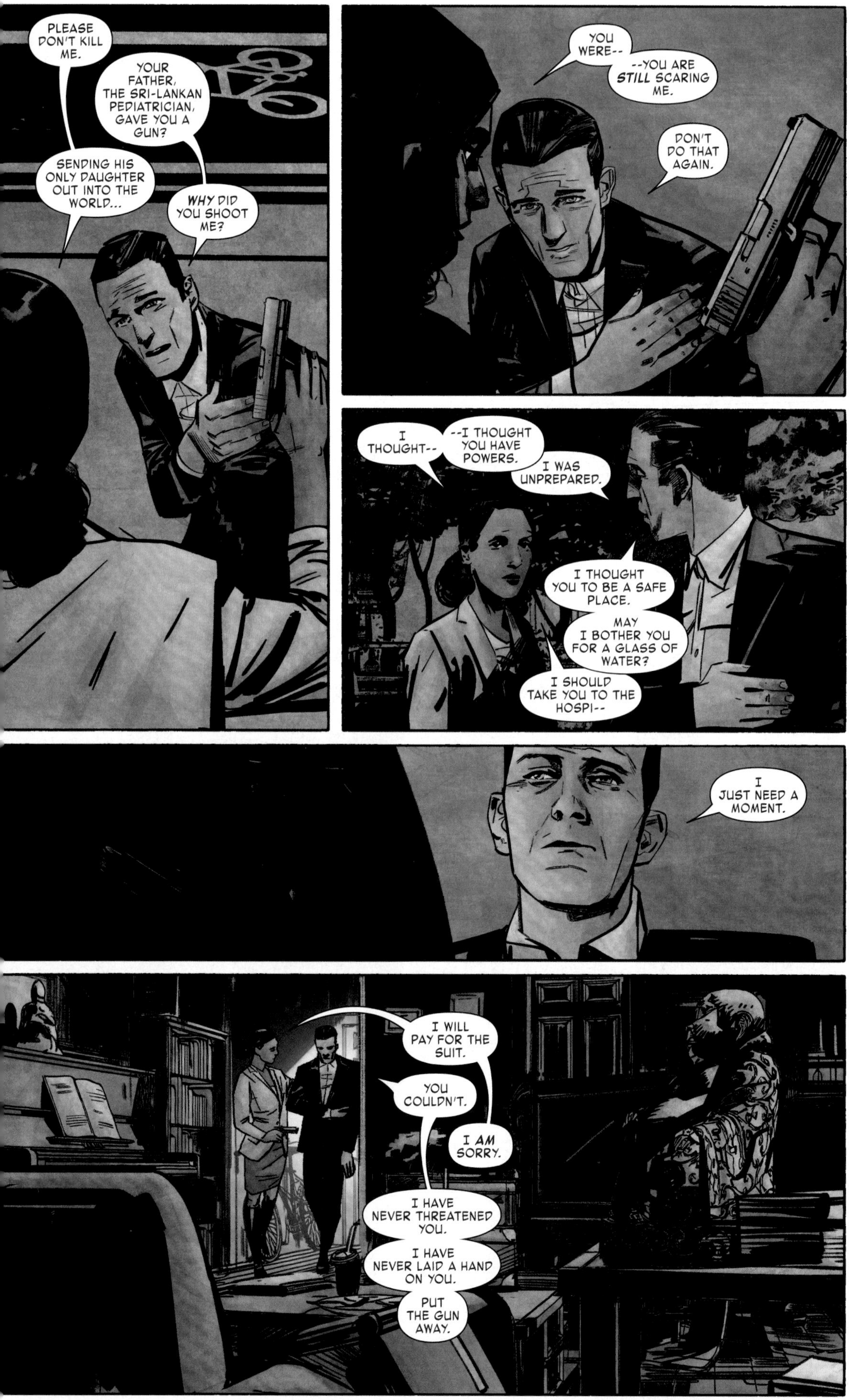
PLEASE DON'T KILL ME.
YOUR FATHER, THE SRI-LANKAN PEDIATRICIAN, GAVE YOU A GUN?
SENDING HIS ONLY DAUGHTER OUT INTO THE WORLD...
WHY DID YOU SHOOT ME?
YOU WERE--
--YOU ARE STILL SCARING ME.
DON'T DO THAT AGAIN.
I THOUGHT--
--I THOUGHT YOU HAVE POWERS.
I WAS UNPREPARED.
I THOUGHT YOU TO BE A SAFE PLACE.
MAY I BOTHER YOU FOR A GLASS OF WATER?
I SHOULD TAKE YOU TO THE HOSPI--
I JUST NEED A MOMENT.
I WILL PAY FOR THE SUIT.
YOU COULDN'T.
I AM SORRY.
I HAVE NEVER THREATENED YOU.
I HAVE NEVER LAID A HAND ON YOU.
PUT THE GUN AWAY.

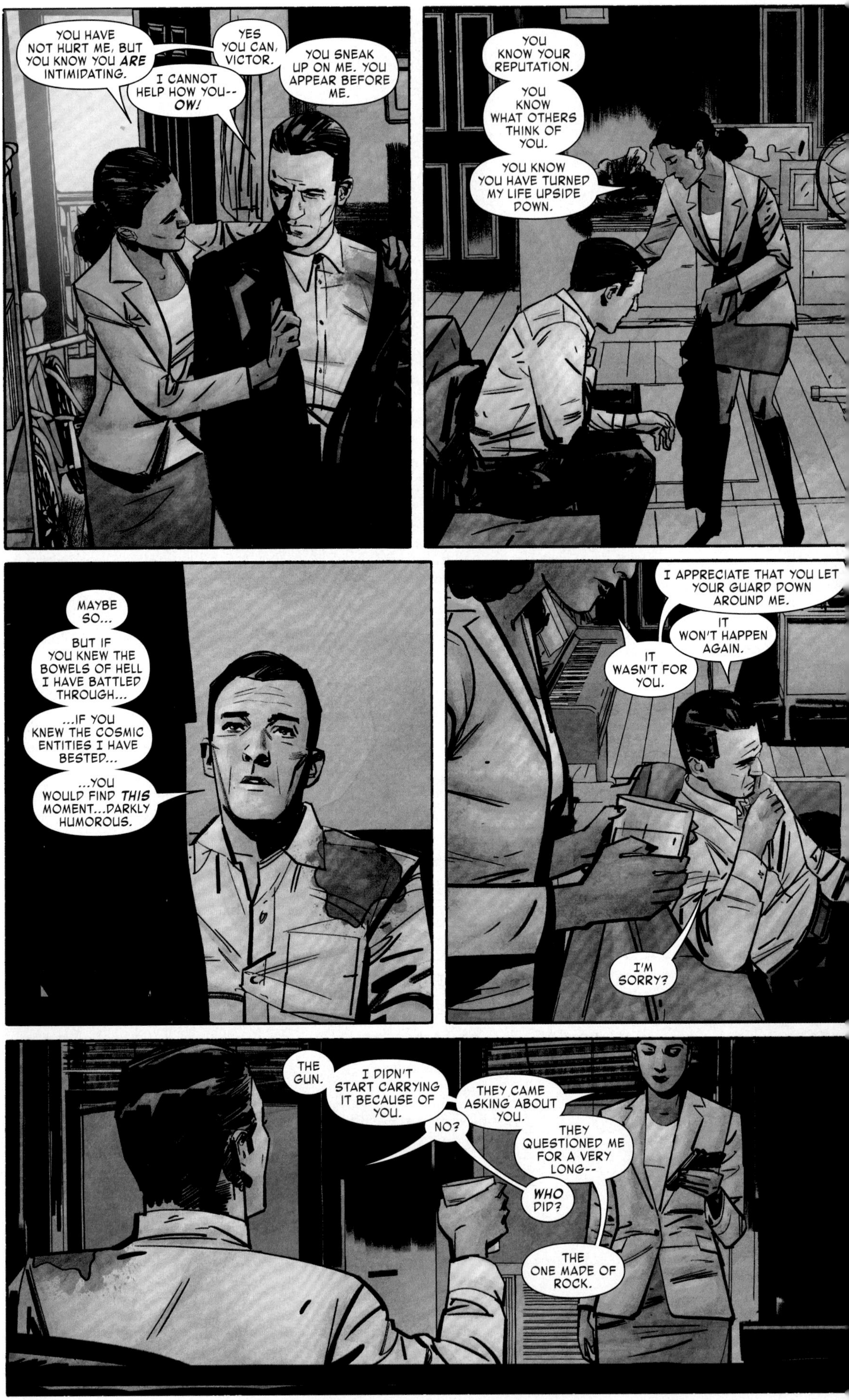
YOU HAVE NOT HURT ME, BUT YOU KNOW YOU ARE INTIMIDATING.
I CANNOT HELP HOW YOU-- OW!
YES YOU CAN, VICTOR.
YOU SNEAK UP ON ME. YOU APPEAR BEFORE ME.
YOU KNOW YOUR REPUTATION.
YOU KNOW WHAT OTHERS THINK OF YOU.
YOU KNOW YOU HAVE TURNED MY LIFE UPSIDE DOWN.
MAYBE SO...
BUT IF YOU KNEW THE BOWELS OF HELL I HAVE BATTLED THROUGH...
...IF YOU KNEW THE COSMIC ENTITIES I HAVE BESTED...
...YOU WOULD FIND THIS MOMENT...DARKLY HUMOROUS.
I APPRECIATE THAT YOU LET YOUR GUARD DOWN AROUND ME.
IT WON'T HAPPEN AGAIN.
IT WASN'T FOR YOU.
I'M SORRY?
THE GUN.
I DIDN'T START CARRYING IT BECAUSE OF YOU.
NO?
THEY CAME ASKING ABOUT YOU.
THEY QUESTIONED ME FOR A VERY LONG--
WHO DID?
THE ONE MADE OF ROCK.

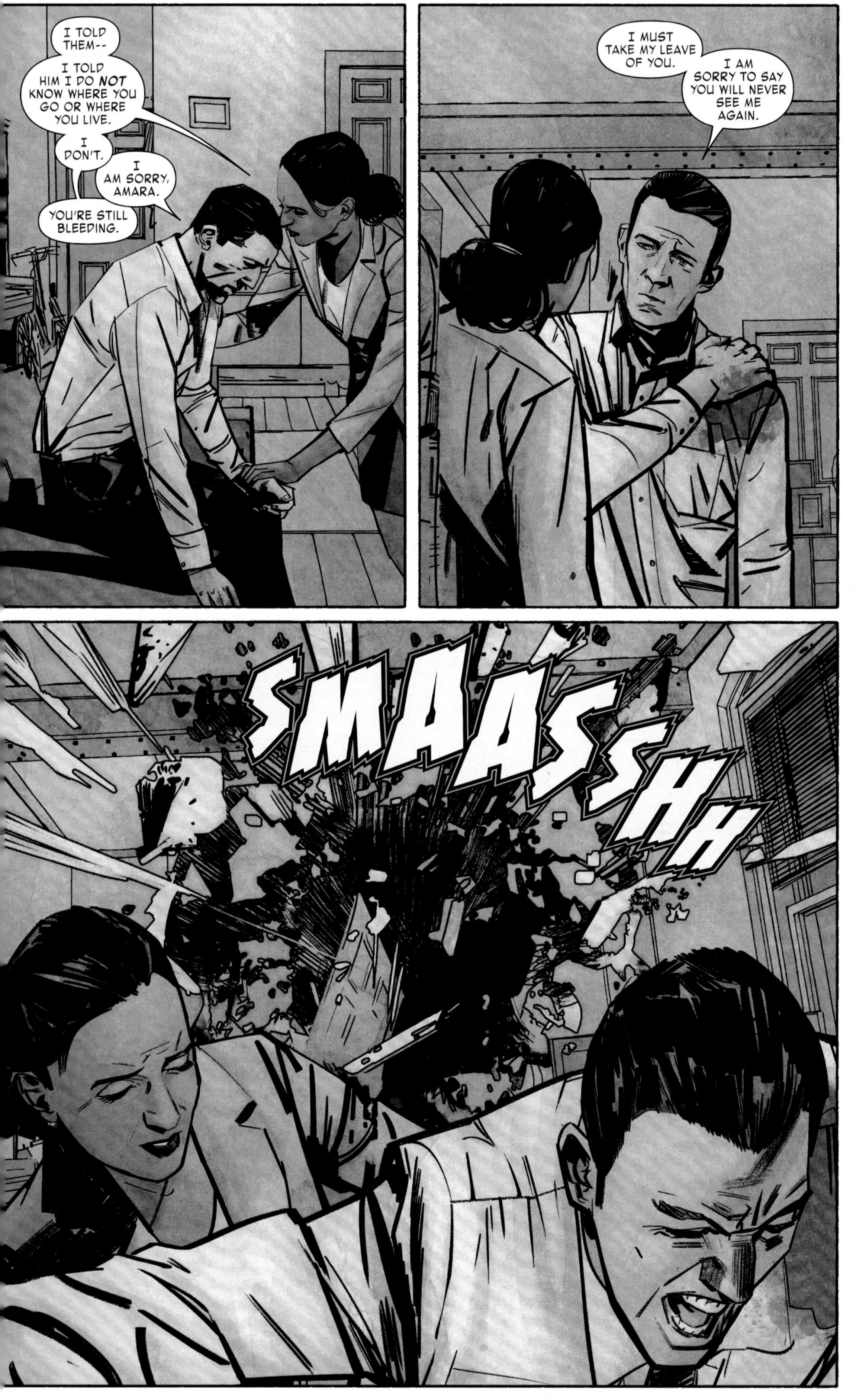
I TOLD THEM--
I TOLD HIM I DO NOT KNOW WHERE YOU GO OR WHERE YOU LIVE.
I DON'T.
I AM SORRY, AMARA.
YOU'RE STILL BLEEDING.
I MUST TAKE MY LEAVE OF YOU.
I AM SORRY TO SAY YOU WILL NEVER SEE ME AGAIN.
SMAASSHH

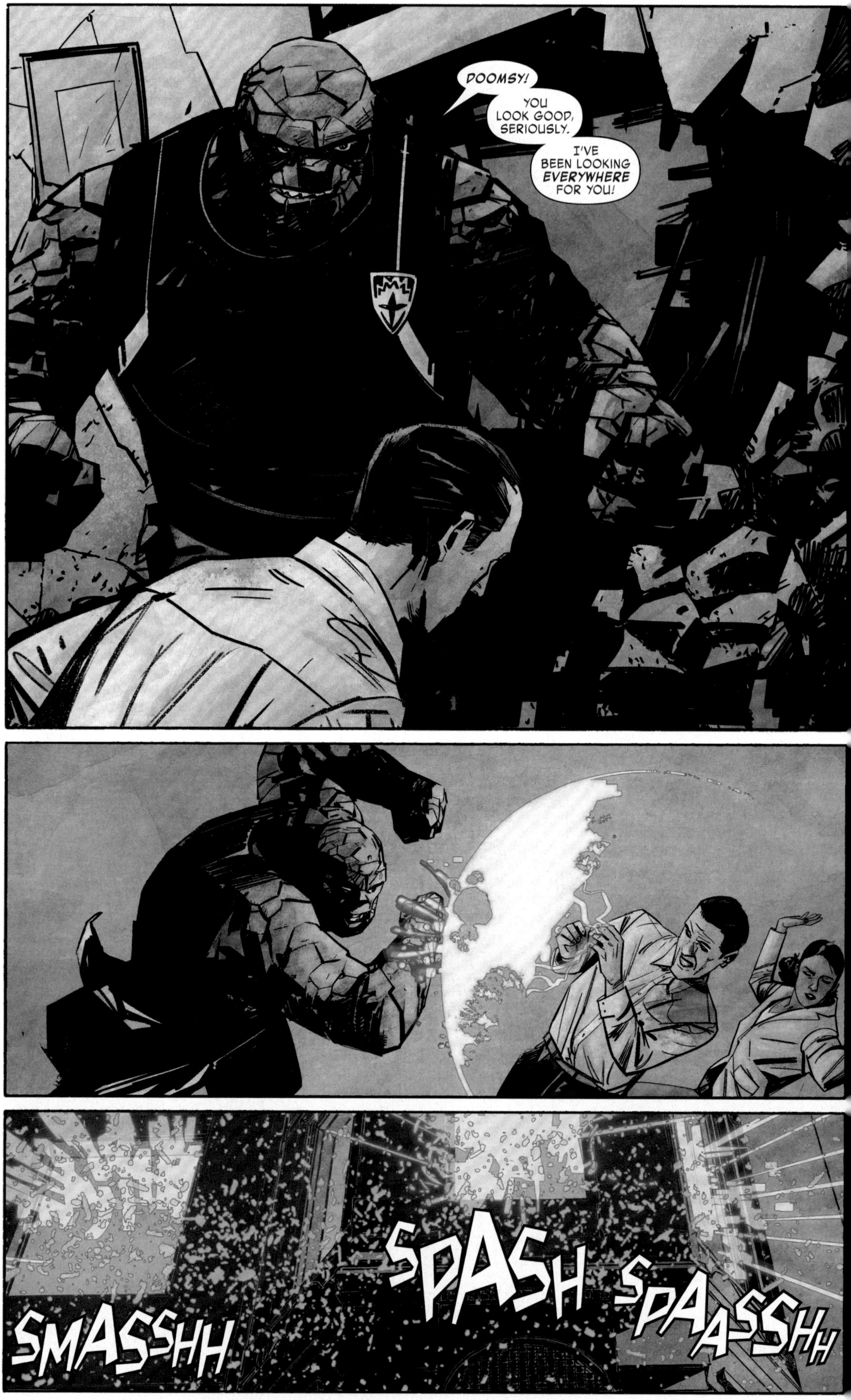
DOOMSY!
YOU LOOK GOOD, SERIOUSLY.
I'VE BEEN LOOKING EVERYWHERE FOR YOU!
SMASSHH
SPASH
SPAASSHH

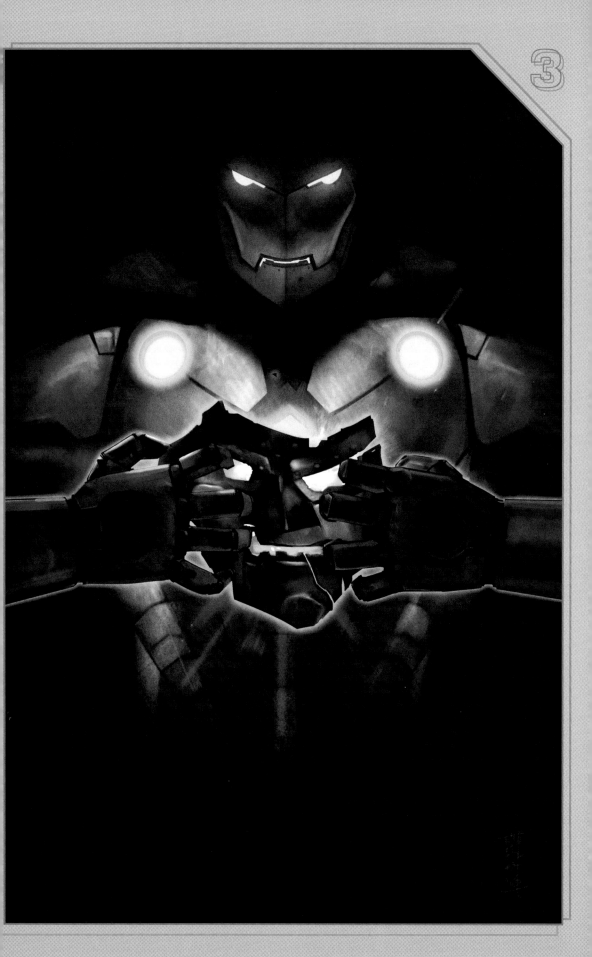

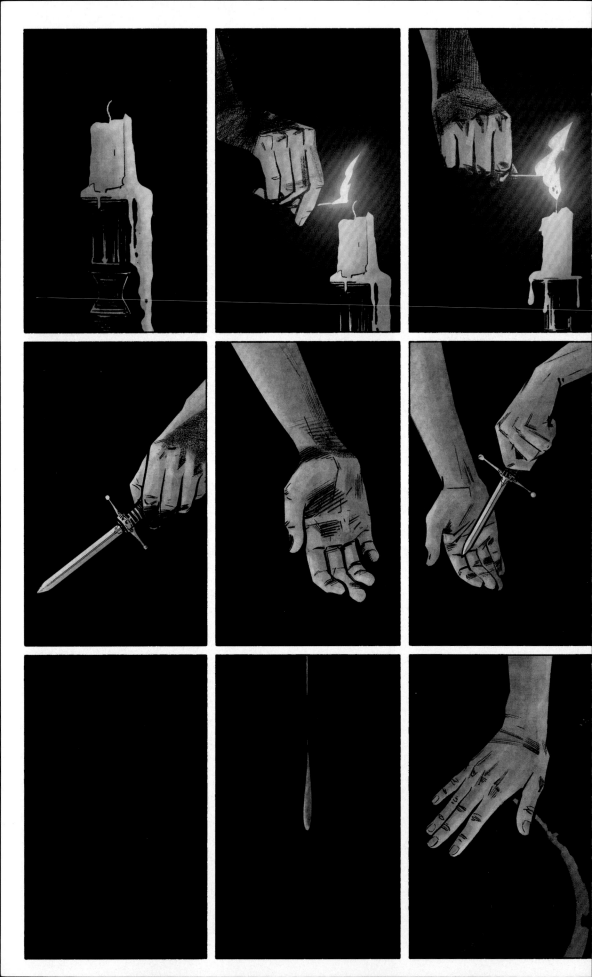

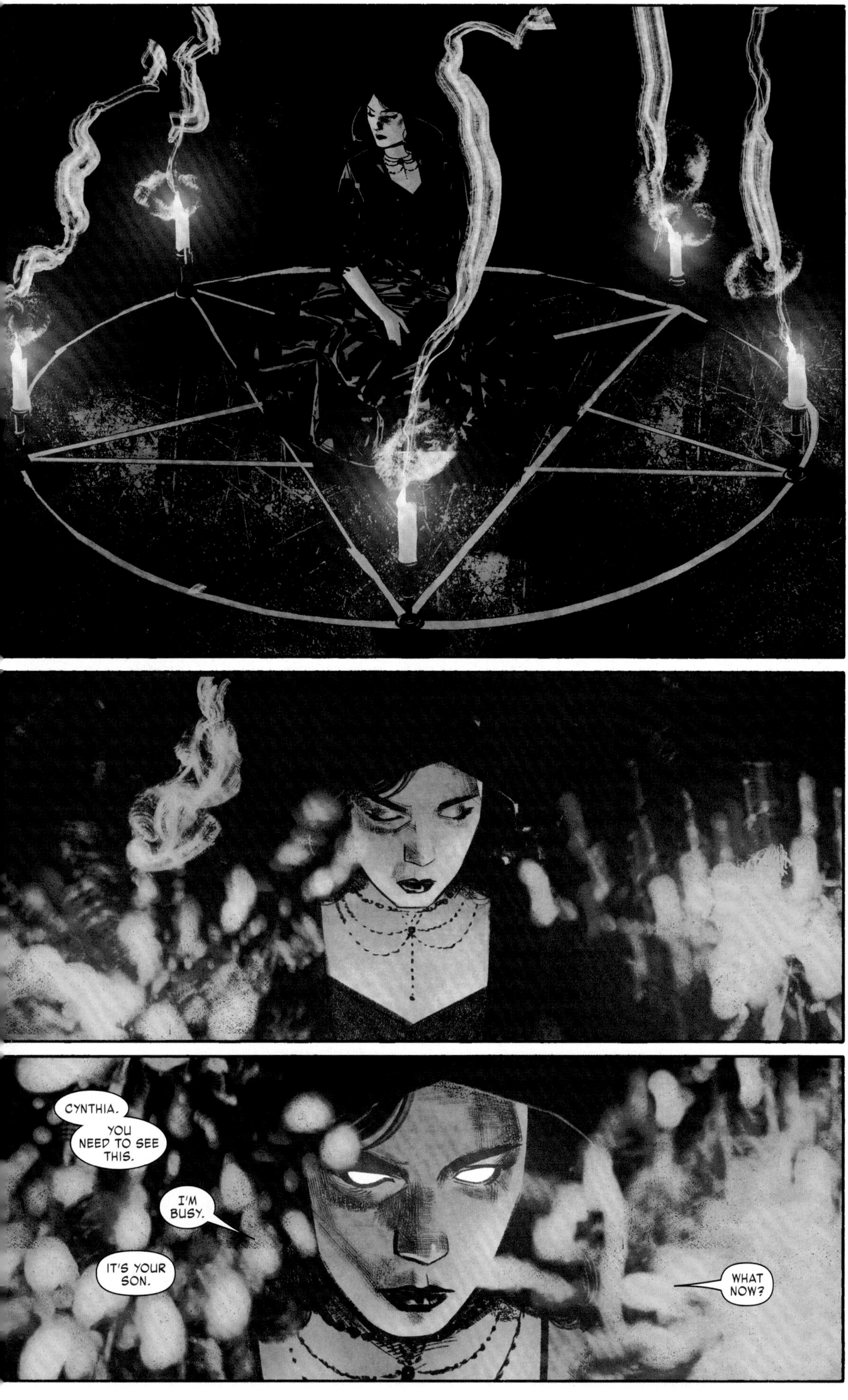
CYNTHIA.
YOU NEED TO SEE THIS.
I'M BUSY.
IT'S YOUR SON.
WHAT NOW?

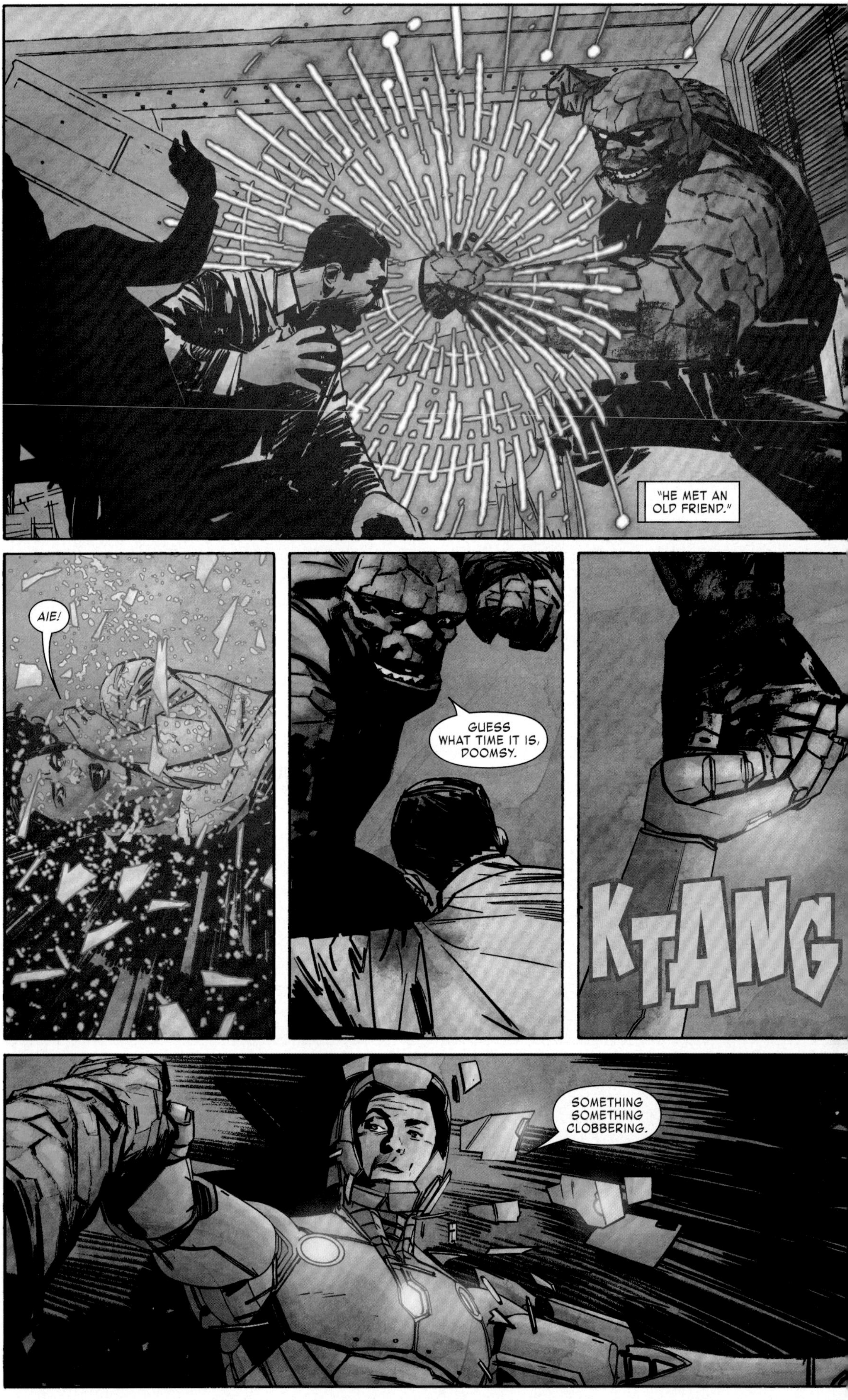
"HE MET AN OLD FRIEND."
AIE!
GUESS WHAT TIME IT IS, DOOMSY.
KTANG
SOMETHING SOMETHING CLOBBERING.

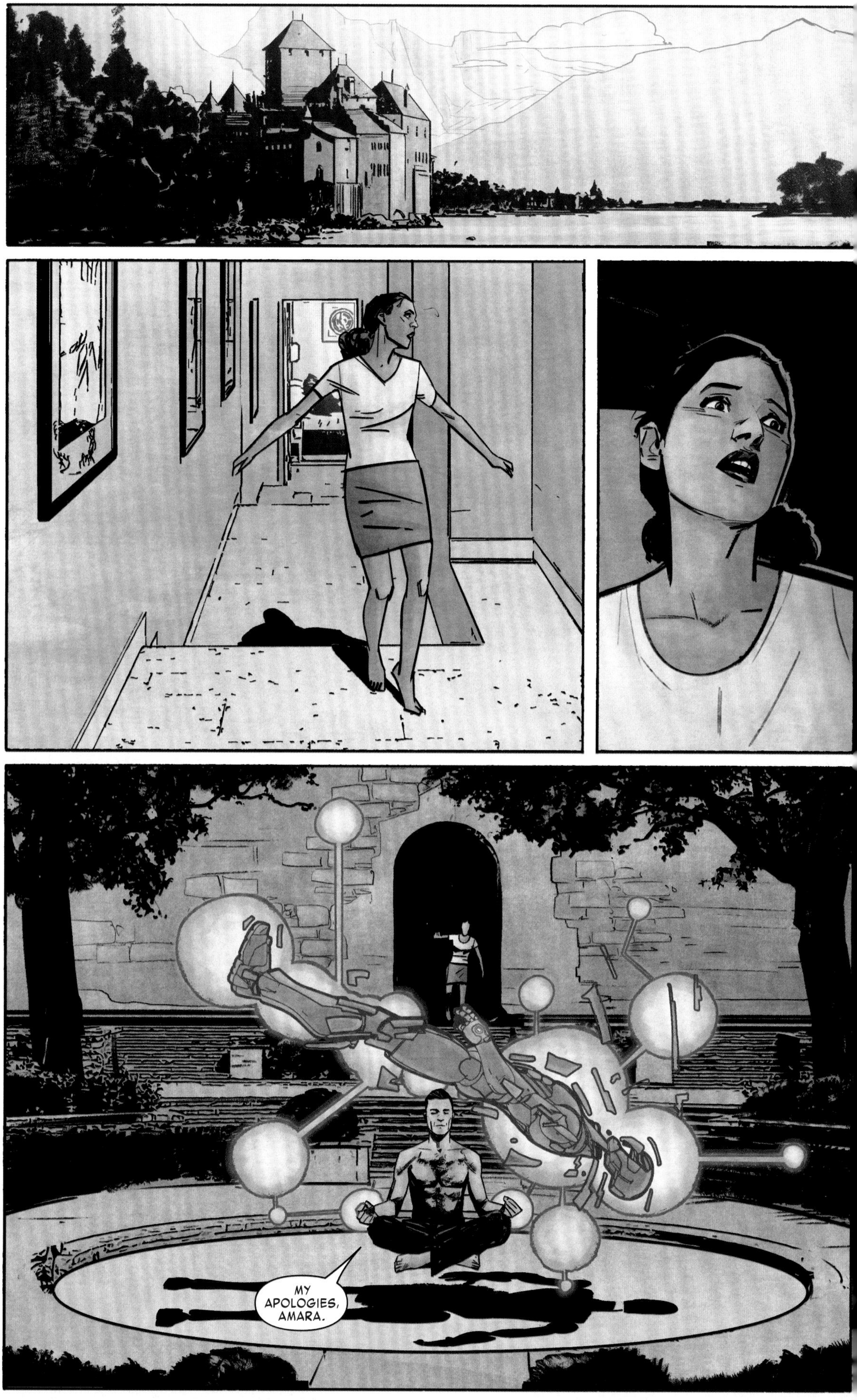
MY APOLOGIES, AMARA.

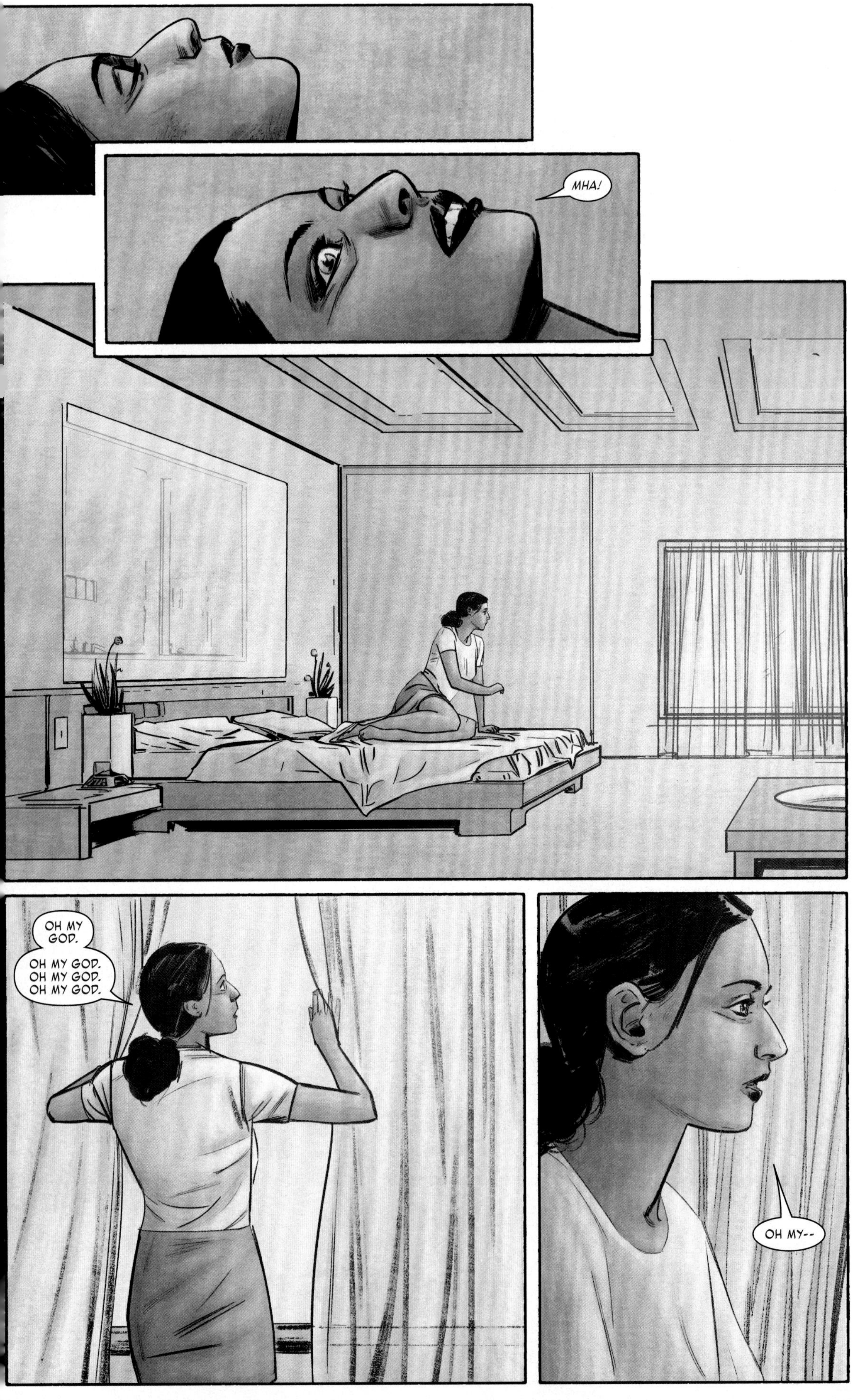
MHA!
OH MY GOD.
OH MY GOD. OH MY GOD. OH MY GOD.
OH MY--

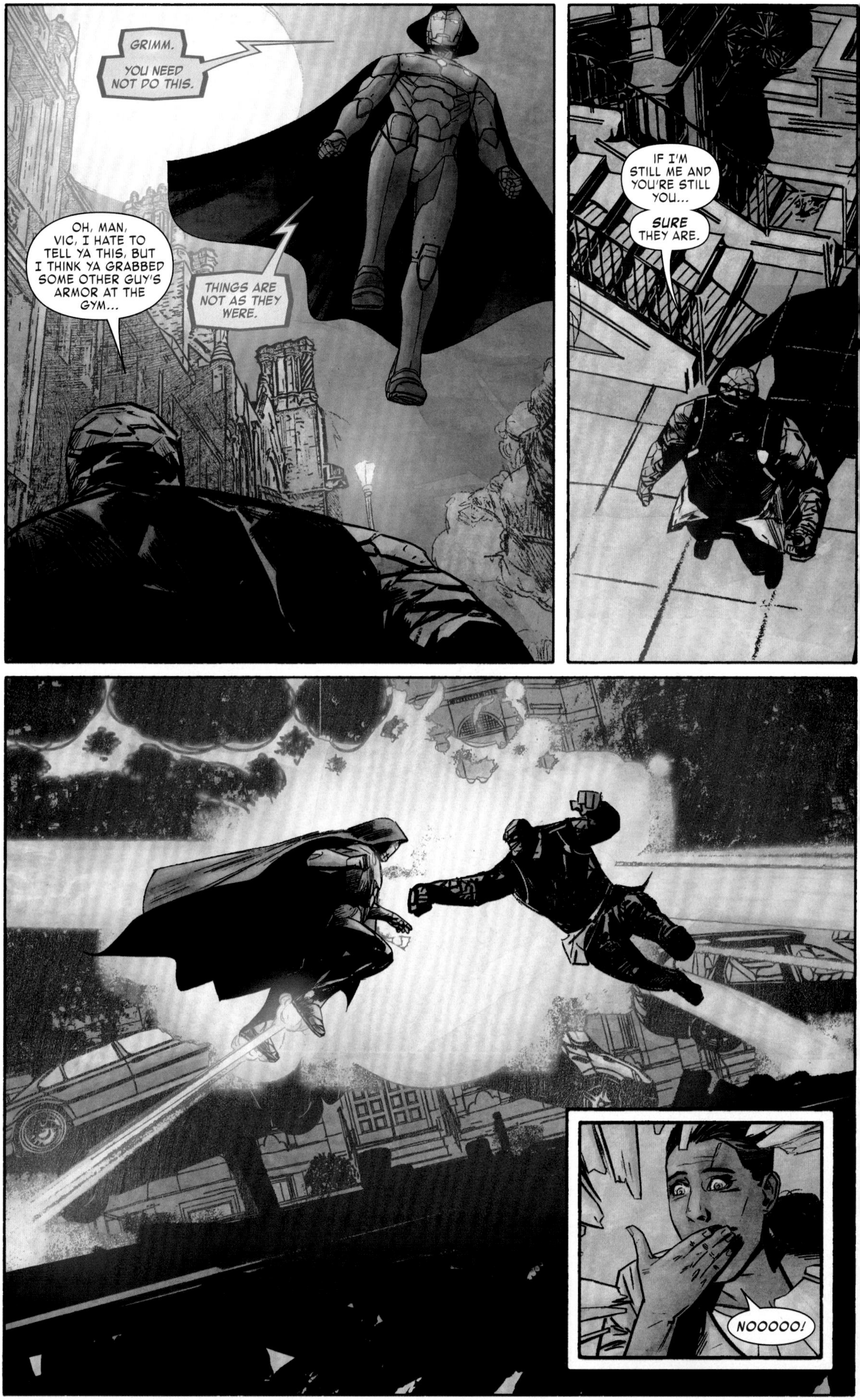
GRIMM.
YOU NEED NOT DO THIS.
OH, MAN, VIC, I HATE TO TELL YA THIS, BUT I THINK YA GRABBED SOME OTHER GUY'S ARMOR AT THE GYM...
THINGS ARE NOT AS THEY WERE.
IF I'M STILL ME AND YOU'RE STILL YOU...
SURE THEY ARE.
NOOOOO!

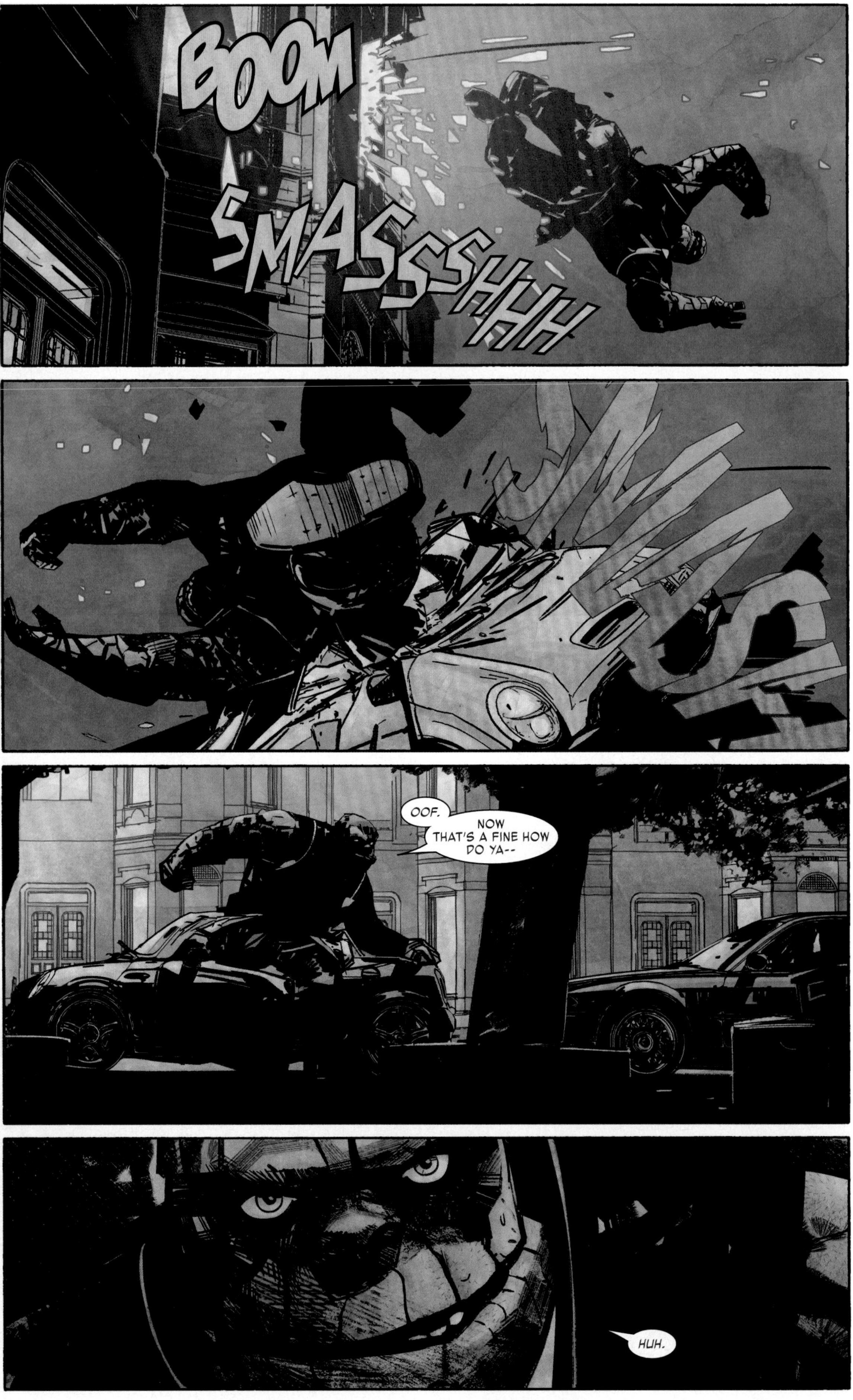
BOOM
SMASSSHHH
OOF.
NOW THAT'S A FINE HOW DO YA--
HUH.

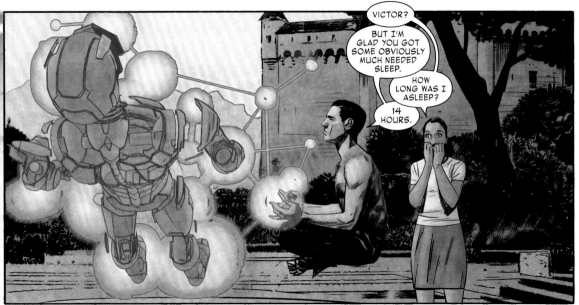

VICTOR?

BUT I'M GLAD YOU GOT SOME OBVIOUSLY MUCH NEEDED SLEEP.

HOW LONG WAS I ASLEEP?

14 HOURS.

WHAT?! WHAT *DAY* IS IT?

WHERE AM I?

YOU ARE SAFE. THIS IS MY HOME.

WHERE *AM* I, VICTOR?

SAFE.

I DEMAND YOU TAKE ME BACK! I *DEMAND* IT!

THERE'S NOTHING BACK THERE FOR YOU.

WAIT!

I WAS-- YOU WERE FIGHTING THE--THE *THING* MAN. MY APARTMENT.

I'M SORRY ABOUT YOUR THINGS.

I KNOW WHAT IT FEELS LIKE TO LOSE EVERYTHING YOU OWN.

YOU *TRASHED* MY HOUSE AND THEN YOU KIDNAPPED ME?

OR...

...I DEFENDED YOUR HOME AND THEN RESCUED YOU FROM ANY HARM.

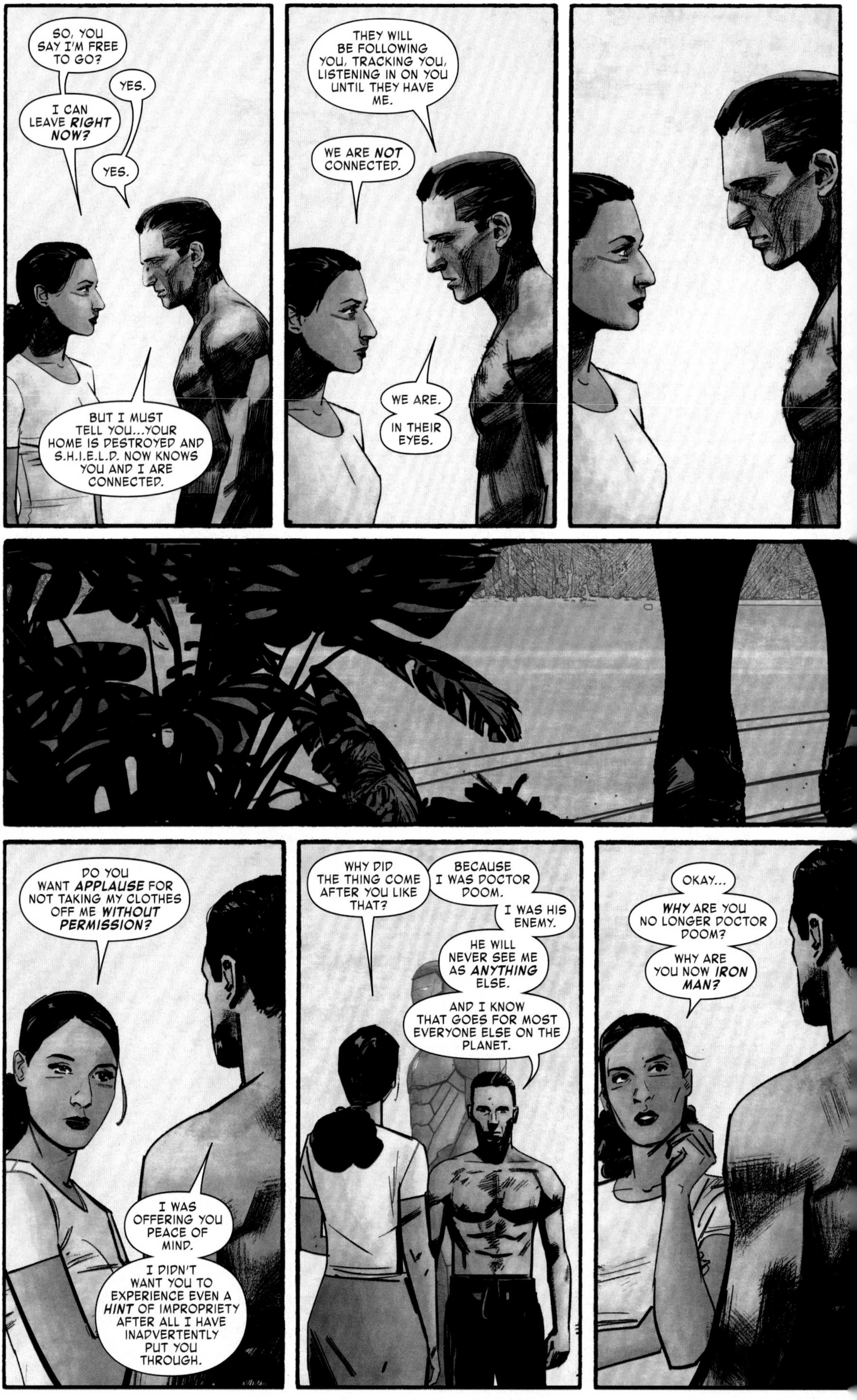
SO, YOU SAY I'M FREE TO GO?
YES.
I CAN LEAVE **RIGHT NOW?**
YES.
BUT I MUST TELL YOU...YOUR HOME IS DESTROYED AND S.H.I.E.L.D. NOW KNOWS YOU AND I ARE CONNECTED.
THEY WILL BE FOLLOWING YOU, TRACKING YOU, LISTENING IN ON YOU UNTIL THEY HAVE ME.
WE ARE **NOT** CONNECTED.
WE ARE.
IN THEIR EYES.
DO YOU WANT **APPLAUSE** FOR NOT TAKING MY CLOTHES OFF ME **WITHOUT PERMISSION?**
I WAS OFFERING YOU PEACE OF MIND.
I DIDN'T WANT YOU TO EXPERIENCE EVEN A **HINT** OF IMPROPRIETY AFTER ALL I HAVE INADVERTENTLY PUT YOU THROUGH.
WHY DID THE THING COME AFTER YOU LIKE THAT?
BECAUSE I WAS DOCTOR DOOM.
I WAS HIS ENEMY.
HE WILL NEVER SEE ME AS **ANYTHING** ELSE.
AND I KNOW THAT GOES FOR MOST EVERYONE ELSE ON THE PLANET.
OKAY...
WHY ARE YOU NO LONGER DOCTOR DOOM?
WHY ARE YOU NOW **IRON MAN?**

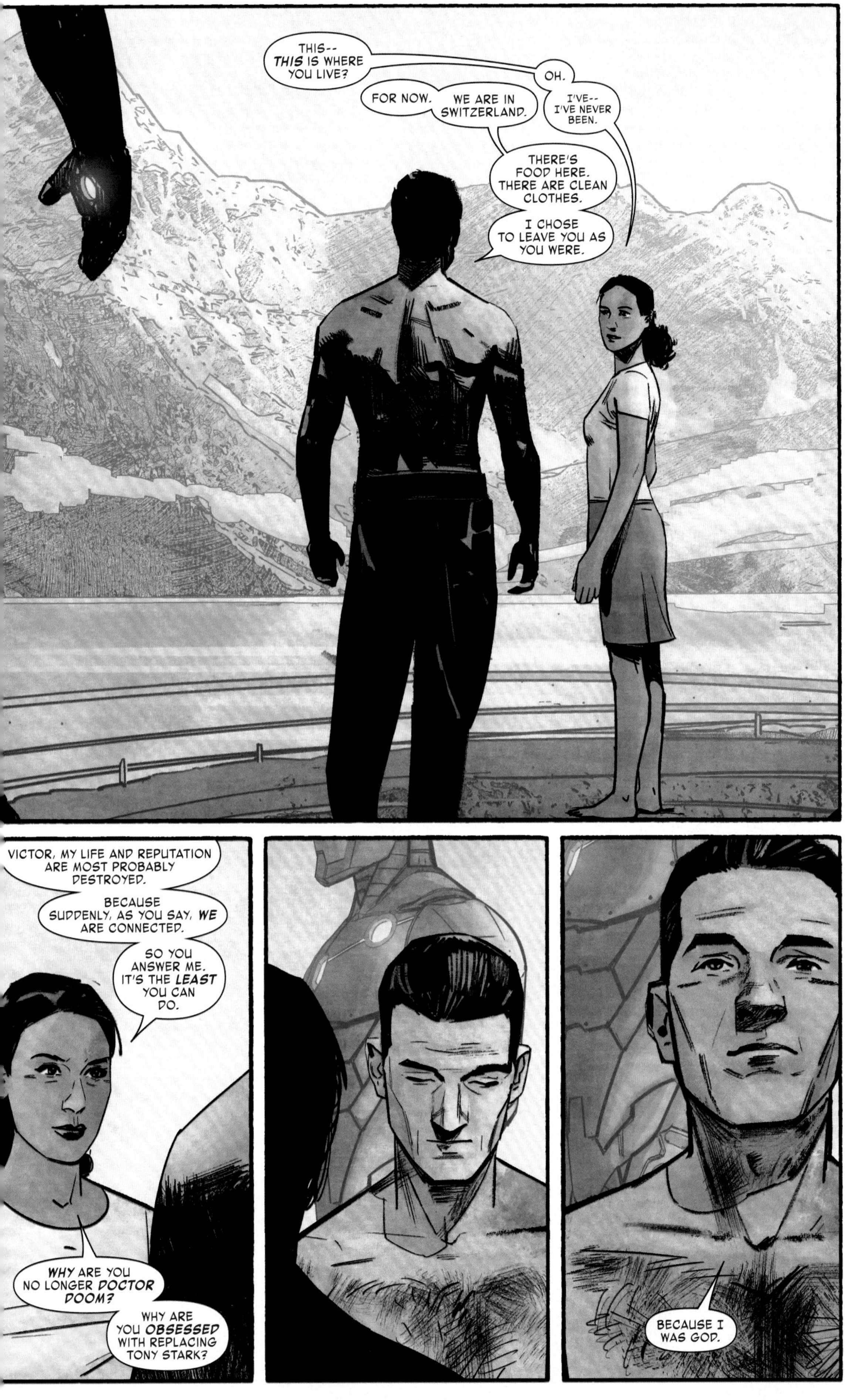
THIS-- THIS IS WHERE YOU LIVE?
OH.
FOR NOW.
WE ARE IN SWITZERLAND.
I'VE-- I'VE NEVER BEEN.
THERE'S FOOD HERE. THERE ARE CLEAN CLOTHES.
I CHOSE TO LEAVE YOU AS YOU WERE.
VICTOR, MY LIFE AND REPUTATION ARE MOST PROBABLY DESTROYED.
BECAUSE SUDDENLY, AS YOU SAY, WE ARE CONNECTED.
SO YOU ANSWER ME. IT'S THE LEAST YOU CAN DO.
WHY ARE YOU NO LONGER DOCTOR DOOM?
WHY ARE YOU OBSESSED WITH REPLACING TONY STARK?
BECAUSE I WAS GOD.

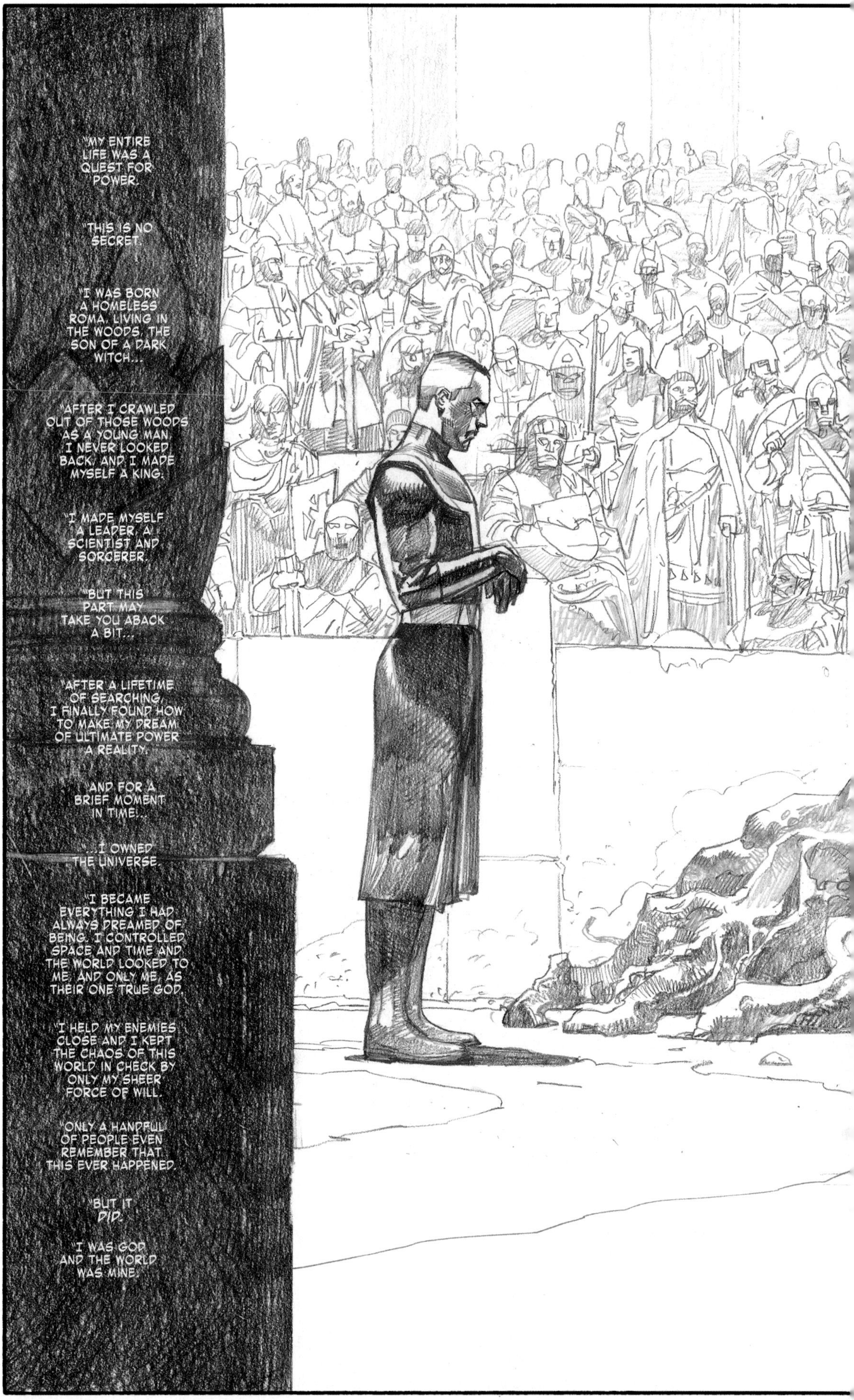
"MY ENTIRE LIFE WAS A QUEST FOR POWER.
"THIS IS NO SECRET.
"I WAS BORN A HOMELESS ROMA, LIVING IN THE WOODS, THE SON OF A DARK WITCH...
"AFTER I CRAWLED OUT OF THOSE WOODS AS A YOUNG MAN, I NEVER LOOKED BACK, AND I MADE MYSELF A KING.
"I MADE MYSELF A LEADER, A SCIENTIST AND SORCERER.
"BUT THIS PART MAY TAKE YOU ABACK A BIT...
"AFTER A LIFETIME OF SEARCHING, I FINALLY FOUND HOW TO MAKE MY DREAM OF ULTIMATE POWER A REALITY.
"AND FOR A BRIEF MOMENT IN TIME...
"...I OWNED THE UNIVERSE.
"I BECAME EVERYTHING I HAD ALWAYS DREAMED OF BEING. I CONTROLLED SPACE AND TIME AND THE WORLD LOOKED TO ME, AND ONLY ME, AS THEIR ONE TRUE GOD.
"I HELD MY ENEMIES CLOSE AND I KEPT THE CHAOS OF THIS WORLD IN CHECK BY ONLY MY SHEER FORCE OF WILL.
"ONLY A HANDFUL OF PEOPLE EVEN REMEMBER THAT THIS EVER HAPPENED.
"BUT IT *DID*.
"I WAS GOD AND THE WORLD WAS MINE.

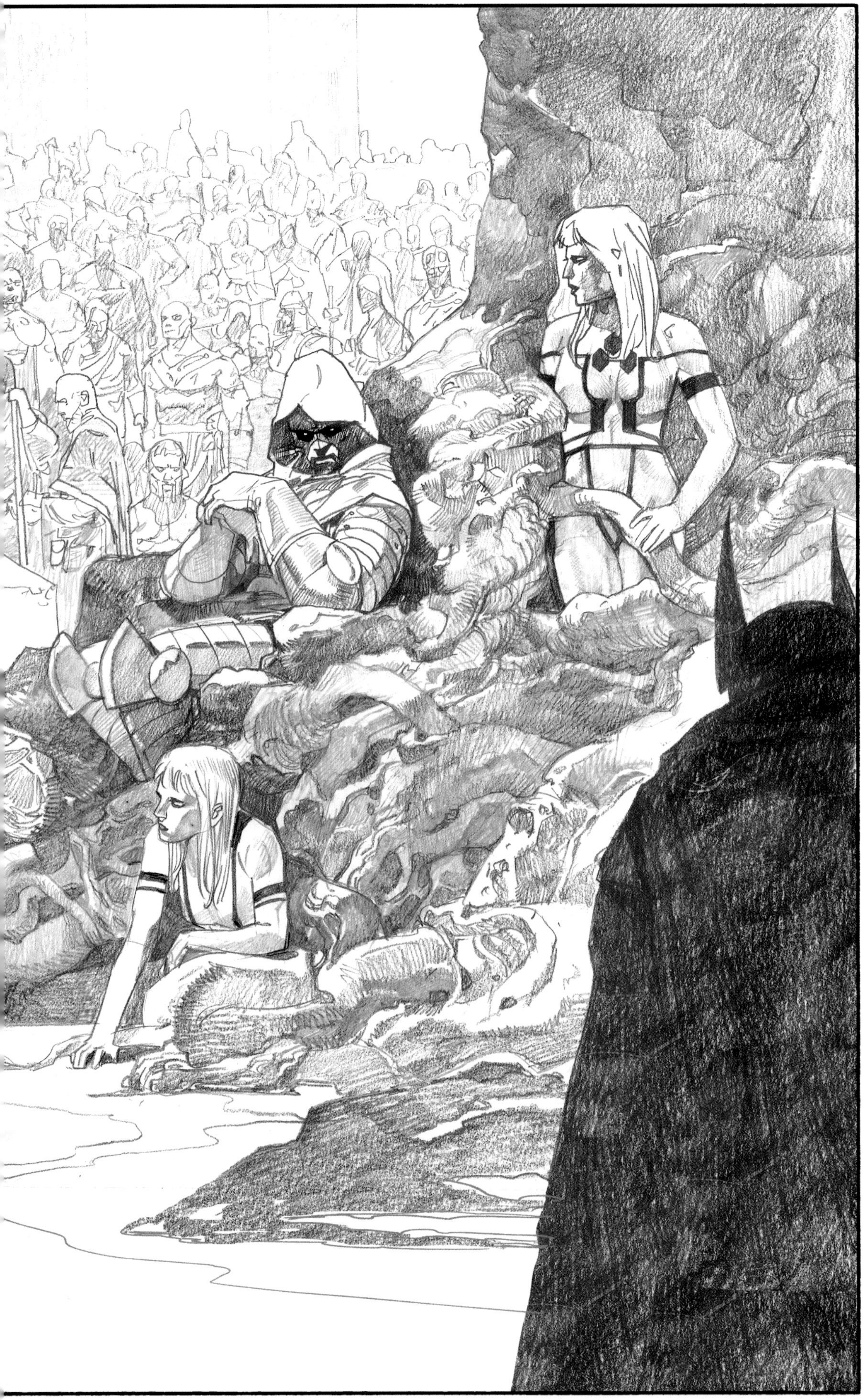

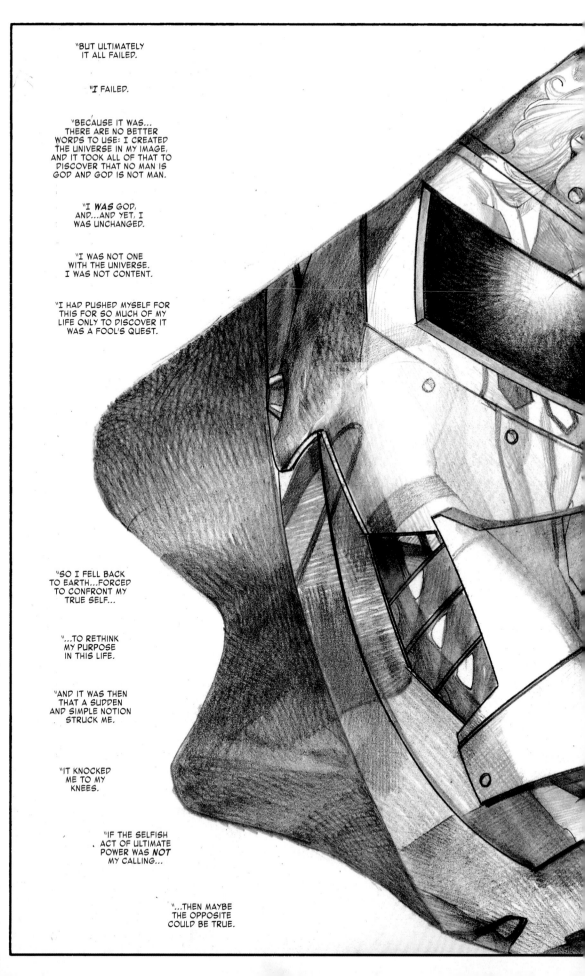

"BUT ULTIMATELY IT ALL FAILED.

"*I* FAILED.

"BECAUSE IT WAS... THERE ARE NO BETTER WORDS TO USE: I CREATED THE UNIVERSE IN MY IMAGE, AND IT TOOK ALL OF THAT TO DISCOVER THAT NO MAN IS GOD AND GOD IS NOT MAN.

"I *WAS* GOD, AND...AND YET, I WAS UNCHANGED.

"I WAS NOT ONE WITH THE UNIVERSE. I WAS NOT CONTENT.

"I HAD PUSHED MYSELF FOR THIS FOR SO MUCH OF MY LIFE ONLY TO DISCOVER IT WAS A FOOL'S QUEST.

"SO I FELL BACK TO EARTH...FORCED TO CONFRONT MY TRUE SELF...

"...TO RETHINK MY PURPOSE IN THIS LIFE.

"AND IT WAS THEN THAT A SUDDEN AND SIMPLE NOTION STRUCK ME.

"IT KNOCKED ME TO MY KNEES.

"IF THE SELFISH ACT OF ULTIMATE POWER WAS *NOT* MY CALLING...

"...THEN MAYBE THE OPPOSITE COULD BE TRUE.

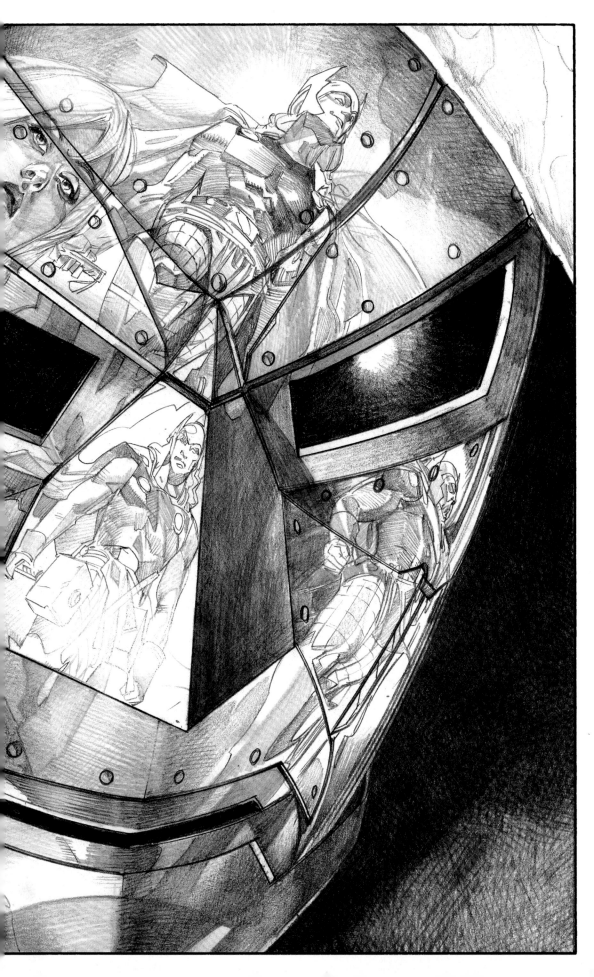

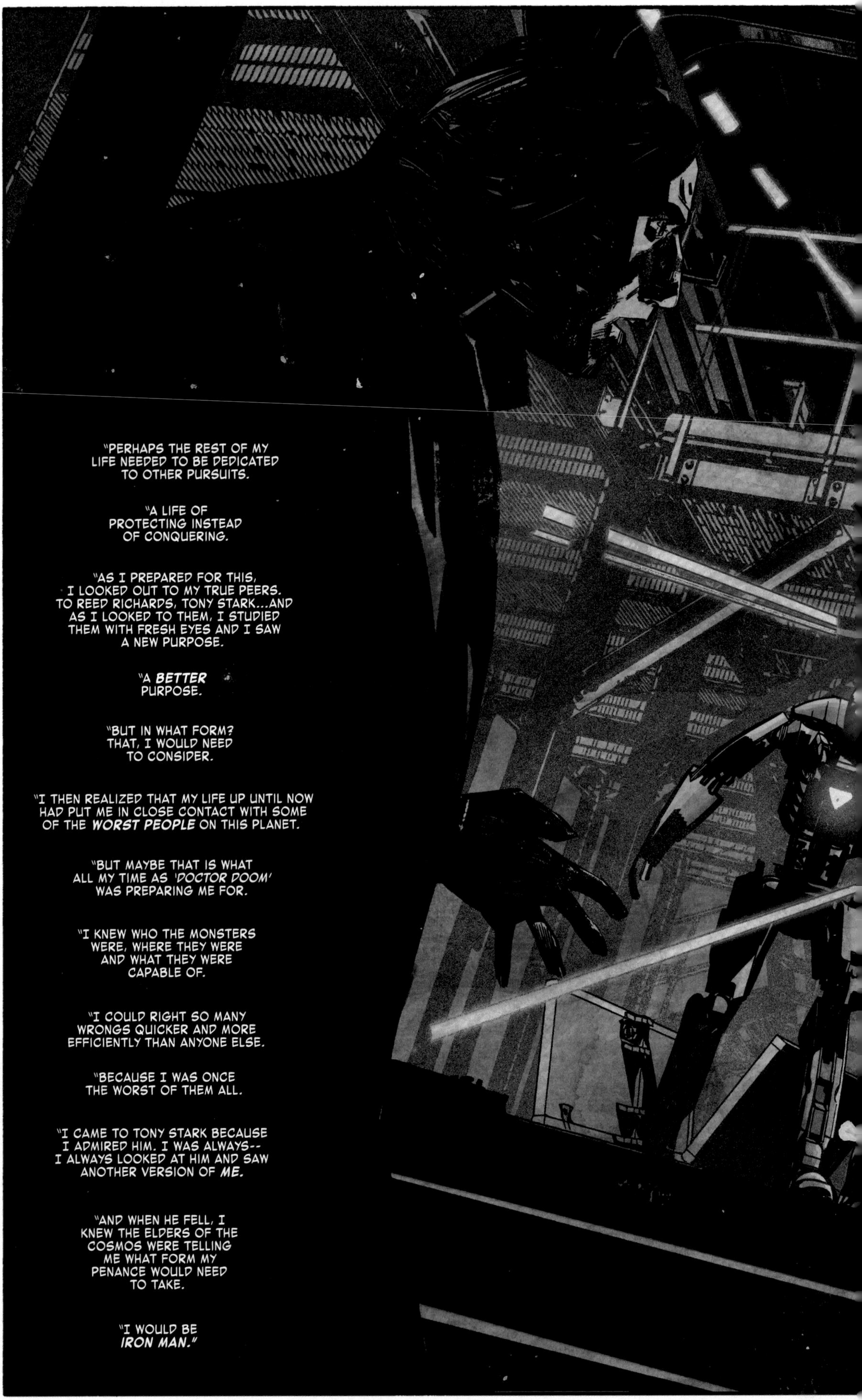
"PERHAPS THE REST OF MY LIFE NEEDED TO BE DEDICATED TO OTHER PURSUITS.
"A LIFE OF PROTECTING INSTEAD OF CONQUERING.
"AS I PREPARED FOR THIS, I LOOKED OUT TO MY TRUE PEERS. TO REED RICHARDS, TONY STARK...AND AS I LOOKED TO THEM, I STUDIED THEM WITH FRESH EYES AND I SAW A NEW PURPOSE.
"A ***BETTER*** PURPOSE.
"BUT IN WHAT FORM? THAT, I WOULD NEED TO CONSIDER.
"I THEN REALIZED THAT MY LIFE UP UNTIL NOW HAD PUT ME IN CLOSE CONTACT WITH SOME OF THE ***WORST PEOPLE*** ON THIS PLANET.
"BUT MAYBE THAT IS WHAT ALL MY TIME AS *'DOCTOR DOOM'* WAS PREPARING ME FOR.
"I KNEW WHO THE MONSTERS WERE, WHERE THEY WERE AND WHAT THEY WERE CAPABLE OF.
"I COULD RIGHT SO MANY WRONGS QUICKER AND MORE EFFICIENTLY THAN ANYONE ELSE.
"BECAUSE I WAS ONCE THE WORST OF THEM ALL.
"I CAME TO TONY STARK BECAUSE I ADMIRED HIM. I WAS ALWAYS-- I ALWAYS LOOKED AT HIM AND SAW ANOTHER VERSION OF ***ME.***
"AND WHEN HE FELL, I KNEW THE ELDERS OF THE COSMOS WERE TELLING ME WHAT FORM MY PENANCE WOULD NEED TO TAKE.
"I WOULD BE ***IRON MAN."***

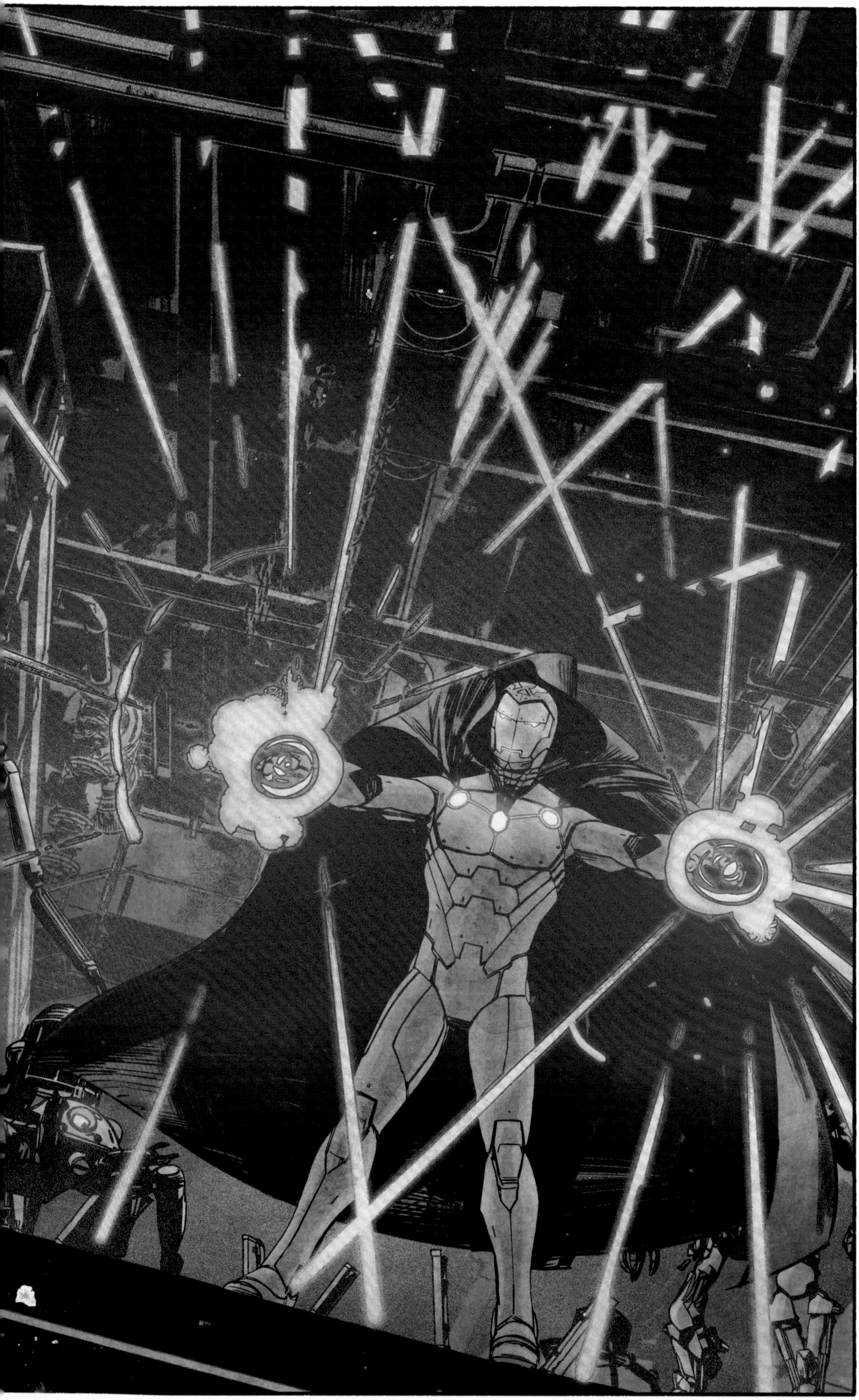

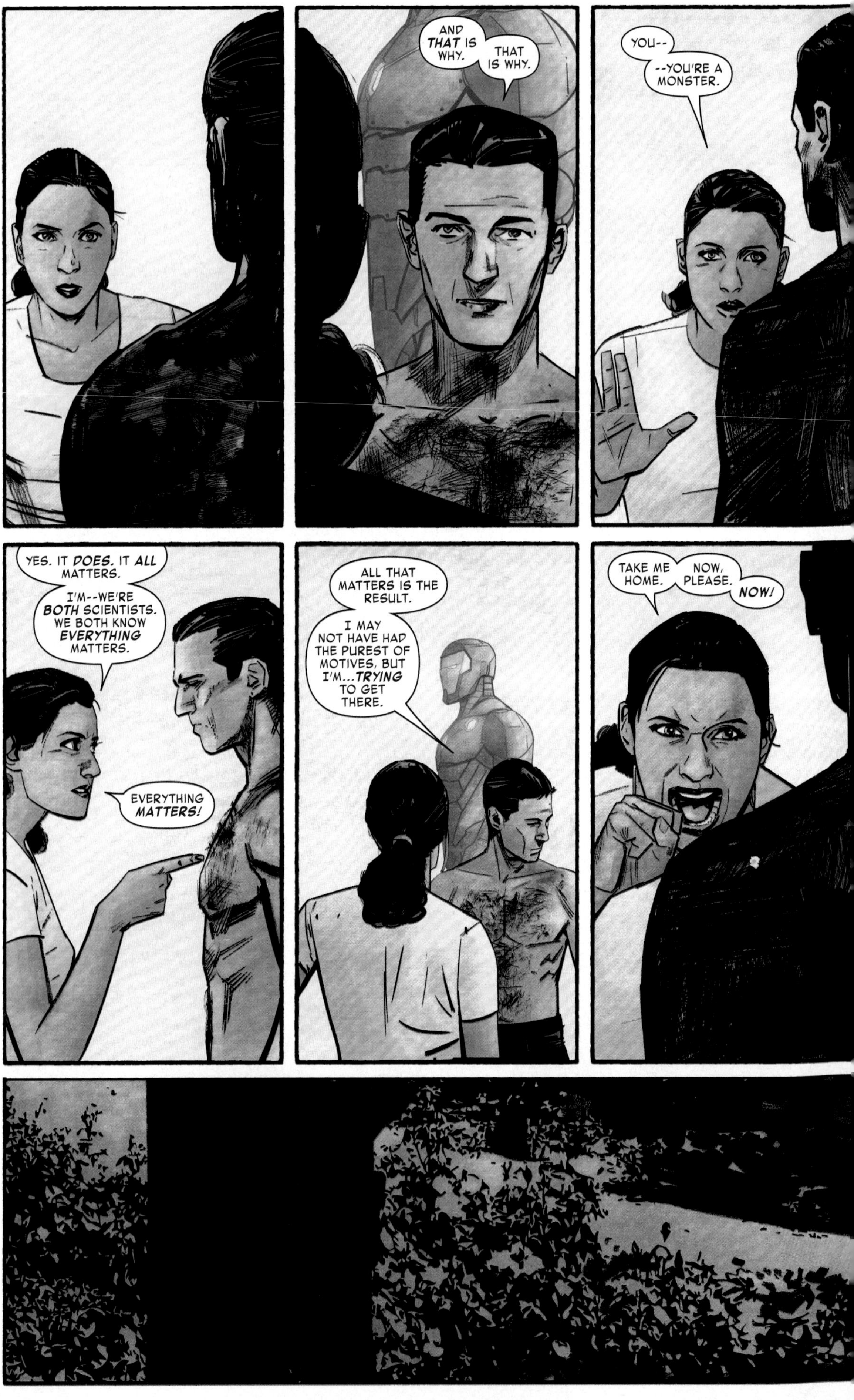
AND THAT IS WHY.
THAT IS WHY.
YOU--
--YOU'RE A MONSTER.
YES. IT DOES. IT ALL MATTERS.
I'M--WE'RE BOTH SCIENTISTS. WE BOTH KNOW EVERYTHING MATTERS.
EVERYTHING MATTERS!
ALL THAT MATTERS IS THE RESULT.
I MAY NOT HAVE HAD THE PUREST OF MOTIVES, BUT I'M...TRYING TO GET THERE.
TAKE ME HOME.
NOW, PLEASE.
NOW!

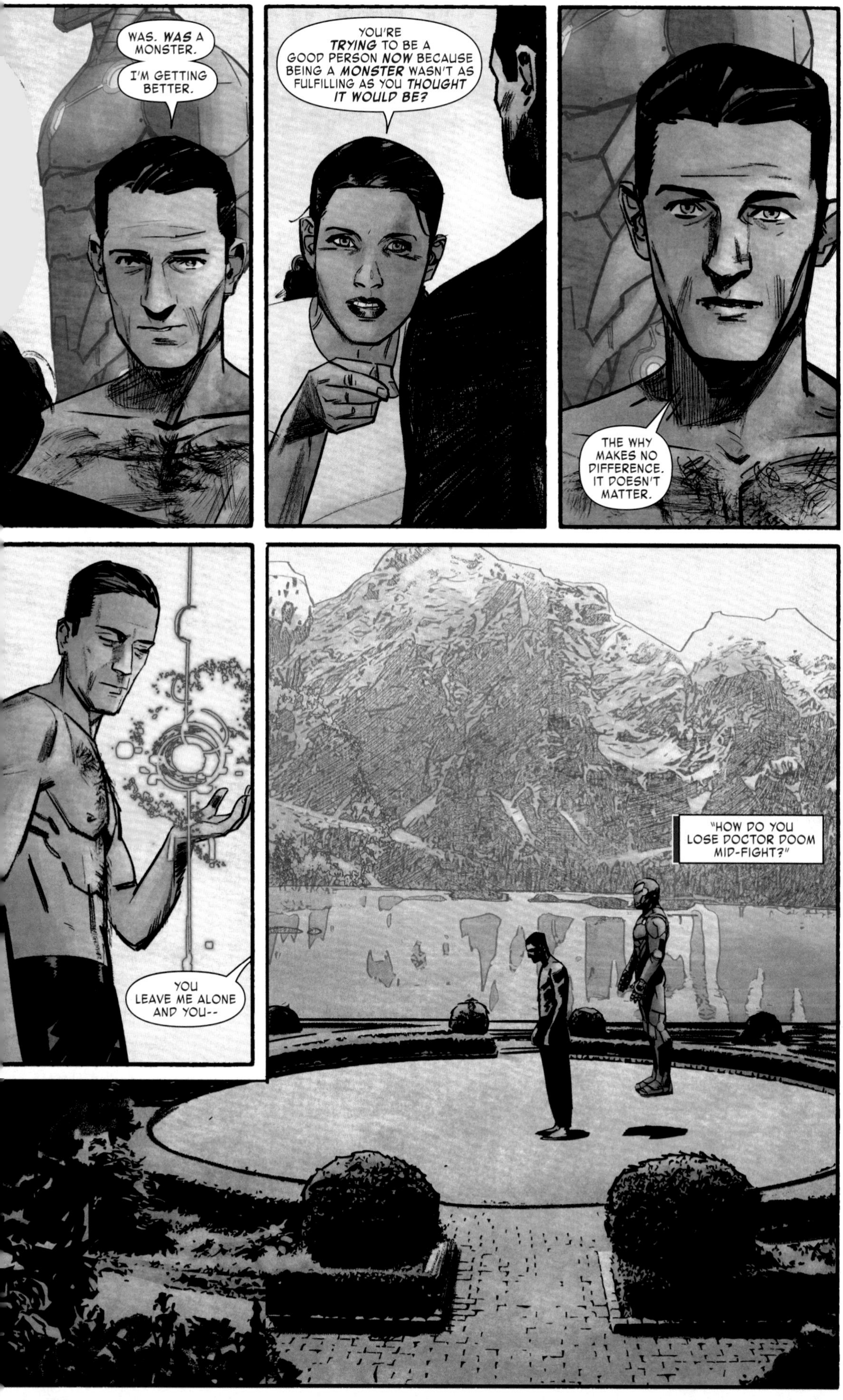
WAS. WAS A MONSTER.
I'M GETTING BETTER.
YOU'RE TRYING TO BE A GOOD PERSON NOW BECAUSE BEING A MONSTER WASN'T AS FULFILLING AS YOU THOUGHT IT WOULD BE?
THE WHY MAKES NO DIFFERENCE. IT DOESN'T MATTER.
YOU LEAVE ME ALONE AND YOU--
"HOW DO YOU LOSE DOCTOR DOOM MID-FIGHT?"

I DIDN'T LOSE HIM, MISS HILL.

HE JUST KINDA SLIPPED OUTTA MY MITTS.

BUT STILL, YOU FOUND HIM PRETTY FAST. I'M IMPRESSED.

HE'S STILL OUT THERE. I'LL FIND HIM AGAIN.

YOU THINK HE'S IN LATVERIA?

HOW DID YOU KNOW I WAS IN-- OH, YEAH, YOU'RE S.H.I.E.L.D.

PLEASE, OF COURSE.

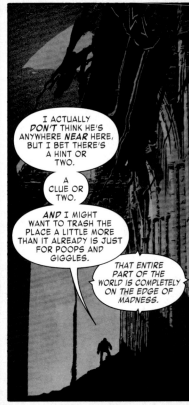

I ACTUALLY *DON'T* THINK HE'S ANYWHERE *NEAR* HERE, BUT I BET THERE'S A HINT OR TWO.

A CLUE OR TWO.

AND I MIGHT WANT TO TRASH THE PLACE A LITTLE MORE THAN IT ALREADY IS JUST FOR POOPS AND GIGGLES.

THAT ENTIRE PART OF THE WORLD IS COMPLETELY ON THE EDGE OF MADNESS.

WATCH OUT FOR INSURGENTS AND PLEASE TRY TO AVOID ANY ⸘ZAKT⸘ INTERNATIONAL INCIDENTS.

I AIN'T MAKIN' NO PROMISES.

I CAN'T ⸘ZAAT⸘ YOU'RE BREAKING ⸘GKTTAA⸘

YEAH, OKAY, BAD RECEPTION. BYE.

OH, MY STARS AND GARTERS...

...WHATEVER THE HELL THAT MEANS...

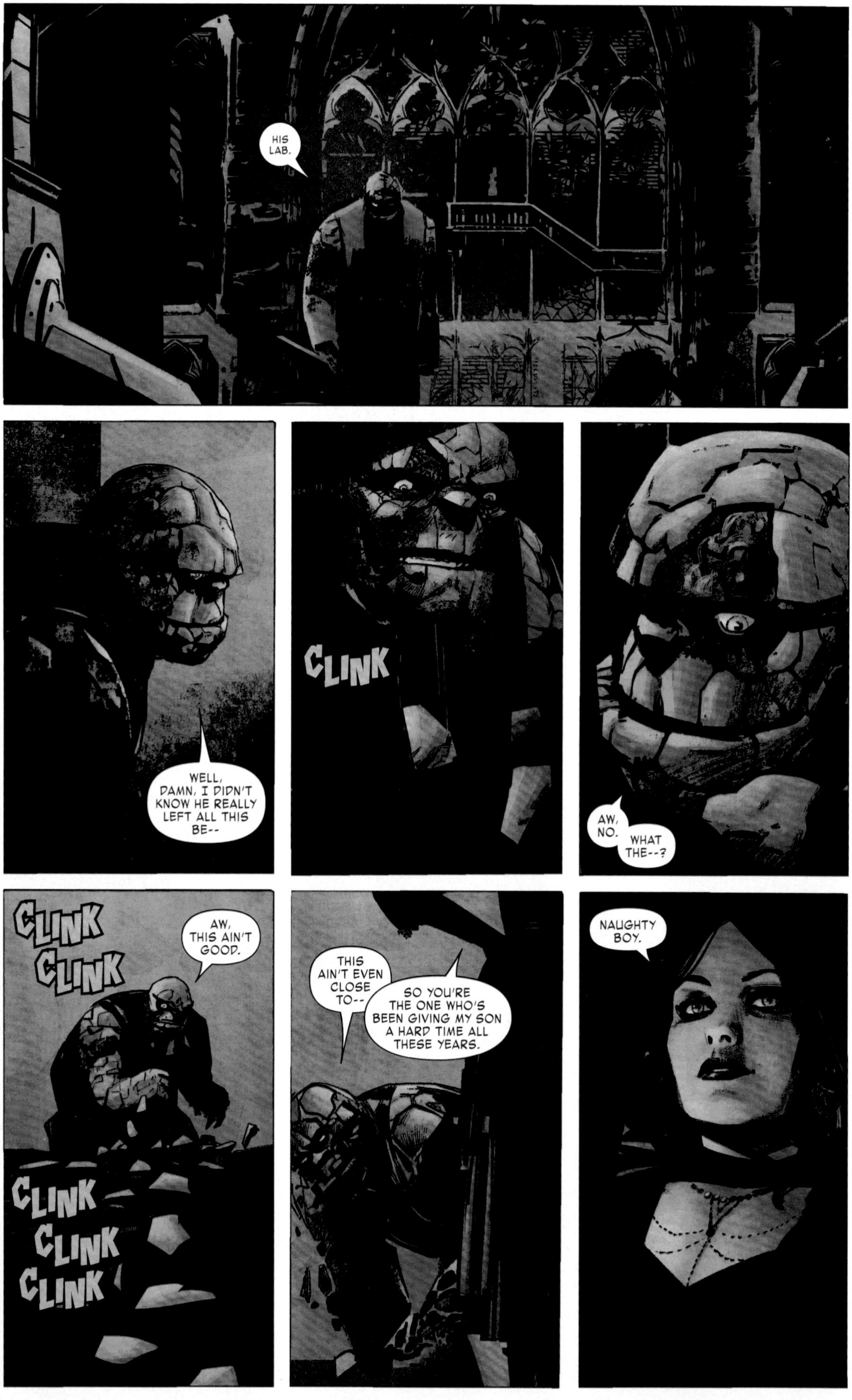
HIS LAB.
WELL, DAMN, I DIDN'T KNOW HE REALLY LEFT ALL THIS BE--
CLINK
AW, NO.
WHAT THE--?
CLINK
CLINK
AW, THIS AIN'T GOOD.
CLINK
CLINK
CLINK
THIS AIN'T EVEN CLOSE TO--
SO YOU'RE THE ONE WHO'S BEEN GIVING MY SON A HARD TIME ALL THESE YEARS.
NAUGHTY BOY.

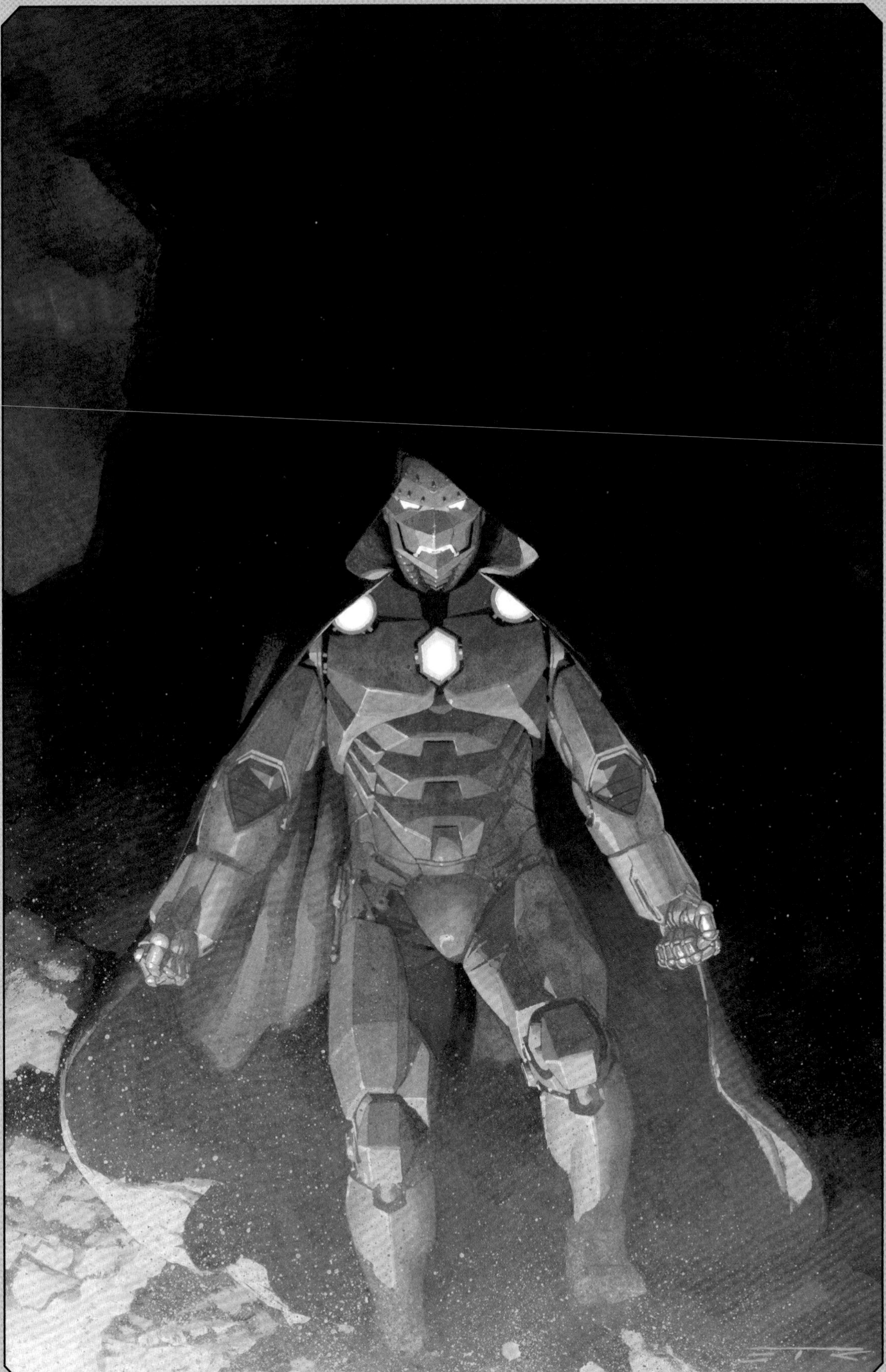

ESAD REBIC
1 VARIANT

4

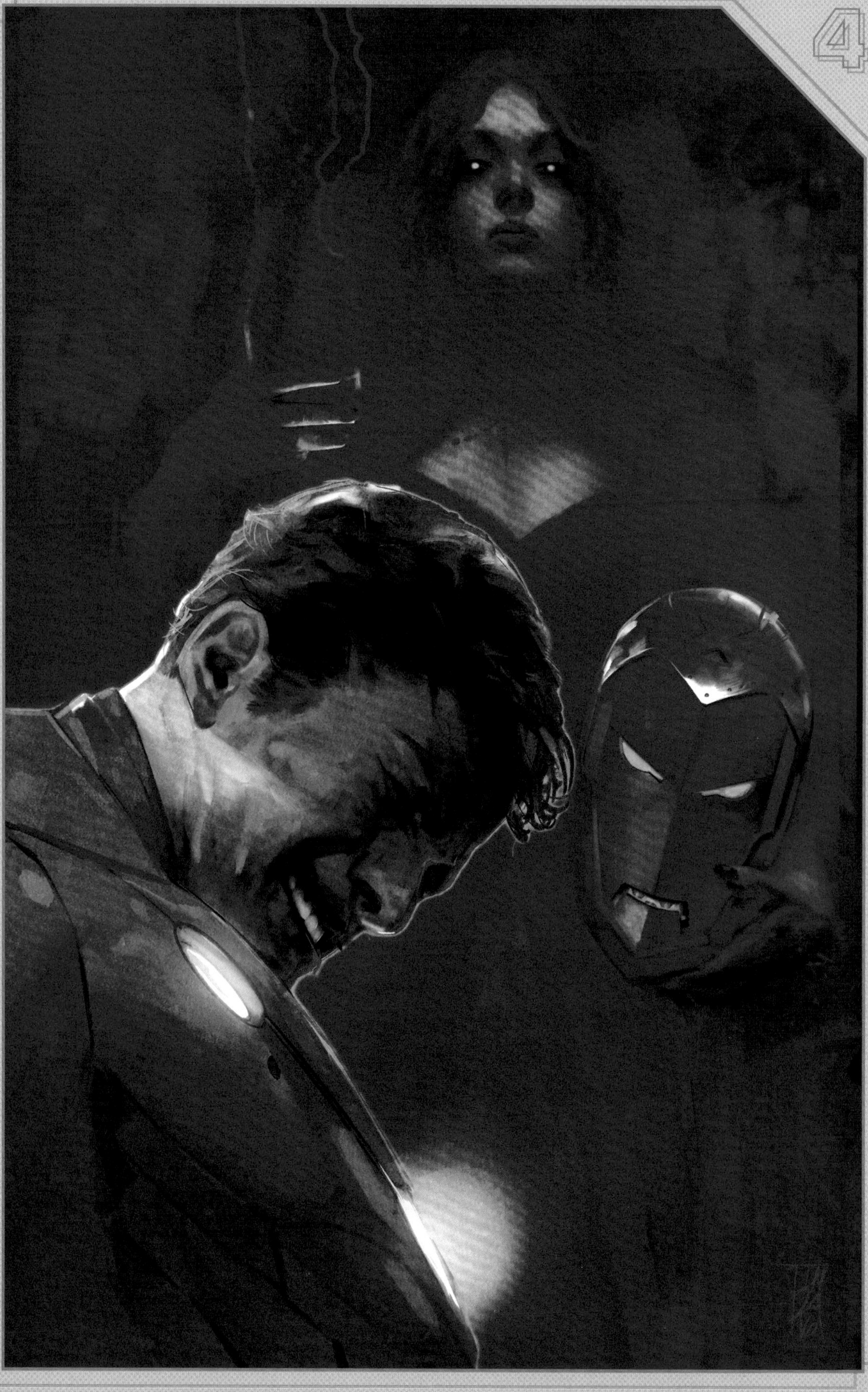

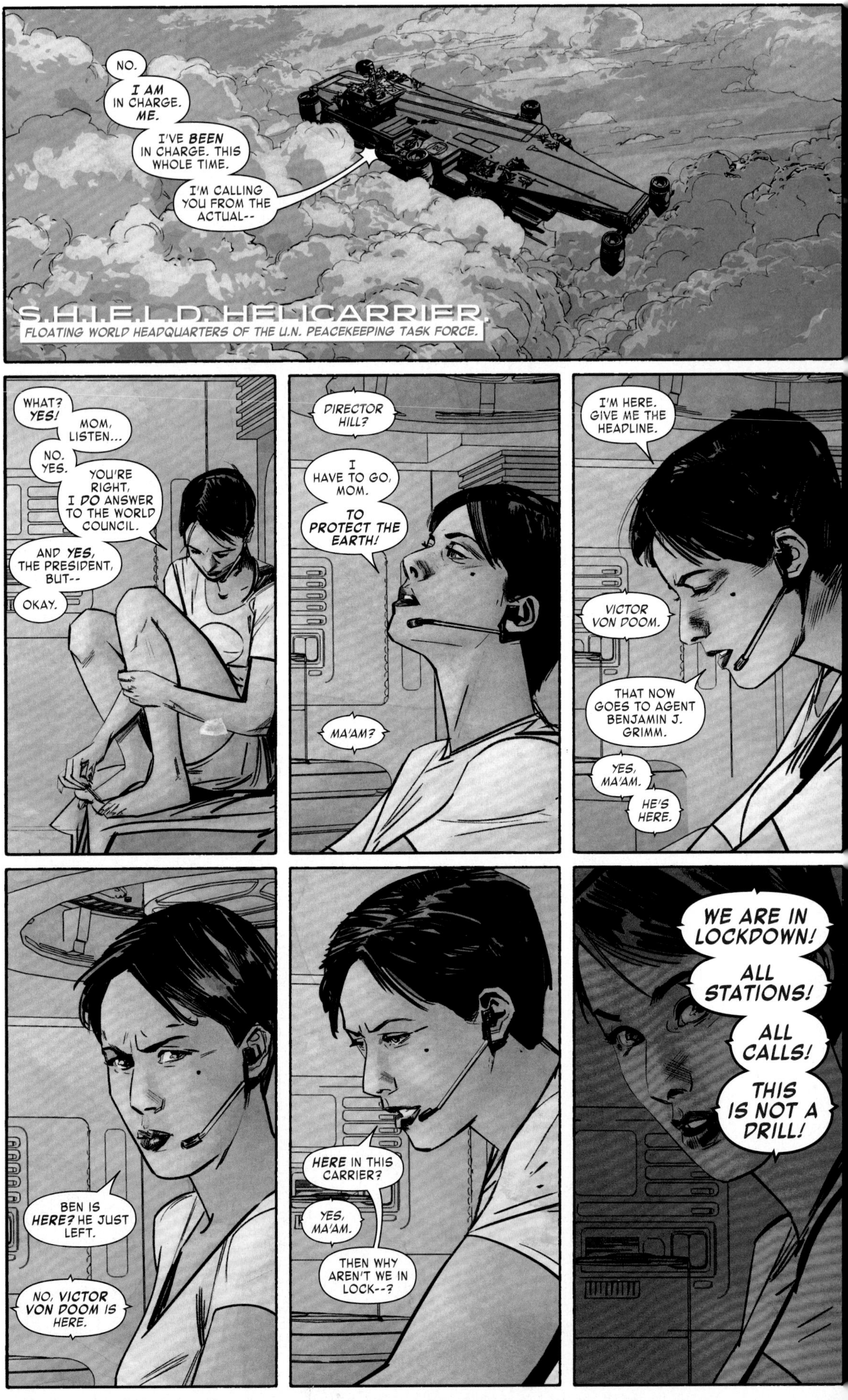
NO.
I AM IN CHARGE. ME.
I'VE BEEN IN CHARGE. THIS WHOLE TIME.
I'M CALLING YOU FROM THE ACTUAL--
S.H.I.E.L.D. HELICARRIER.
FLOATING WORLD HEADQUARTERS OF THE U.N. PEACEKEEPING TASK FORCE.
WHAT? YES!
MOM, LISTEN...
NO. YES.
YOU'RE RIGHT, I DO ANSWER TO THE WORLD COUNCIL.
AND YES, THE PRESIDENT, BUT--
OKAY.
DIRECTOR HILL?
I HAVE TO GO, MOM.
TO PROTECT THE EARTH!
MA'AM?
I'M HERE. GIVE ME THE HEADLINE.
VICTOR VON DOOM.
THAT NOW GOES TO AGENT BENJAMIN J. GRIMM.
YES, MA'AM.
HE'S HERE.
BEN IS HERE? HE JUST LEFT.
NO, VICTOR VON DOOM IS HERE.
HERE IN THIS CARRIER?
YES, MA'AM.
THEN WHY AREN'T WE IN LOCK--?
WE ARE IN LOCKDOWN!
ALL STATIONS!
ALL CALLS!
THIS IS NOT A DRILL!

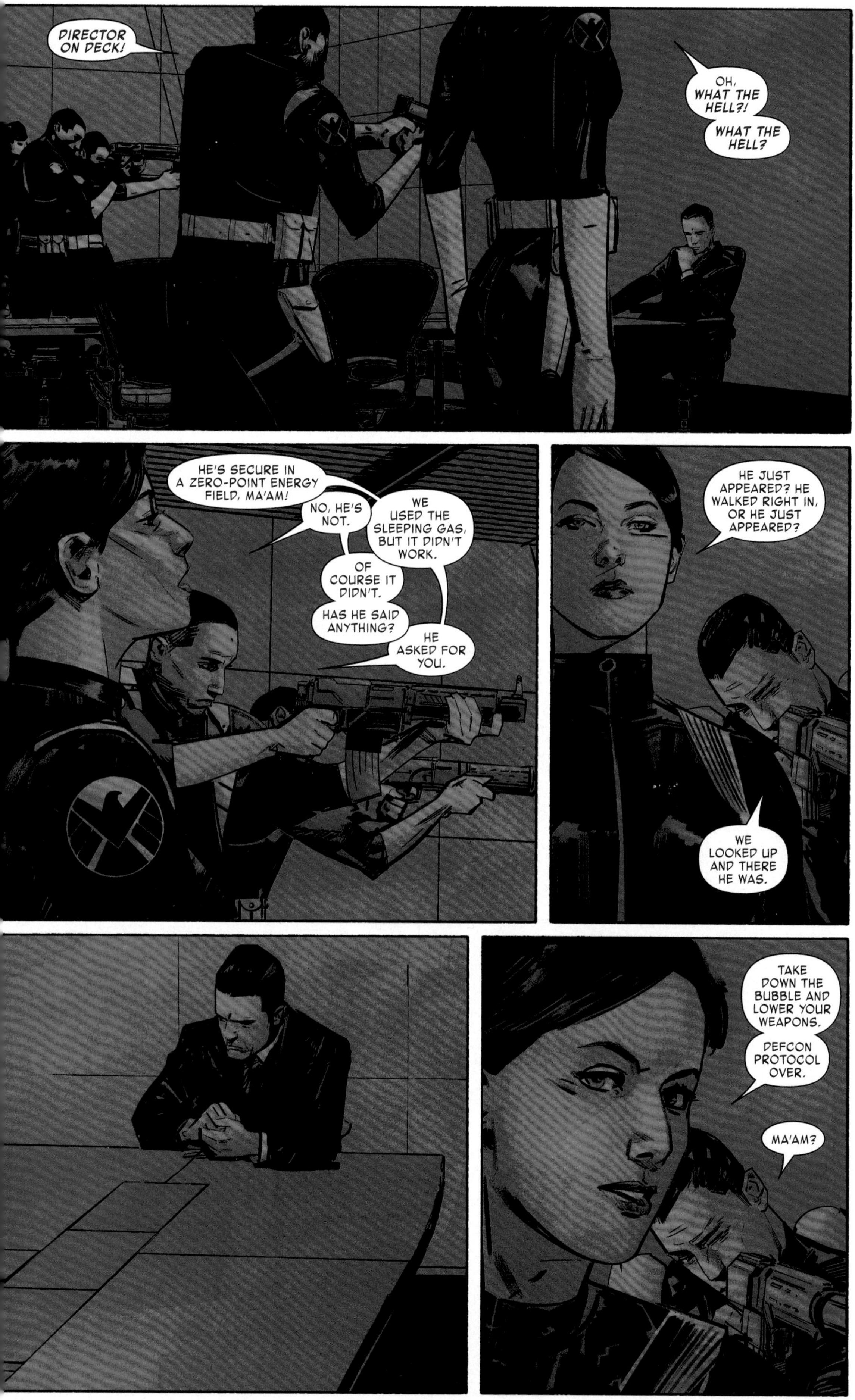

DIRECTOR ON DECK!
OH, WHAT THE HELL?!
WHAT THE HELL?
HE'S SECURE IN A ZERO-POINT ENERGY FIELD, MA'AM!
NO, HE'S NOT.
WE USED THE SLEEPING GAS, BUT IT DIDN'T WORK.
OF COURSE IT DIDN'T.
HAS HE SAID ANYTHING?
HE ASKED FOR YOU.
HE JUST APPEARED? HE WALKED RIGHT IN, OR HE JUST APPEARED?
WE LOOKED UP AND THERE HE WAS.
TAKE DOWN THE BUBBLE AND LOWER YOUR WEAPONS.
DEFCON PROTOCOL OVER.
MA'AM?

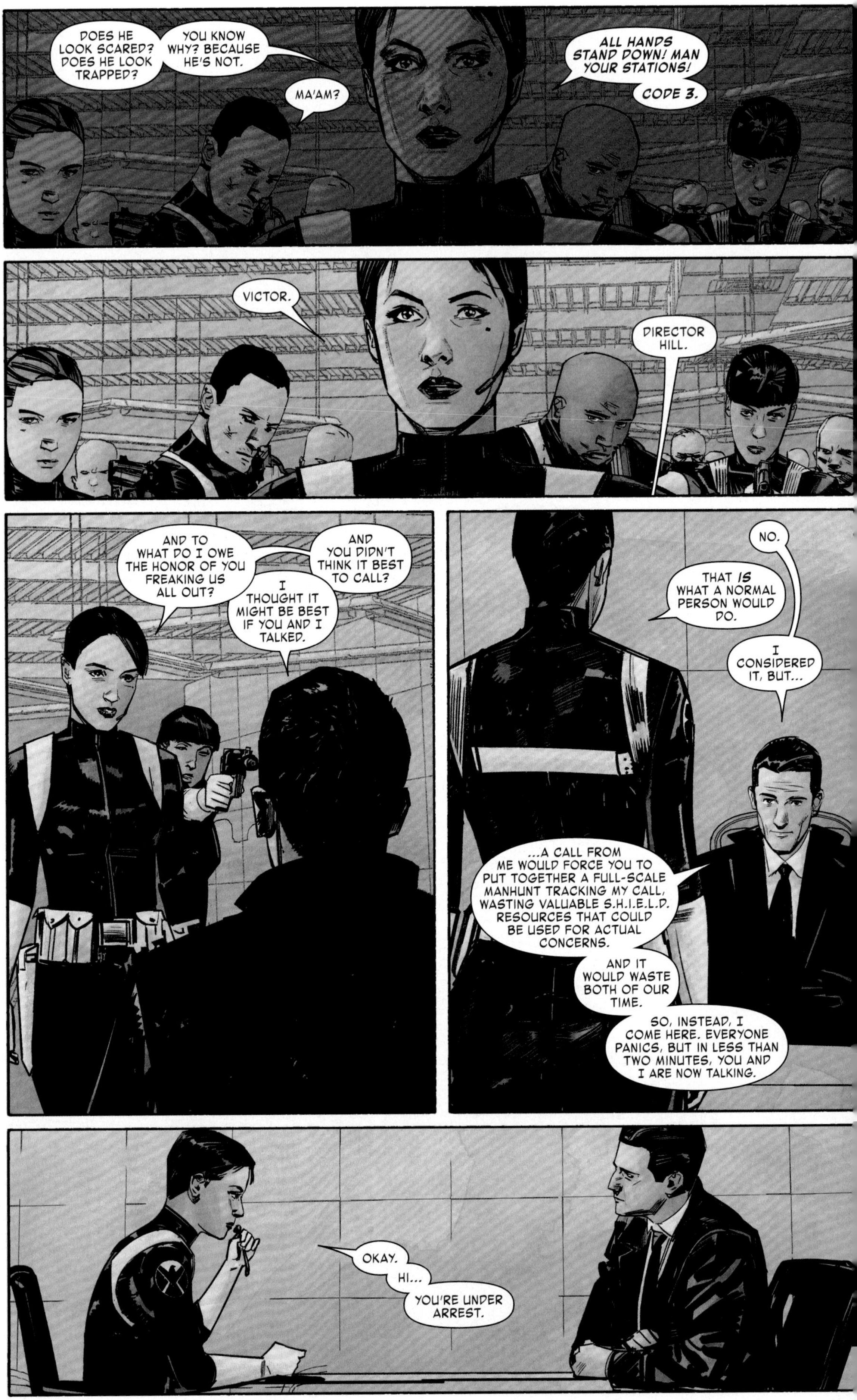
DOES HE LOOK SCARED? DOES HE LOOK TRAPPED?
YOU KNOW WHY? BECAUSE HE'S NOT.
MA'AM?
ALL HANDS STAND DOWN! MAN YOUR STATIONS!
CODE 3.
VICTOR.
DIRECTOR HILL.
AND TO WHAT DO I OWE THE HONOR OF YOU FREAKING US ALL OUT?
AND YOU DIDN'T THINK IT BEST TO CALL?
I THOUGHT IT MIGHT BE BEST IF YOU AND I TALKED.
NO.
THAT IS WHAT A NORMAL PERSON WOULD DO.
I CONSIDERED IT, BUT...
...A CALL FROM ME WOULD FORCE YOU TO PUT TOGETHER A FULL-SCALE MANHUNT TRACKING MY CALL, WASTING VALUABLE S.H.I.E.L.D. RESOURCES THAT COULD BE USED FOR ACTUAL CONCERNS.
AND IT WOULD WASTE BOTH OF OUR TIME.
SO, INSTEAD, I COME HERE. EVERYONE PANICS, BUT IN LESS THAN TWO MINUTES, YOU AND I ARE NOW TALKING.
OKAY.
HI...
YOU'RE UNDER ARREST.

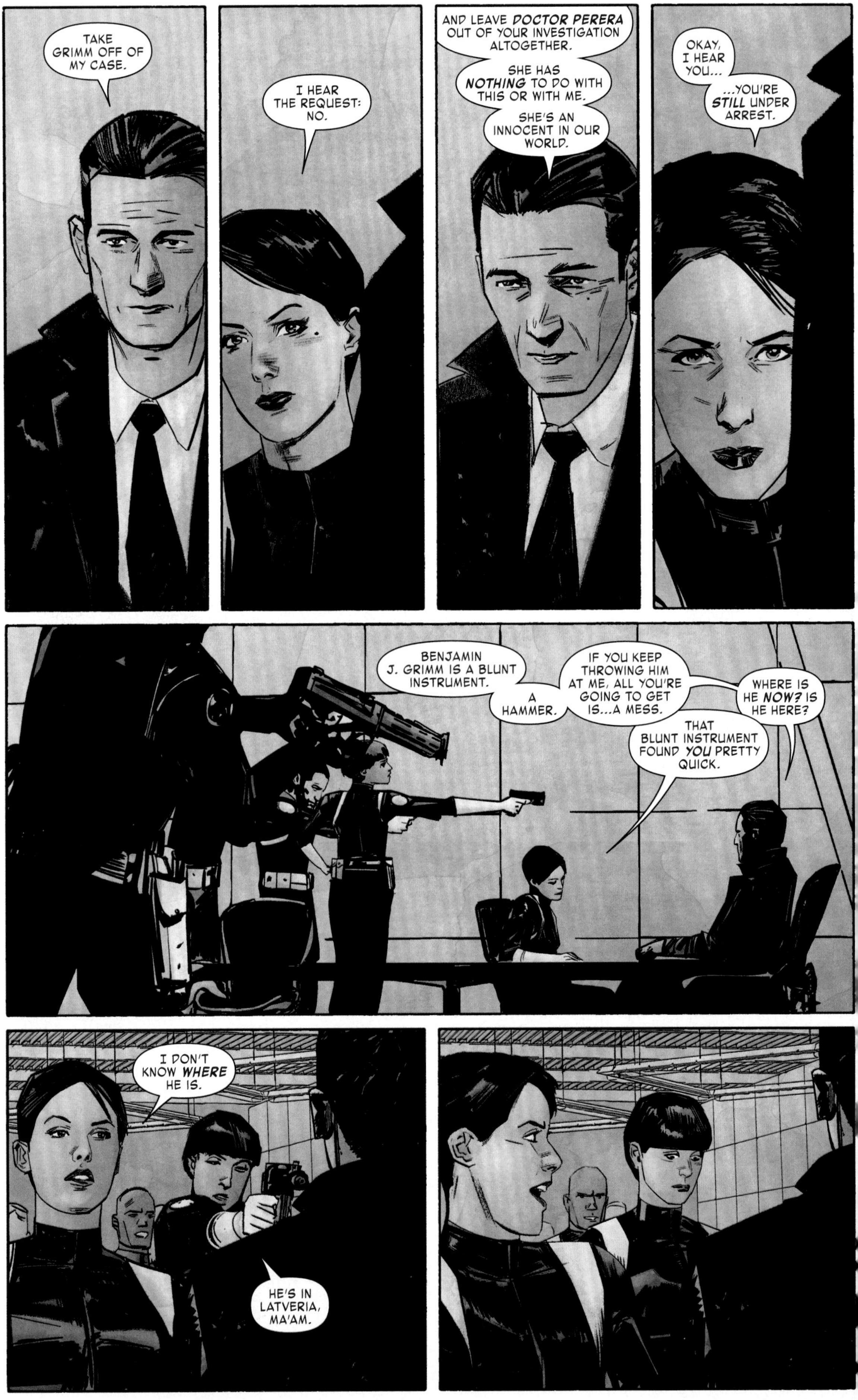
TAKE GRIMM OFF OF MY CASE.
I HEAR THE REQUEST: NO.
AND LEAVE DOCTOR PERERA OUT OF YOUR INVESTIGATION ALTOGETHER.
SHE HAS NOTHING TO DO WITH THIS OR WITH ME.
SHE'S AN INNOCENT IN OUR WORLD.
OKAY, I HEAR YOU...
...YOU'RE STILL UNDER ARREST.
BENJAMIN J. GRIMM IS A BLUNT INSTRUMENT.
A HAMMER.
IF YOU KEEP THROWING HIM AT ME, ALL YOU'RE GOING TO GET IS...A MESS.
THAT BLUNT INSTRUMENT FOUND YOU PRETTY QUICK.
WHERE IS HE NOW? IS HE HERE?
I DON'T KNOW WHERE HE IS.
HE'S IN LATVERIA, MA'AM.

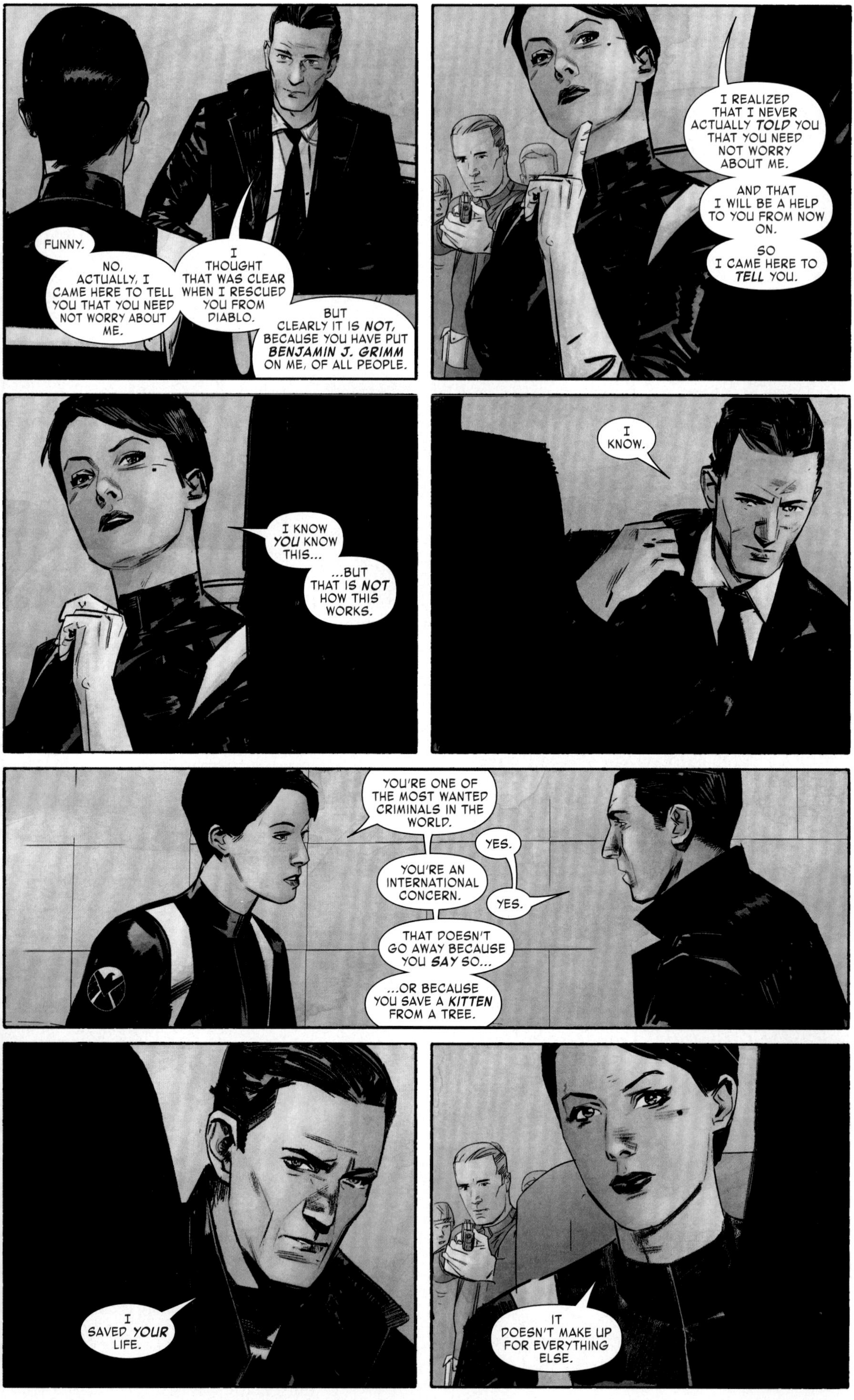

FUNNY.
NO, ACTUALLY, I CAME HERE TO TELL YOU THAT YOU NEED NOT WORRY ABOUT ME.
I THOUGHT THAT WAS CLEAR WHEN I RESCUED YOU FROM DIABLO.
BUT CLEARLY IT IS NOT, BECAUSE YOU HAVE PUT BENJAMIN J. GRIMM ON ME, OF ALL PEOPLE.
I REALIZED THAT I NEVER ACTUALLY TOLD YOU THAT YOU NEED NOT WORRY ABOUT ME.
AND THAT I WILL BE A HELP TO YOU FROM NOW ON.
SO I CAME HERE TO TELL YOU.
I KNOW YOU KNOW THIS...
...BUT THAT IS NOT HOW THIS WORKS.
I KNOW.
YOU'RE ONE OF THE MOST WANTED CRIMINALS IN THE WORLD.
YES.
YOU'RE AN INTERNATIONAL CONCERN.
YES.
THAT DOESN'T GO AWAY BECAUSE YOU SAY SO...
...OR BECAUSE YOU SAVE A KITTEN FROM A TREE.
I SAVED YOUR LIFE.
IT DOESN'T MAKE UP FOR EVERYTHING ELSE.

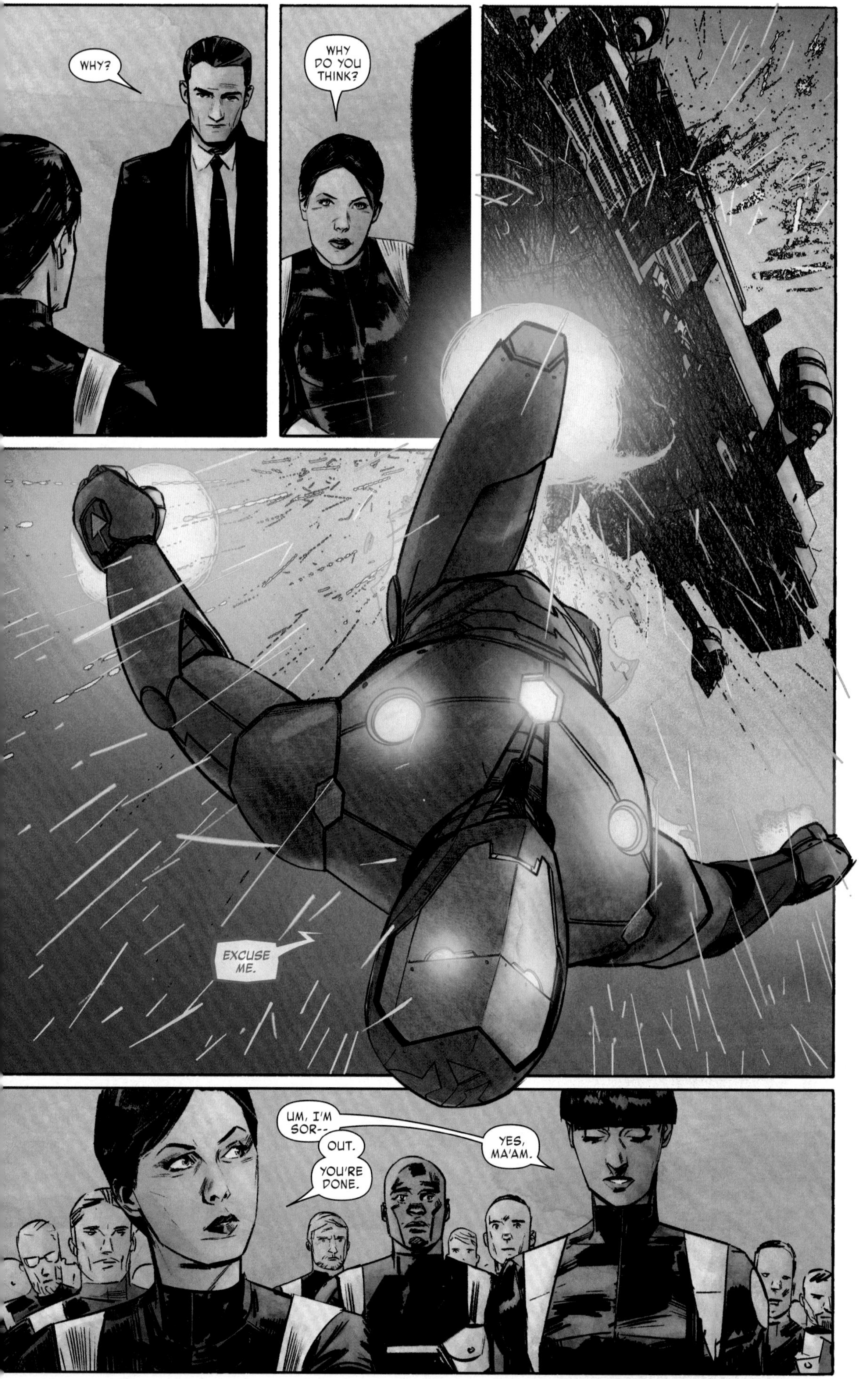
WHY?
WHY DO YOU THINK?
EXCUSE ME.
UM, I'M SOR--
OUT.
YOU'RE DONE.
YES, MA'AM.

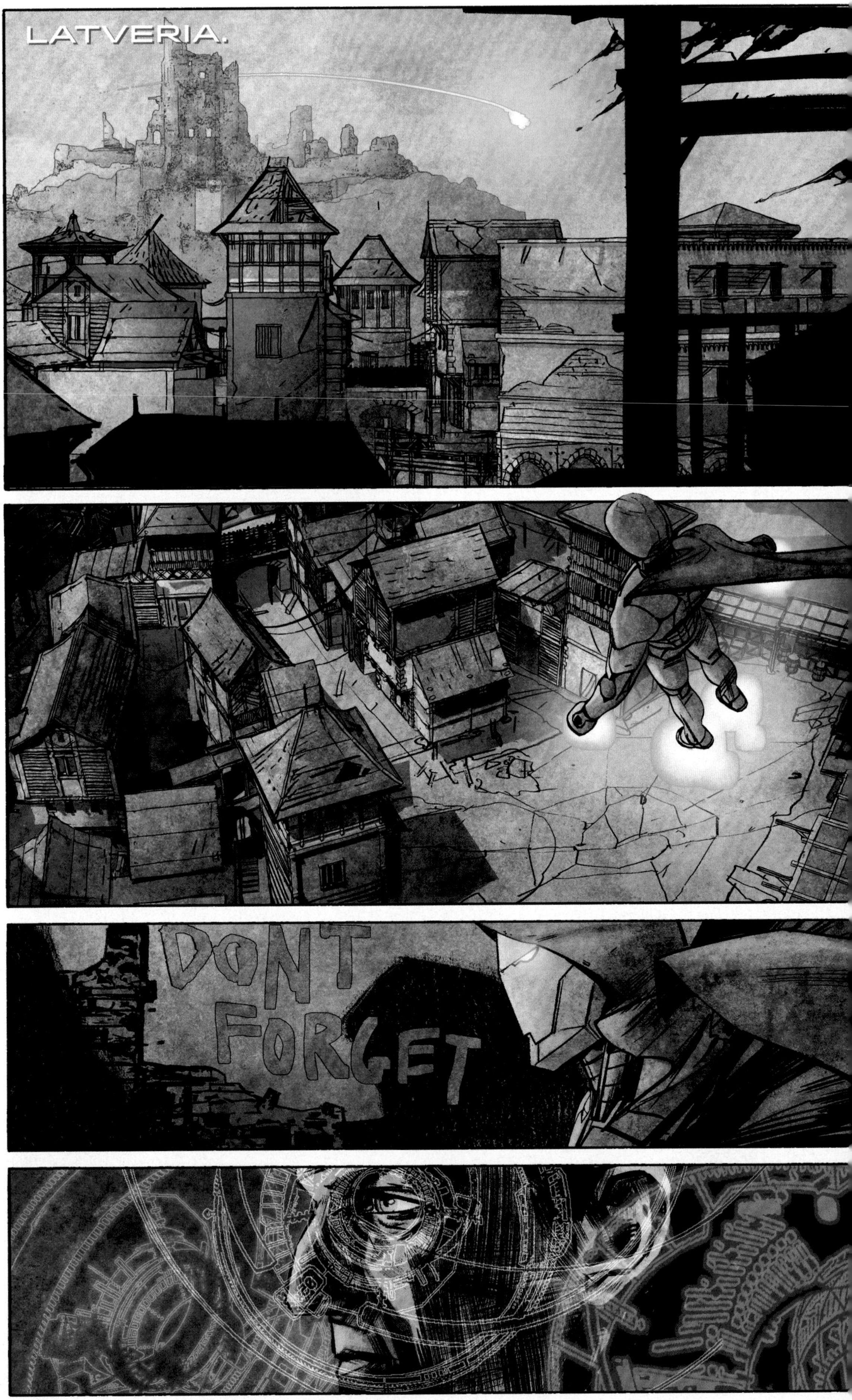
LATVERIA.
DONT FORGET

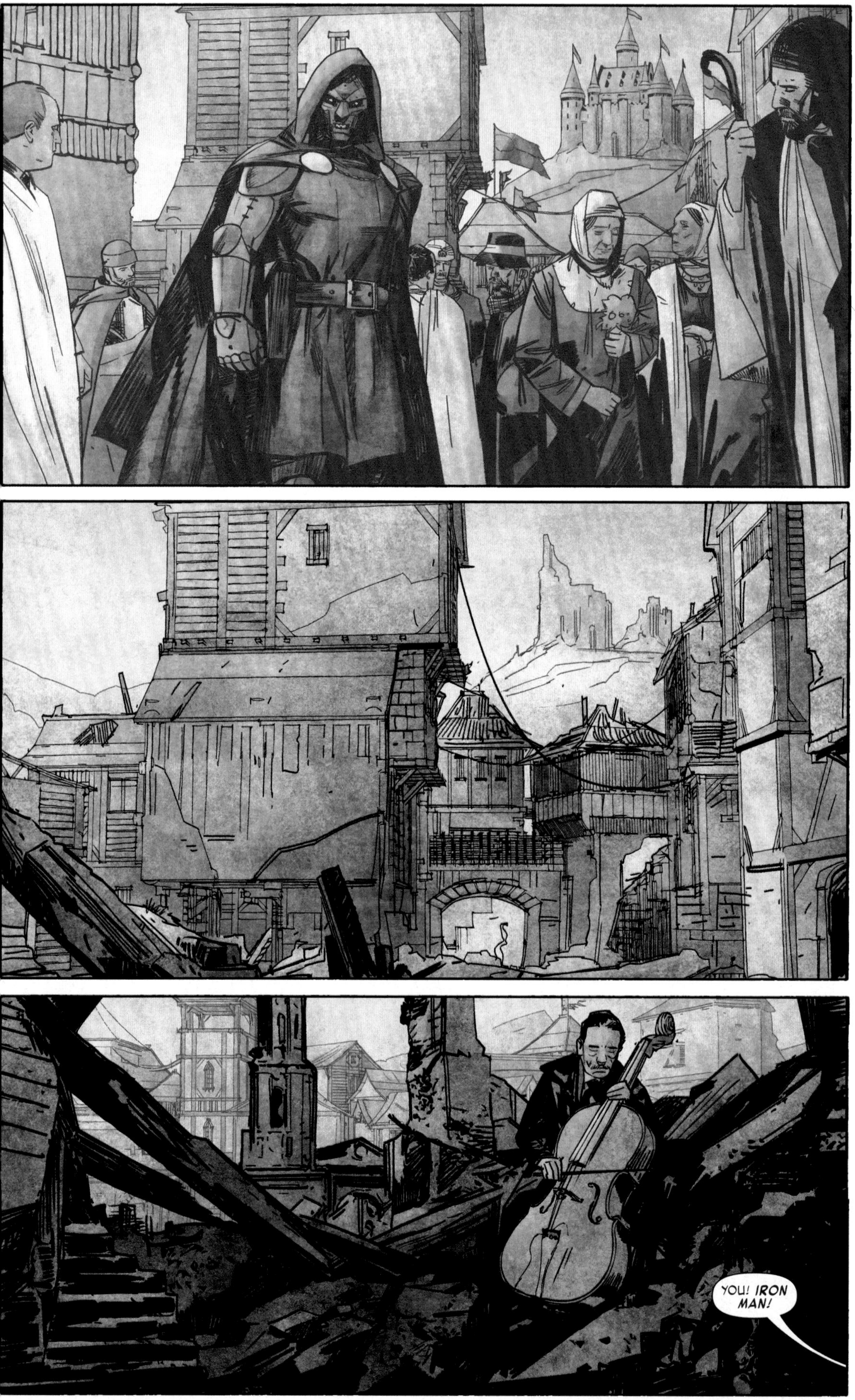
YOU! IRON MAN!

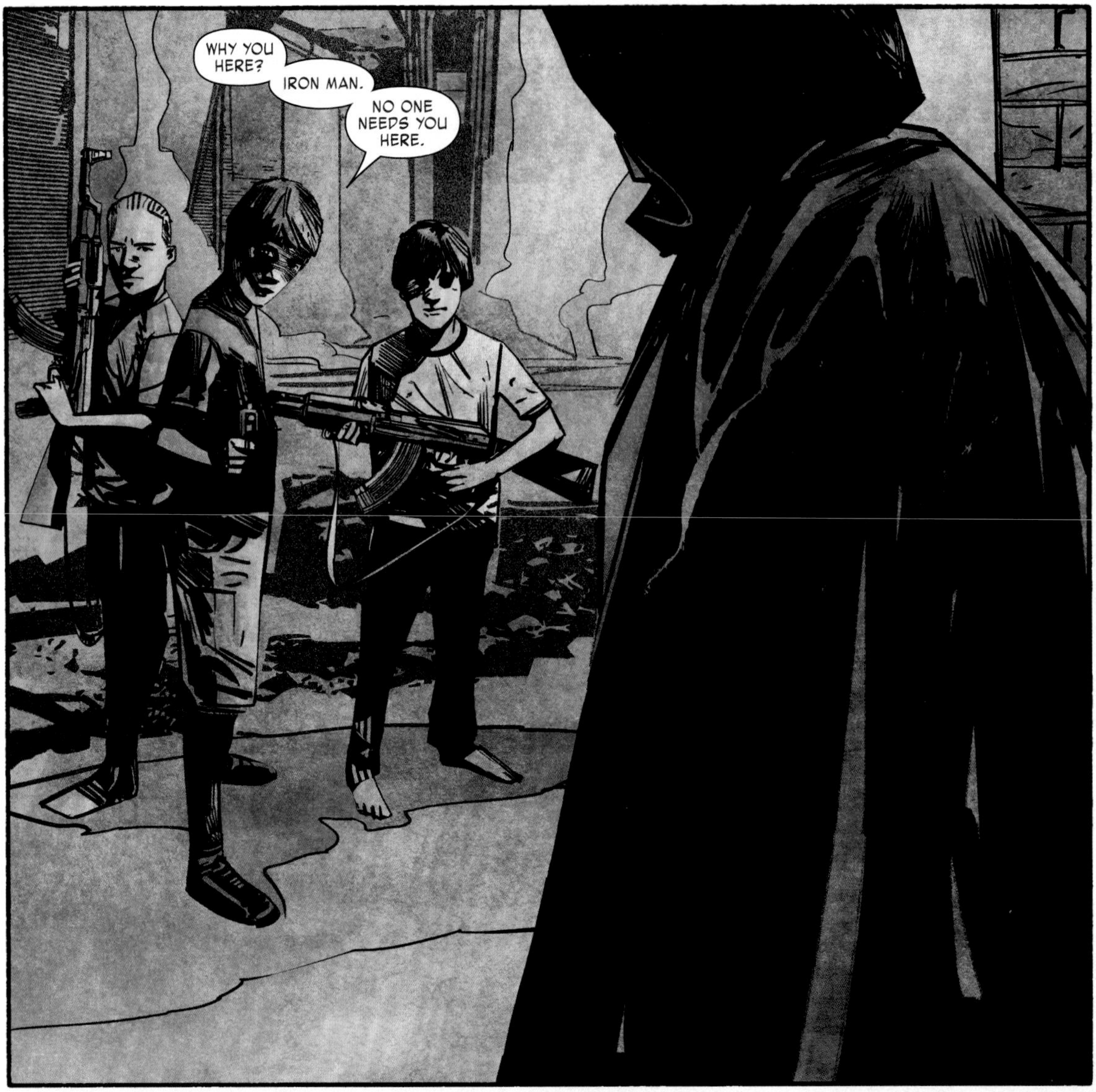
WHY YOU HERE?
IRON MAN.
NO ONE NEEDS YOU HERE.

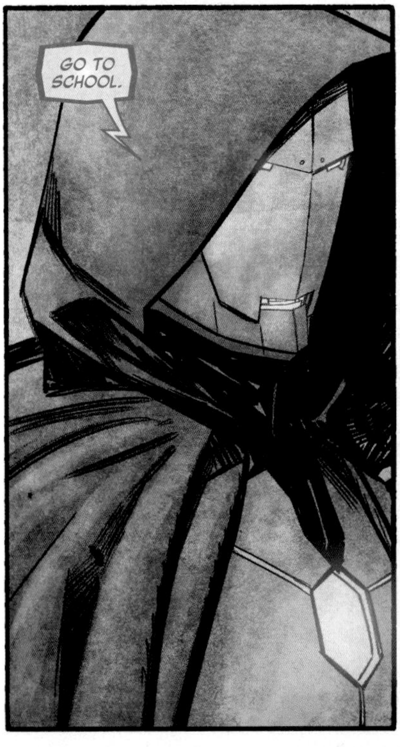
GO TO SCHOOL.

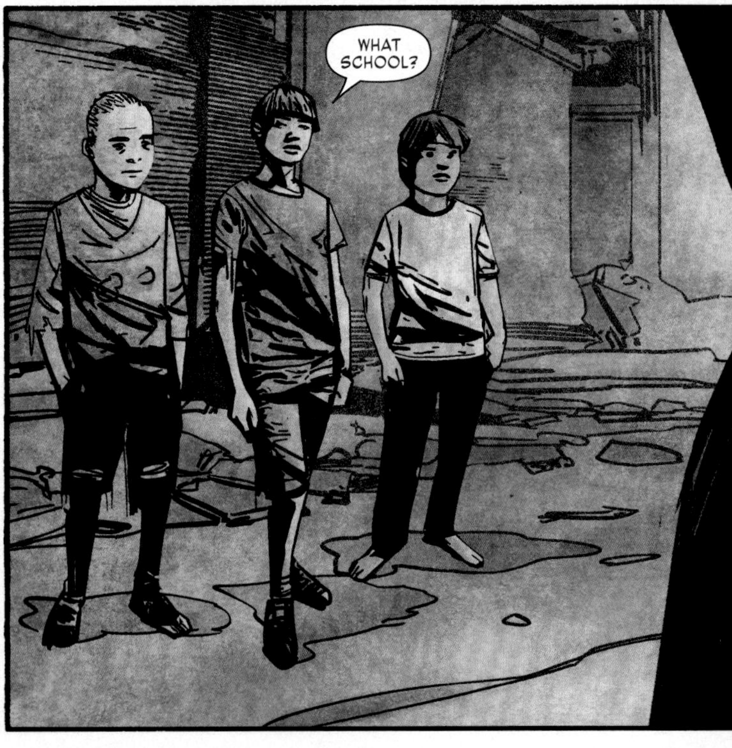
WHAT SCHOOL?

OH!
VHAT!
CLANG
CLUMP
BOOM

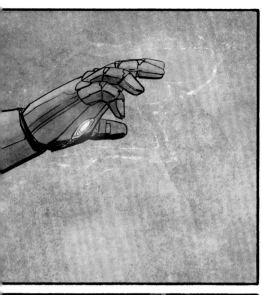

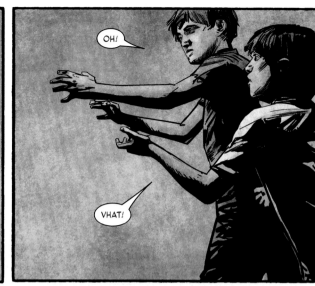

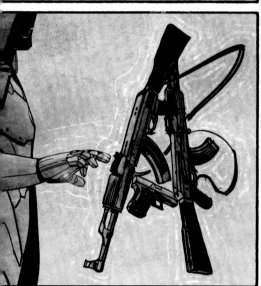

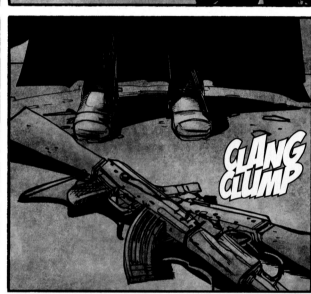

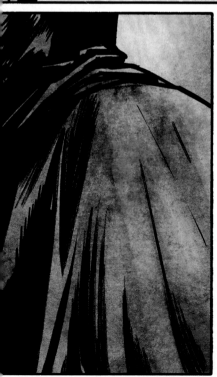

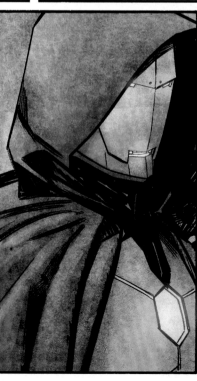

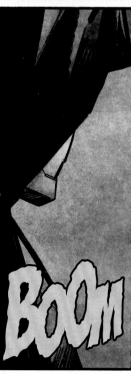

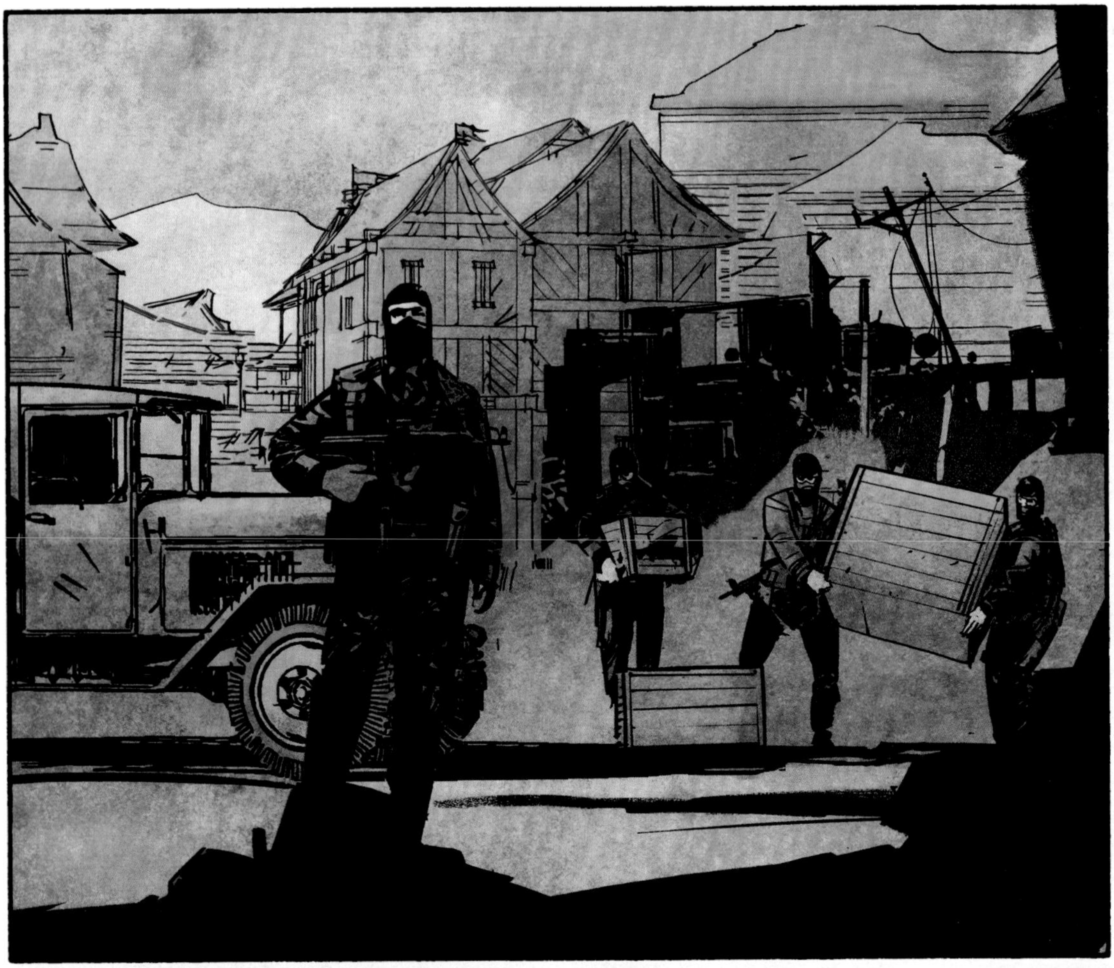

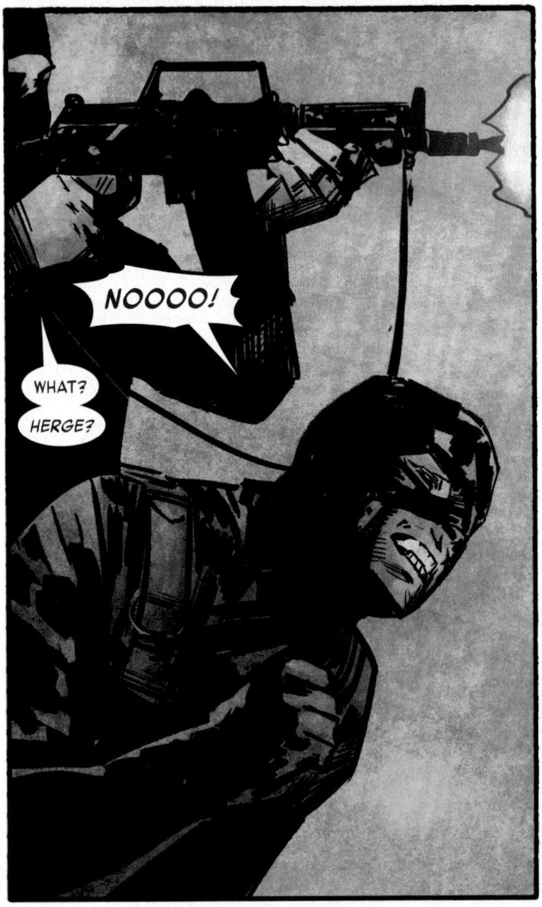
NOOOO!
WHAT? HERGE?

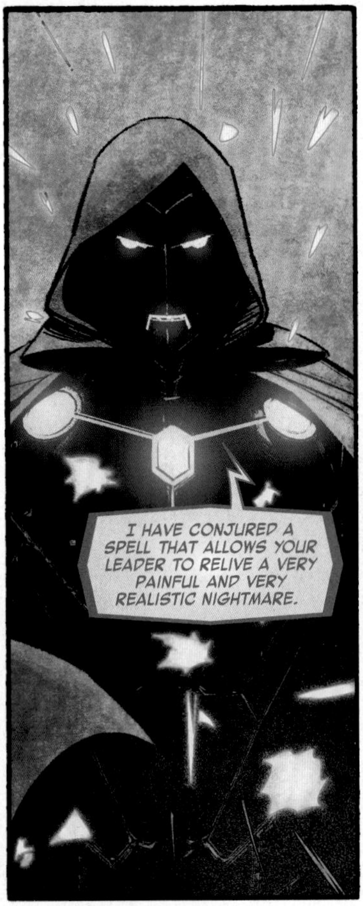
I HAVE CONJURED A SPELL THAT ALLOWS YOUR LEADER TO RELIVE A VERY PAINFUL AND VERY REALISTIC NIGHTMARE.

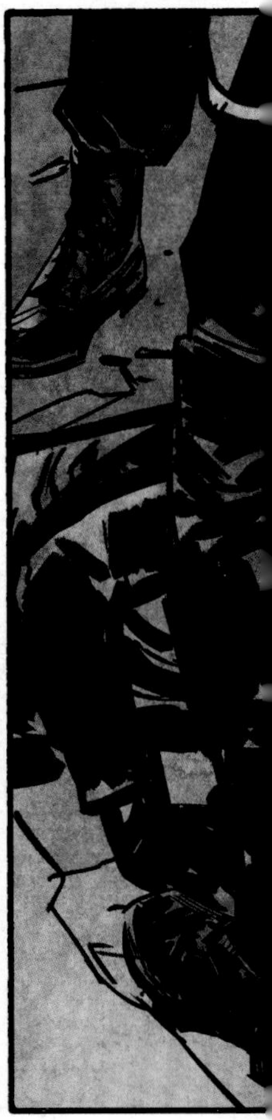

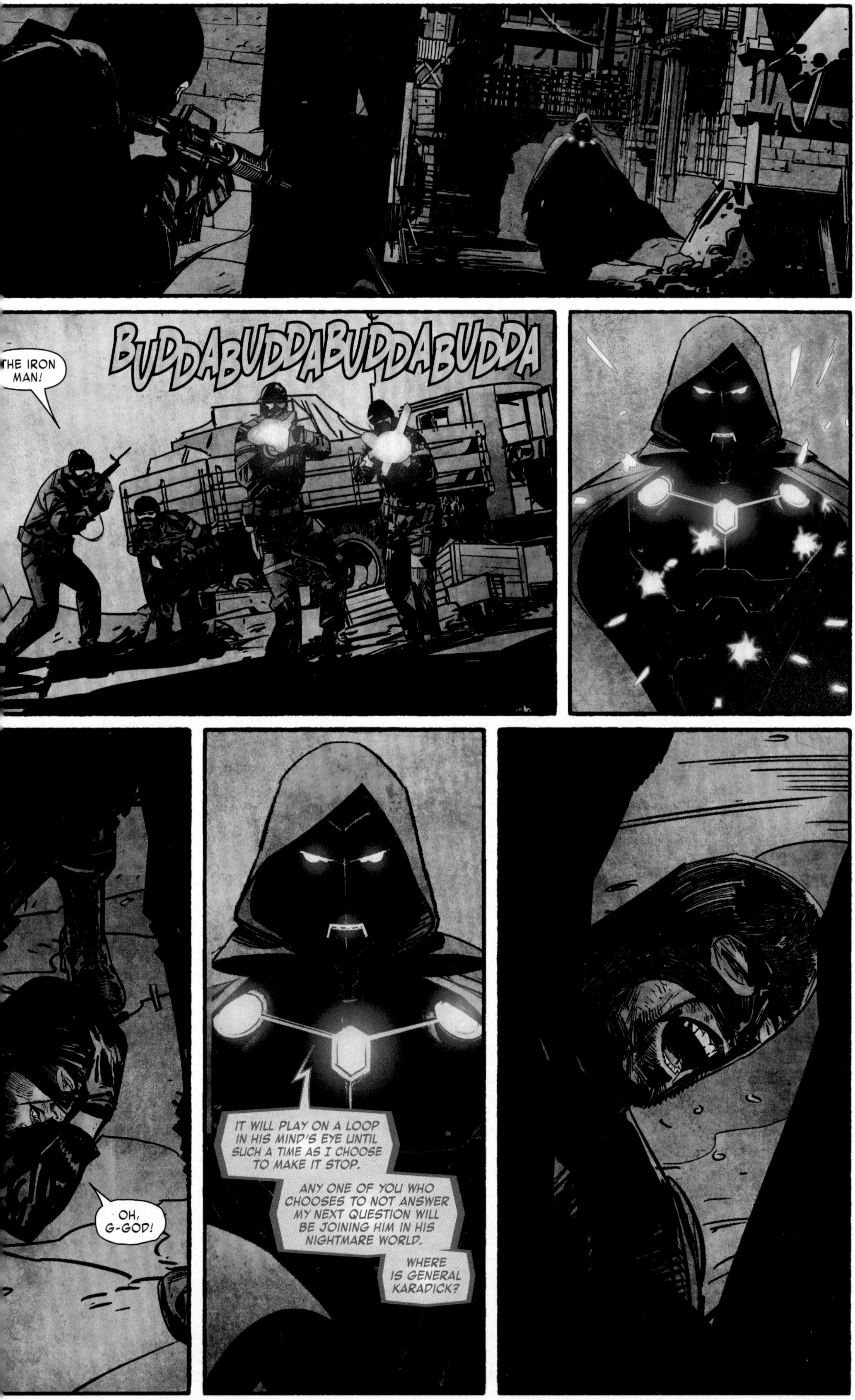

BUDDABUDDABUDDABUDDA
THE IRON MAN!
OH, G-GOD!
IT WILL PLAY ON A LOOP IN HIS MIND'S EYE UNTIL SUCH A TIME AS I CHOOSE TO MAKE IT STOP.
ANY ONE OF YOU WHO CHOOSES TO NOT ANSWER MY NEXT QUESTION WILL BE JOINING HIM IN HIS NIGHTMARE WORLD.
WHERE IS GENERAL KARADICK?

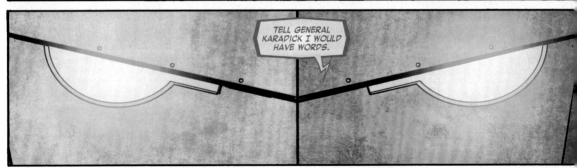

TELL GENERAL
KARADICK I WOULD
HAVE WORDS.

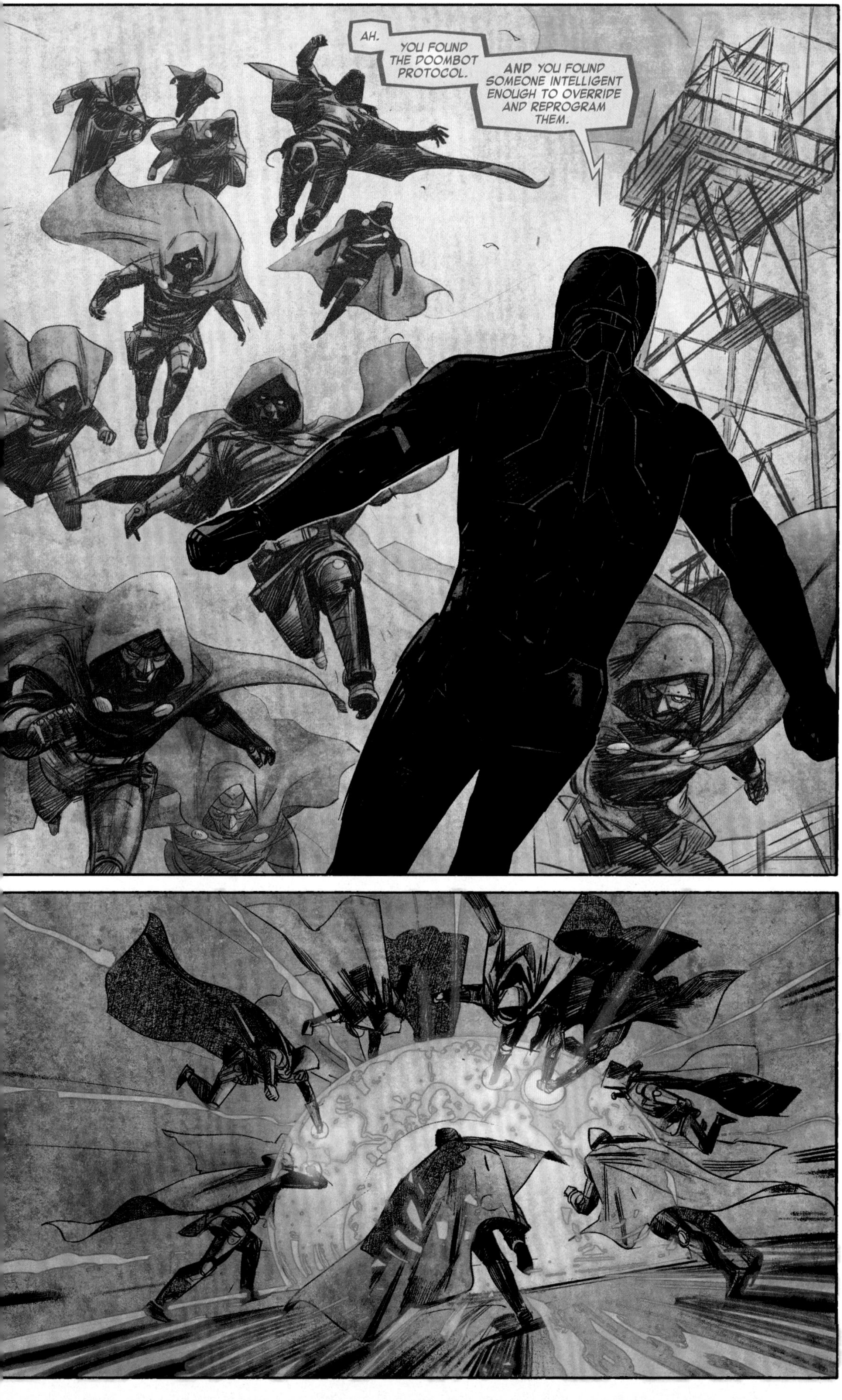
AH.
YOU FOUND THE DOOMBOT PROTOCOL.
AND YOU FOUND SOMEONE INTELLIGENT ENOUGH TO OVERRIDE AND REPROGRAM THEM.

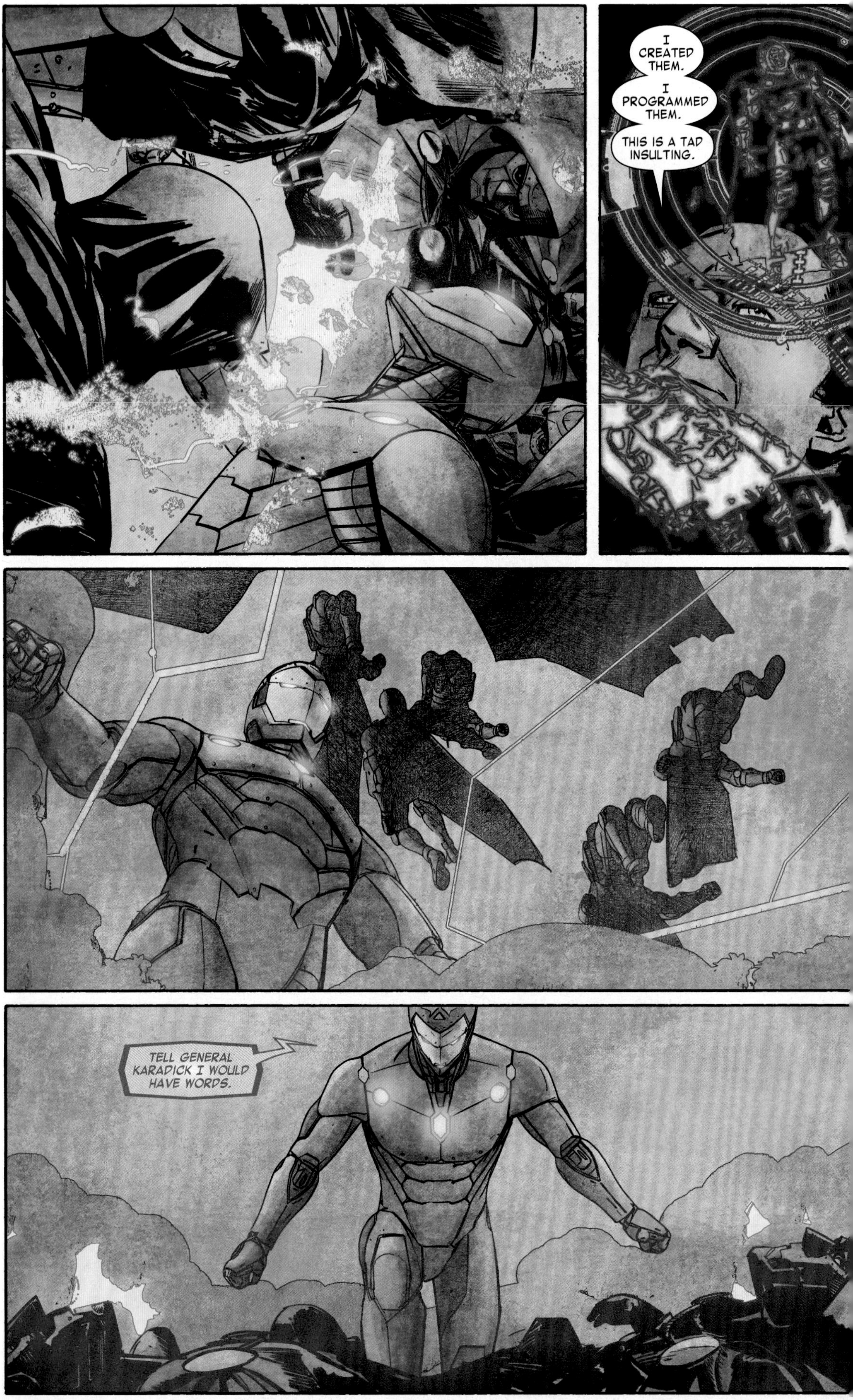
I CREATED THEM.
I PROGRAMMED THEM.
THIS IS A TAD INSULTING.
TELL GENERAL KARADICK I WOULD HAVE WORDS.

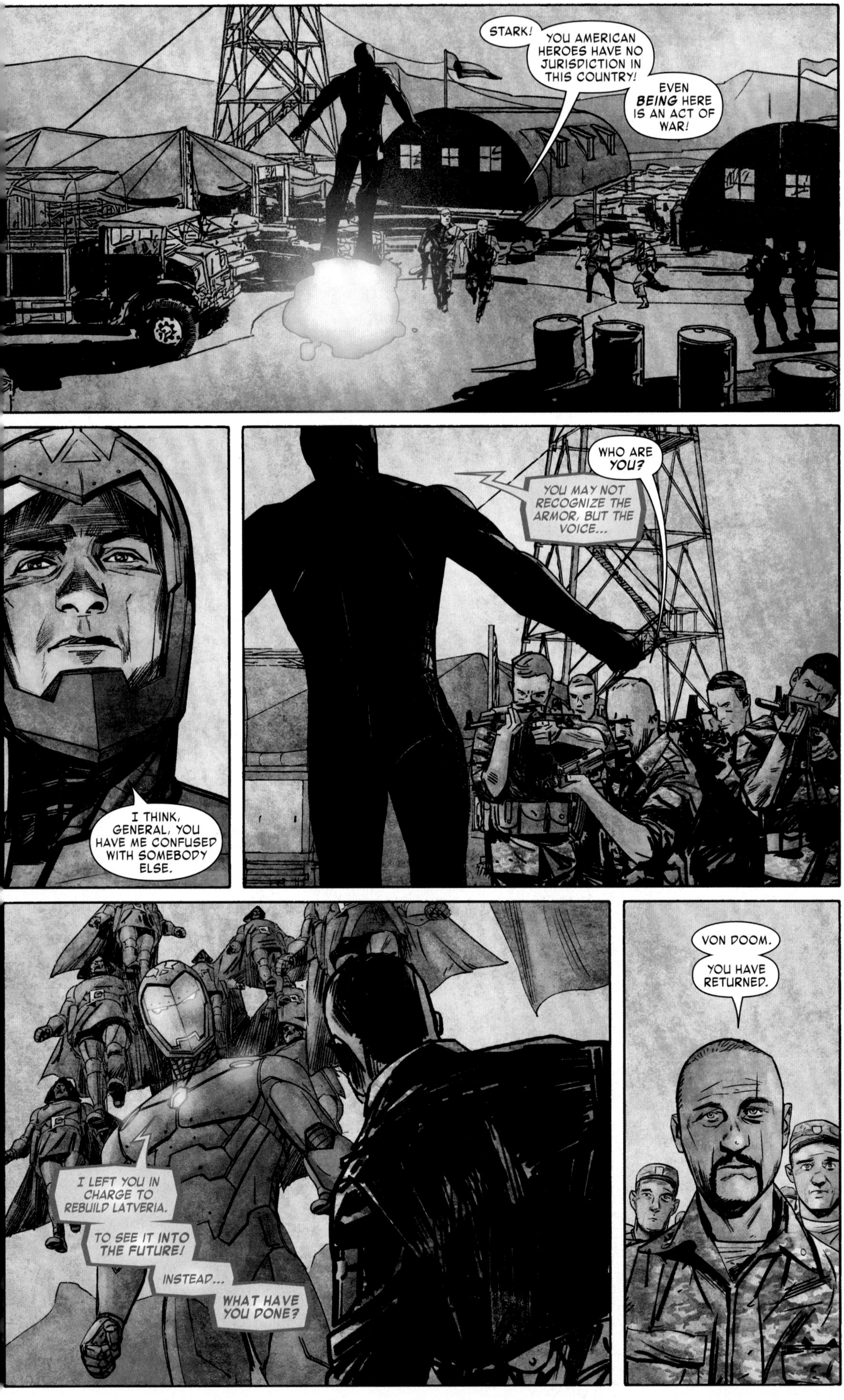
STARK!
YOU AMERICAN HEROES HAVE NO JURISDICTION IN THIS COUNTRY!
EVEN BEING HERE IS AN ACT OF WAR!
WHO ARE YOU?
YOU MAY NOT RECOGNIZE THE ARMOR, BUT THE VOICE...
I THINK, GENERAL, YOU HAVE ME CONFUSED WITH SOMEBODY ELSE.
I LEFT YOU IN CHARGE TO REBUILD LATVERIA.
TO SEE IT INTO THE FUTURE!
INSTEAD...
WHAT HAVE YOU DONE?
VON DOOM.
YOU HAVE RETURNED.

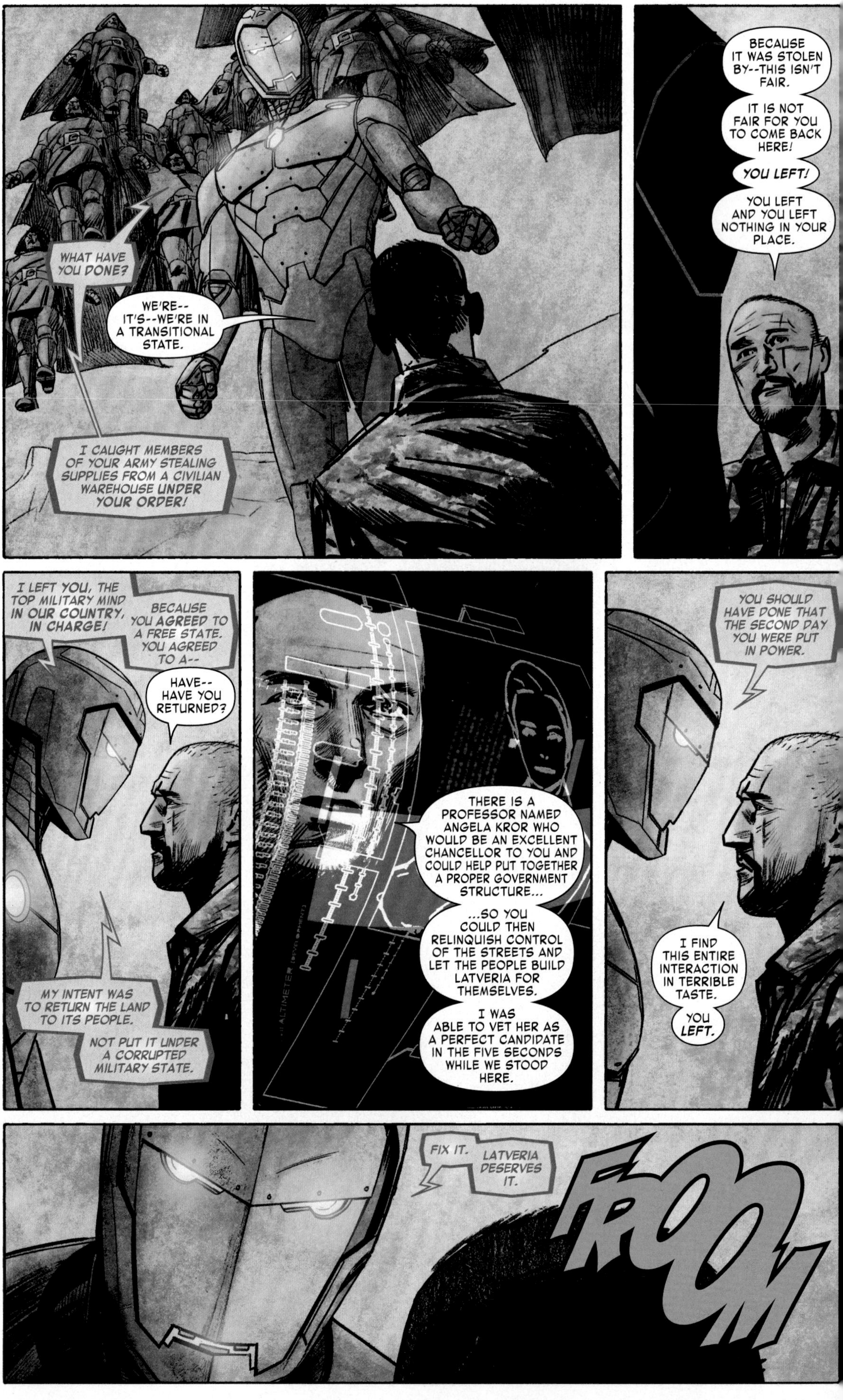
WHAT HAVE YOU DONE?
WE'RE-- IT'S--WE'RE IN A TRANSITIONAL STATE.
I CAUGHT MEMBERS OF YOUR ARMY STEALING SUPPLIES FROM A CIVILIAN WAREHOUSE UNDER YOUR ORDER!
BECAUSE IT WAS STOLEN BY--THIS ISN'T FAIR.
IT IS NOT FAIR FOR YOU TO COME BACK HERE!
YOU LEFT!
YOU LEFT AND YOU LEFT NOTHING IN YOUR PLACE.
I LEFT YOU, THE TOP MILITARY MIND IN OUR COUNTRY, IN CHARGE!
BECAUSE YOU AGREED TO A FREE STATE. YOU AGREED TO A--
HAVE-- HAVE YOU RETURNED?
MY INTENT WAS TO RETURN THE LAND TO ITS PEOPLE.
NOT PUT IT UNDER A CORRUPTED MILITARY STATE.
THERE IS A PROFESSOR NAMED ANGELA KROR WHO WOULD BE AN EXCELLENT CHANCELLOR TO YOU AND COULD HELP PUT TOGETHER A PROPER GOVERNMENT STRUCTURE...
...SO YOU COULD THEN RELINQUISH CONTROL OF THE STREETS AND LET THE PEOPLE BUILD LATVERIA FOR THEMSELVES.
I WAS ABLE TO VET HER AS A PERFECT CANDIDATE IN THE FIVE SECONDS WHILE WE STOOD HERE.
ALTIMETER
YOU SHOULD HAVE DONE THAT THE SECOND DAY YOU WERE PUT IN POWER.
I FIND THIS ENTIRE INTERACTION IN TERRIBLE TASTE.
YOU LEFT.
FIX IT.
LATVERIA DESERVES IT.
FROOM

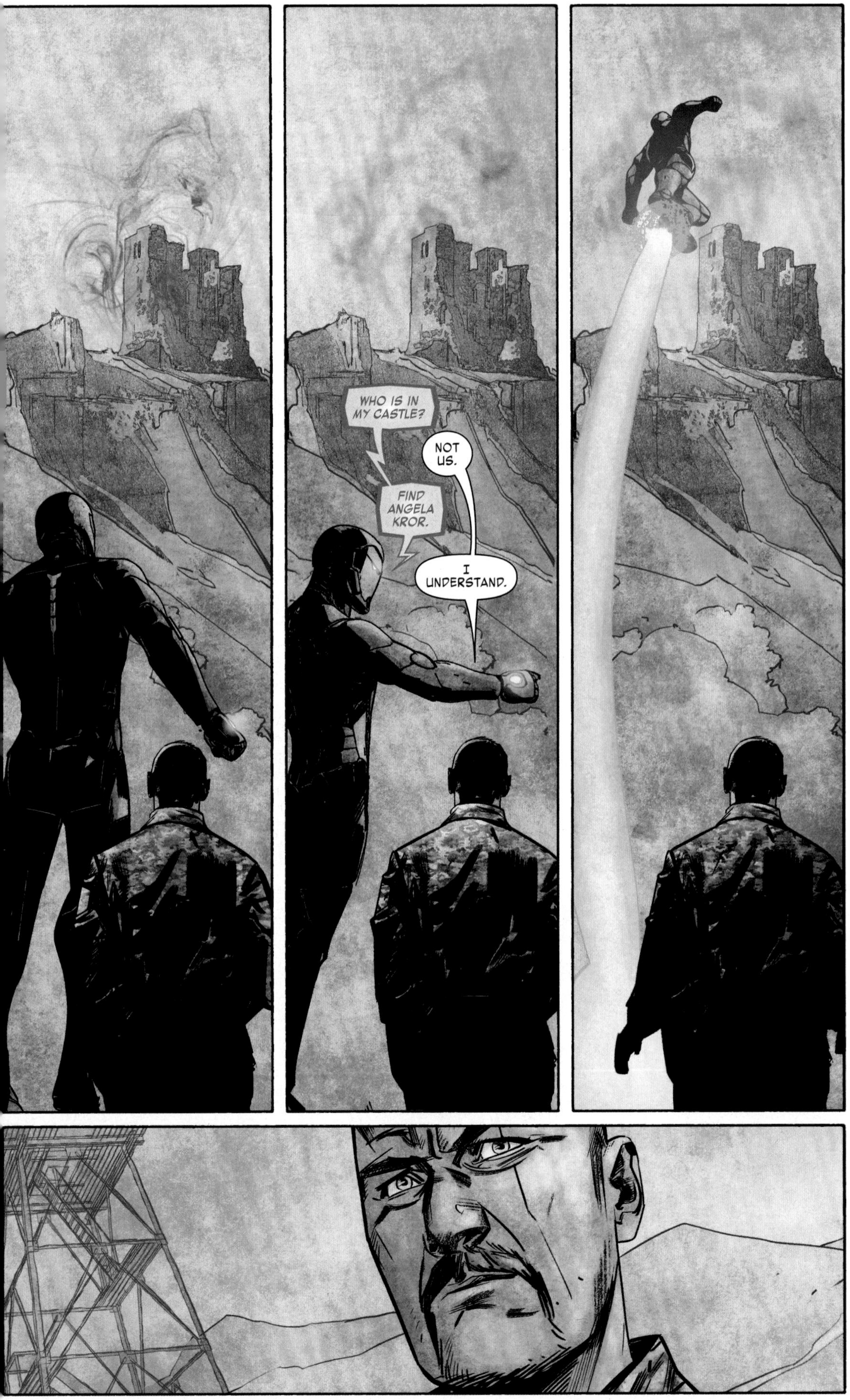
WHO IS IN MY CASTLE?
NOT US.
FIND ANGELA KROR.
I UNDERSTAND.

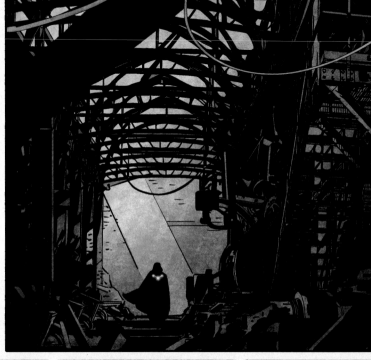

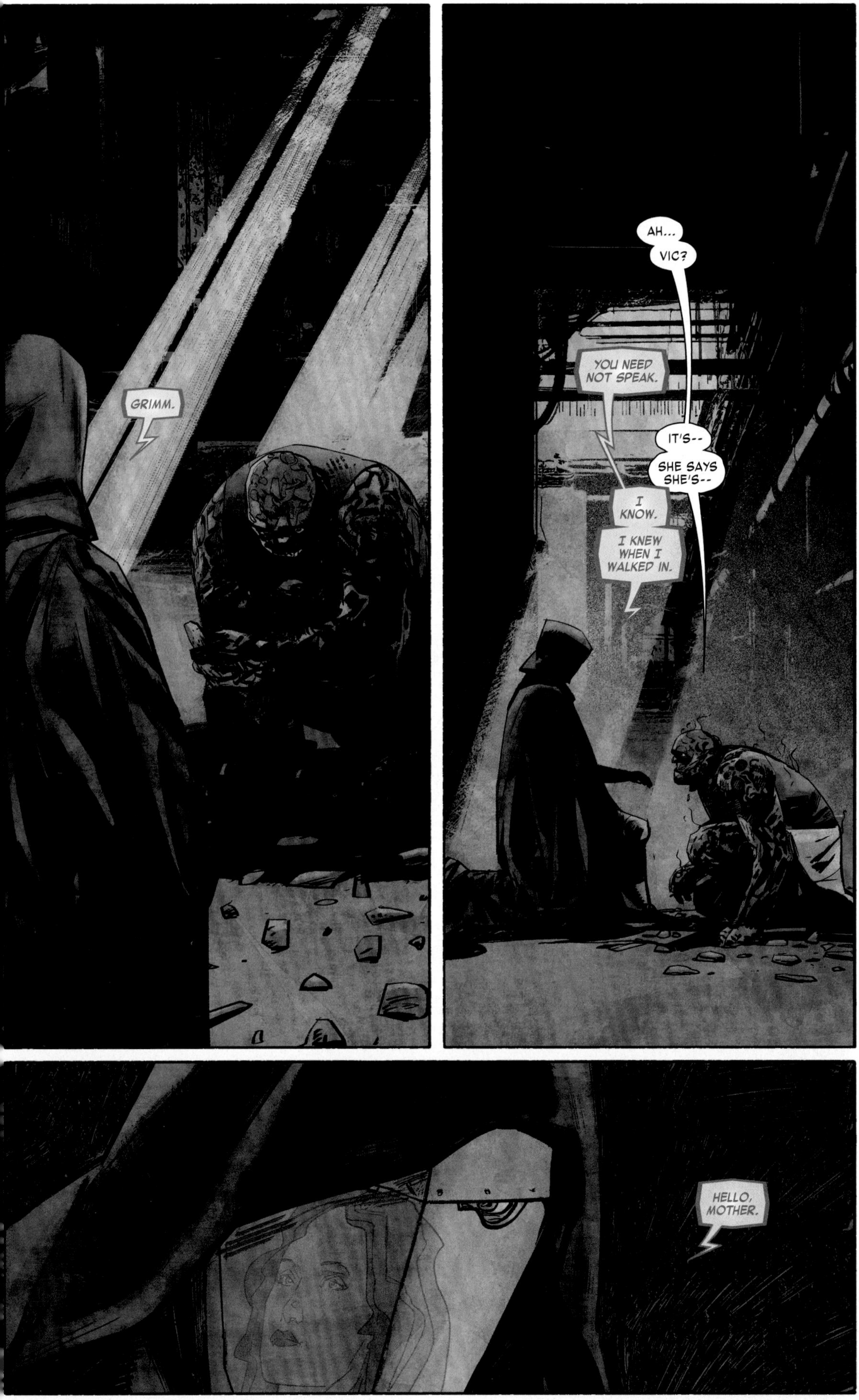
GRIMM.
AH...
VIC?
YOU NEED NOT SPEAK.
IT'S--
SHE SAYS SHE'S--
I KNOW.
I KNEW WHEN I WALKED IN.
HELLO, MOTHER.

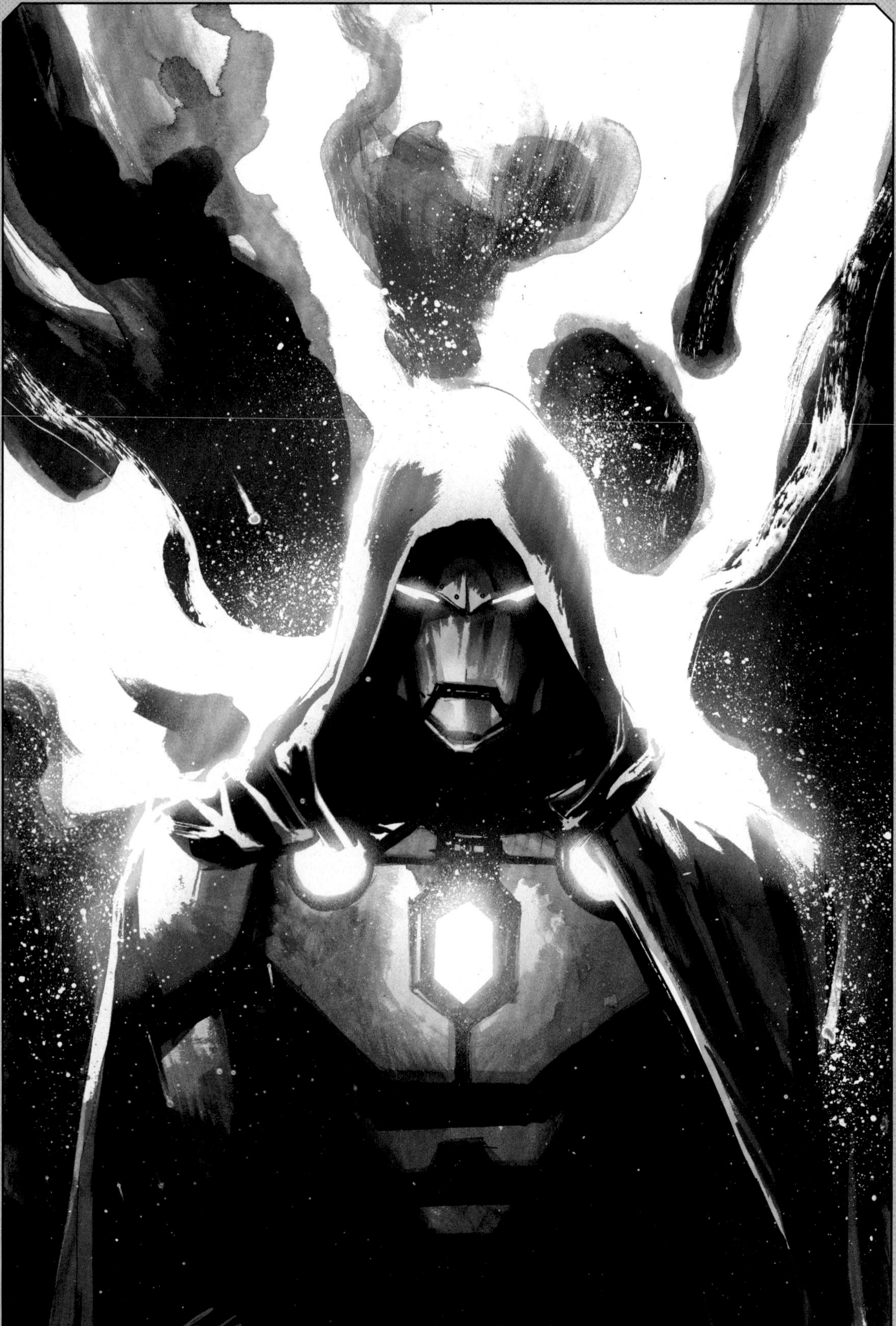
2016

RAFAEL ALBUQUERQUE
2 VARIANT

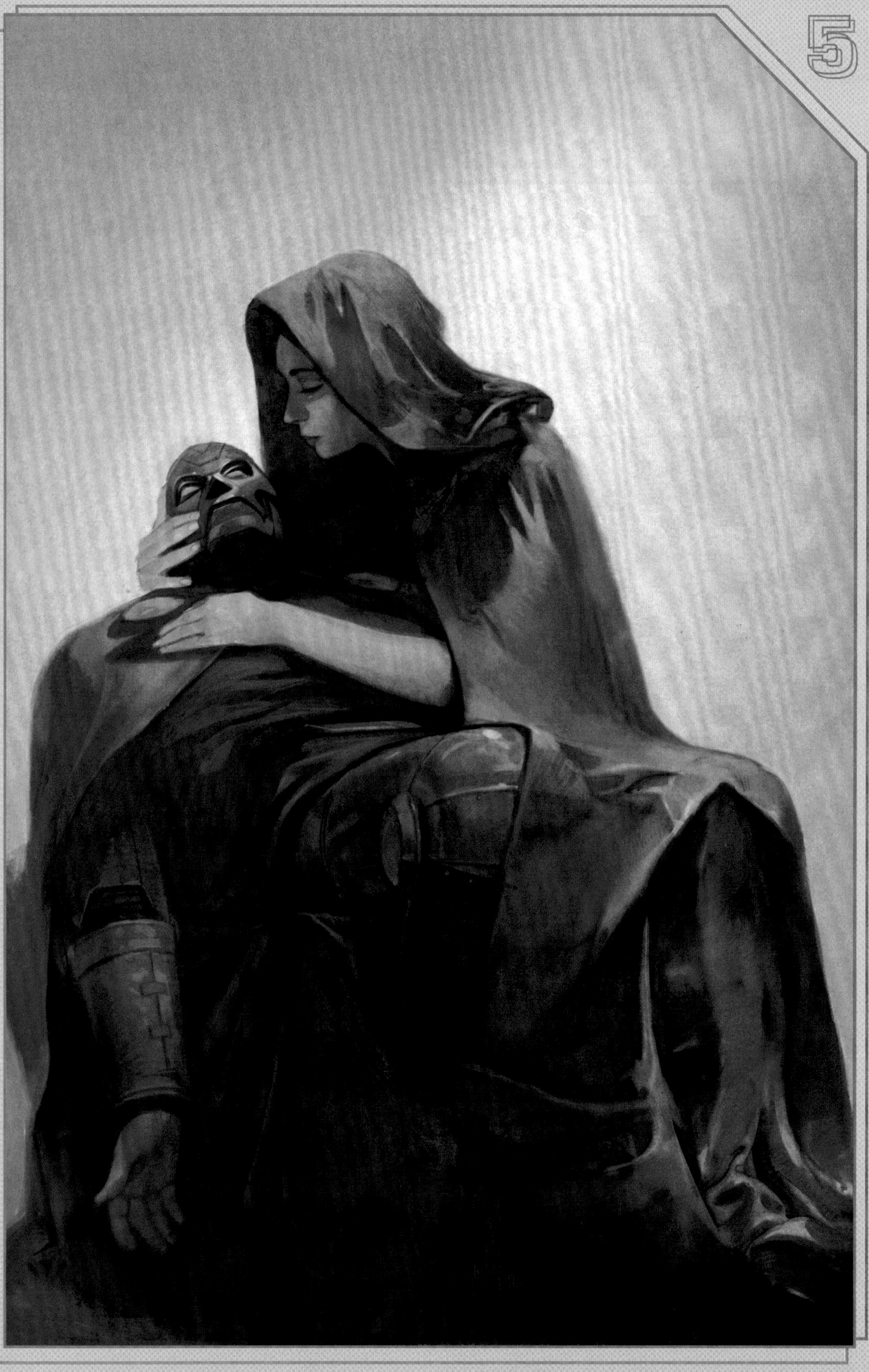
5

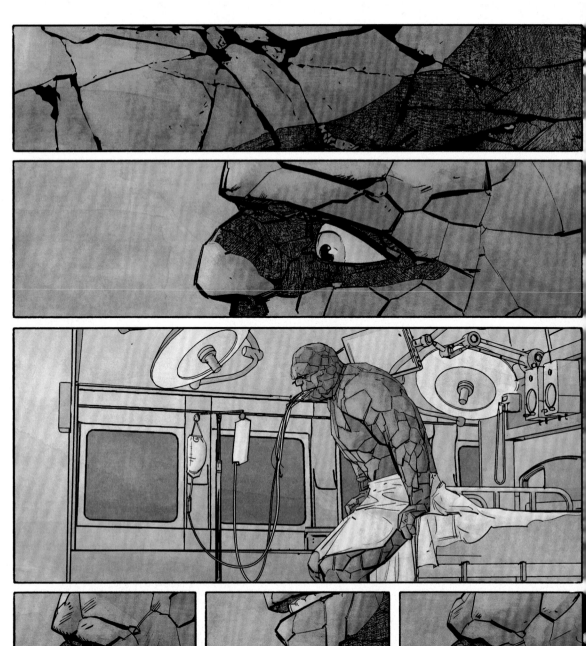

UGG!

M'OKAY?

ALL MY ROCKS ARE WHERE DEY GO?

DID I DREAM THAT WHOLE THING?

I WISH.

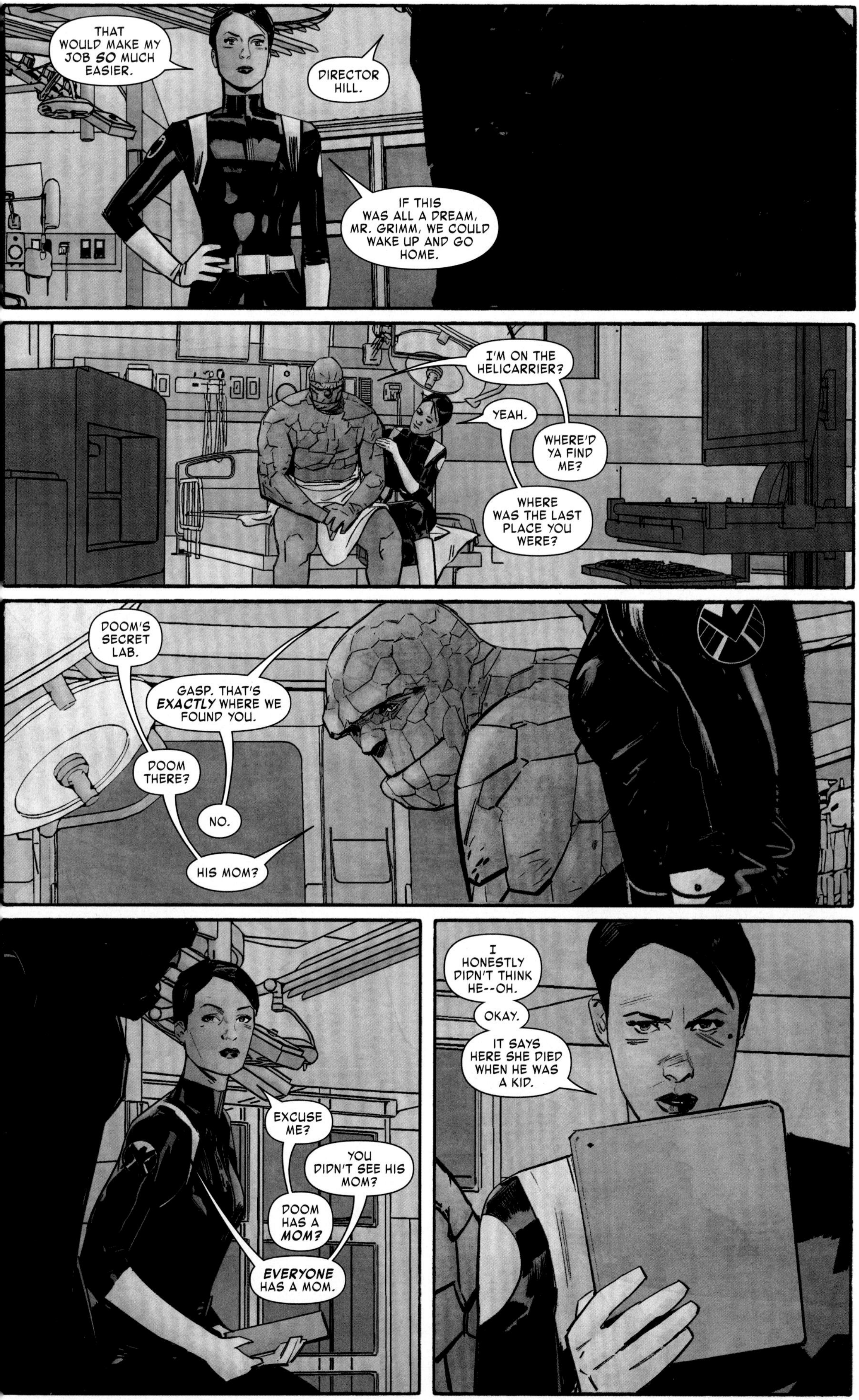
THAT WOULD MAKE MY JOB *SO* MUCH EASIER.
DIRECTOR HILL.
IF THIS WAS ALL A DREAM, MR. GRIMM, WE COULD WAKE UP AND GO HOME.
I'M ON THE HELICARRIER?
YEAH.
WHERE'D YA FIND ME?
WHERE WAS THE LAST PLACE YOU WERE?
DOOM'S SECRET LAB.
GASP. THAT'S *EXACTLY* WHERE WE FOUND YOU.
DOOM THERE?
NO.
HIS MOM?
EXCUSE ME?
YOU DIDN'T SEE HIS MOM?
DOOM HAS A *MOM?*
EVERYONE HAS A MOM.
I HONESTLY DIDN'T THINK HE--OH.
OKAY.
IT SAYS HERE SHE DIED WHEN HE WAS A KID.

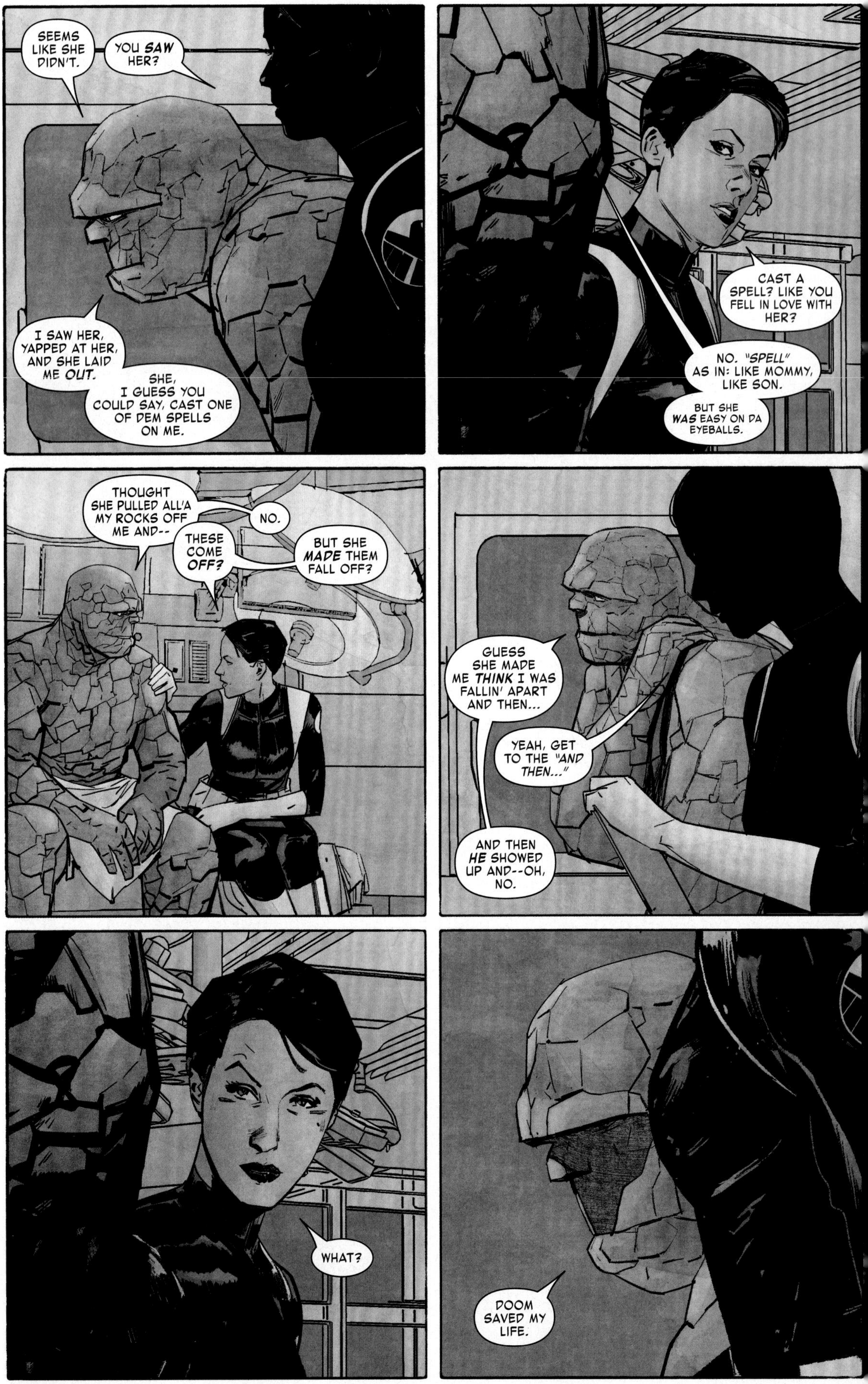
SEEMS LIKE SHE DIDN'T.
YOU SAW HER?
I SAW HER, YAPPED AT HER, AND SHE LAID ME OUT.
SHE, I GUESS YOU COULD SAY, CAST ONE OF DEM SPELLS ON ME.
CAST A SPELL? LIKE YOU FELL IN LOVE WITH HER?
NO. "SPELL" AS IN: LIKE MOMMY, LIKE SON.
BUT SHE WAS EASY ON DA EYEBALLS.
THOUGHT SHE PULLED ALL'A MY ROCKS OFF ME AND--
NO.
THESE COME OFF?
BUT SHE MADE THEM FALL OFF?
GUESS SHE MADE ME THINK I WAS FALLIN' APART AND THEN...
YEAH, GET TO THE "AND THEN..."
AND THEN HE SHOWED UP AND--OH, NO.
WHAT?
DOOM SAVED MY LIFE.

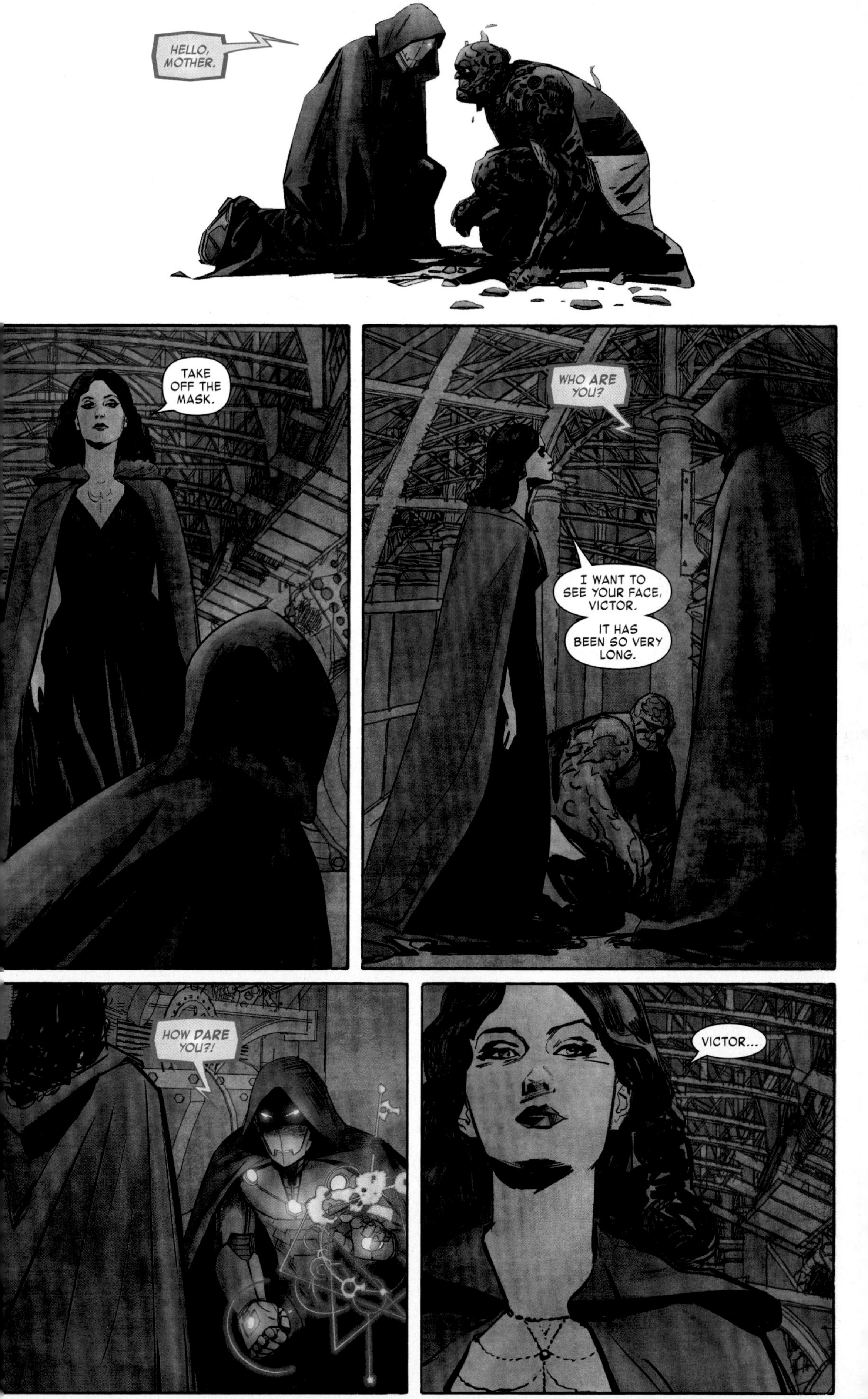
HELLO, MOTHER.
TAKE OFF THE MASK.
WHO ARE YOU?
I WANT TO SEE YOUR FACE, VICTOR.
IT HAS BEEN SO VERY LONG.
HOW DARE YOU?!
VICTOR...

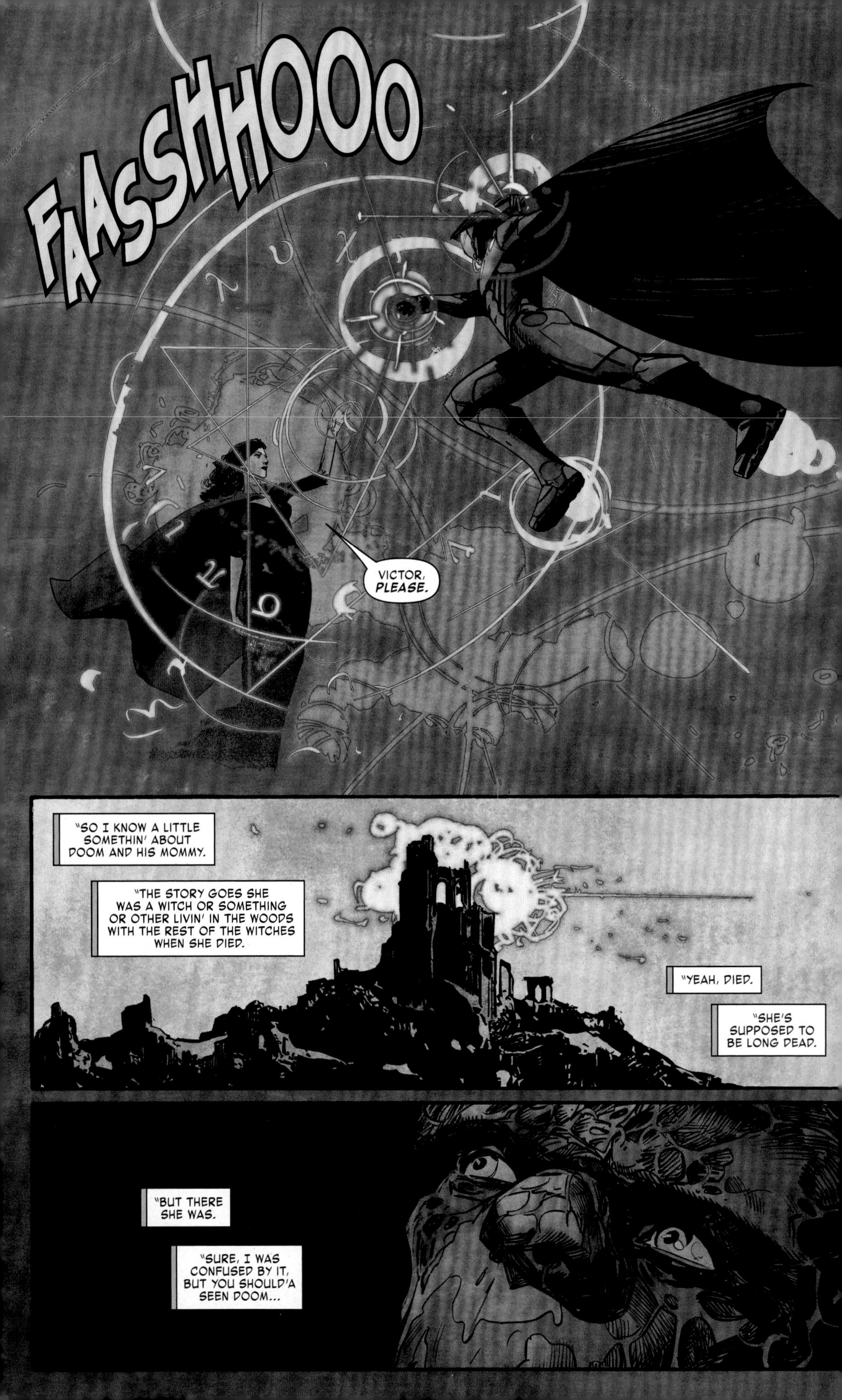
FAASSHHOOO
VICTOR, PLEASE.
"SO I KNOW A LITTLE SOMETHIN' ABOUT DOOM AND HIS MOMMY.
"THE STORY GOES SHE WAS A WITCH OR SOMETHING OR OTHER LIVIN' IN THE WOODS WITH THE REST OF THE WITCHES WHEN SHE DIED.
"YEAH, DIED.
"SHE'S SUPPOSED TO BE LONG DEAD.
"BUT THERE SHE WAS.
"SURE, I WAS CONFUSED BY IT, BUT YOU SHOULD'A SEEN DOOM...

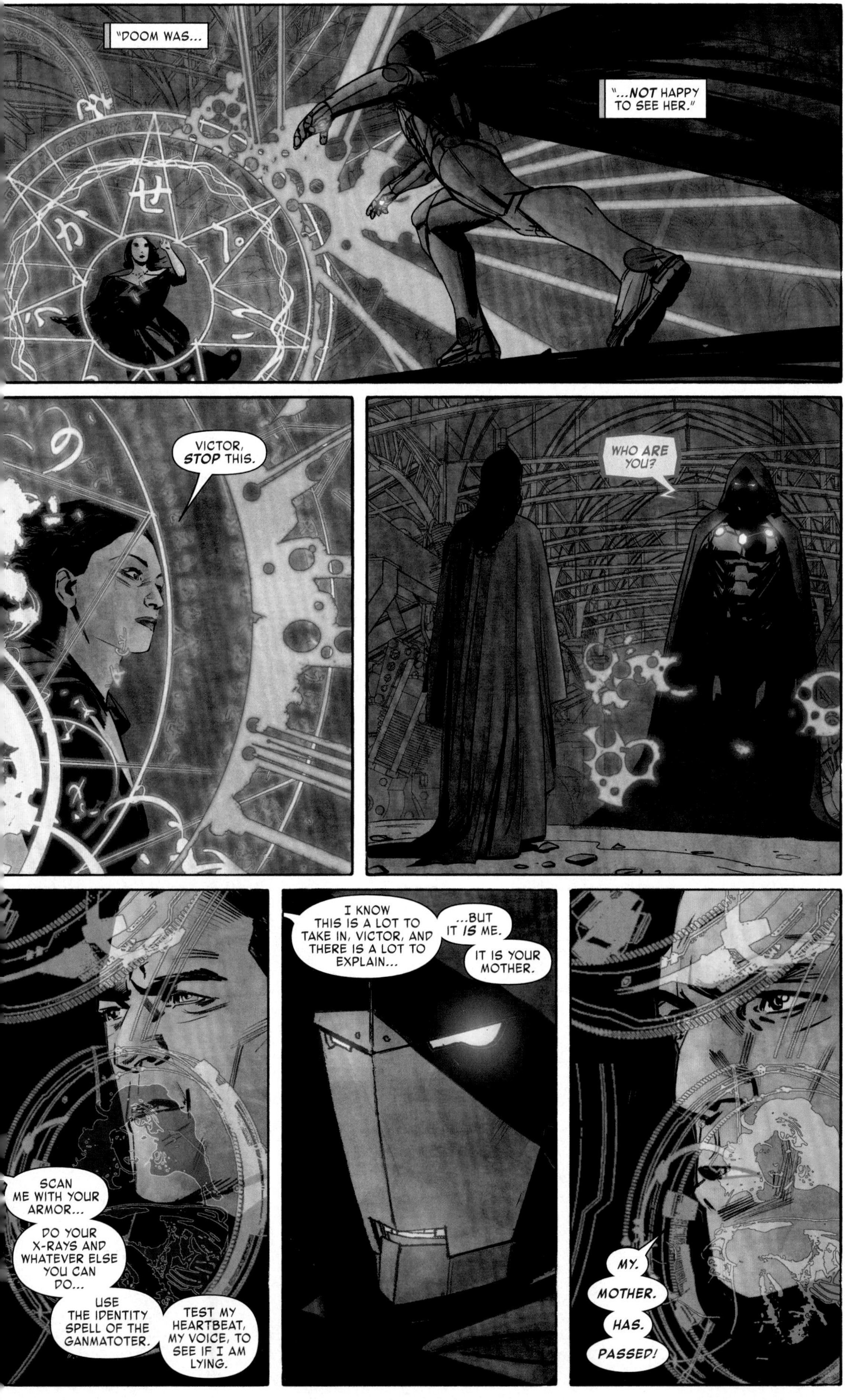
"DOOM WAS...
"...NOT HAPPY TO SEE HER."
VICTOR, STOP THIS.
WHO ARE YOU?
SCAN ME WITH YOUR ARMOR...
DO YOUR X-RAYS AND WHATEVER ELSE YOU CAN DO...
USE THE IDENTITY SPELL OF THE GANMATOTER.
TEST MY HEARTBEAT, MY VOICE, TO SEE IF I AM LYING.
I KNOW THIS IS A LOT TO TAKE IN, VICTOR, AND THERE IS A LOT TO EXPLAIN...
...BUT IT IS ME.
IT IS YOUR MOTHER.
MY.
MOTHER.
HAS.
PASSED!

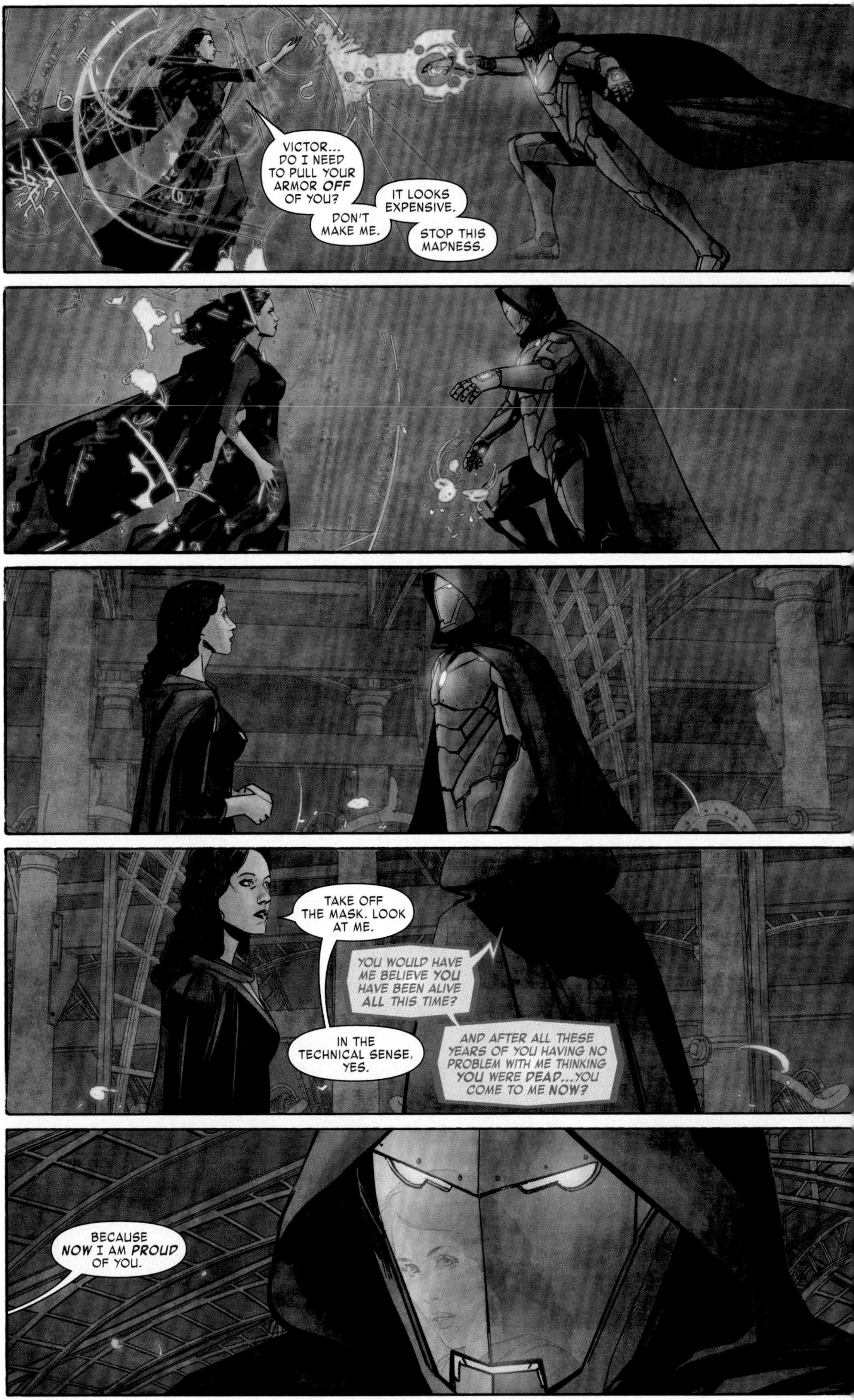

VICTOR... DO I NEED TO PULL YOUR ARMOR OFF OF YOU?
DON'T MAKE ME.
IT LOOKS EXPENSIVE.
STOP THIS MADNESS.
TAKE OFF THE MASK. LOOK AT ME.
YOU WOULD HAVE ME BELIEVE YOU HAVE BEEN ALIVE ALL THIS TIME?
IN THE TECHNICAL SENSE, YES.
AND AFTER ALL THESE YEARS OF YOU HAVING NO PROBLEM WITH ME THINKING YOU WERE DEAD...YOU COME TO ME NOW?
BECAUSE NOW I AM PROUD OF YOU.

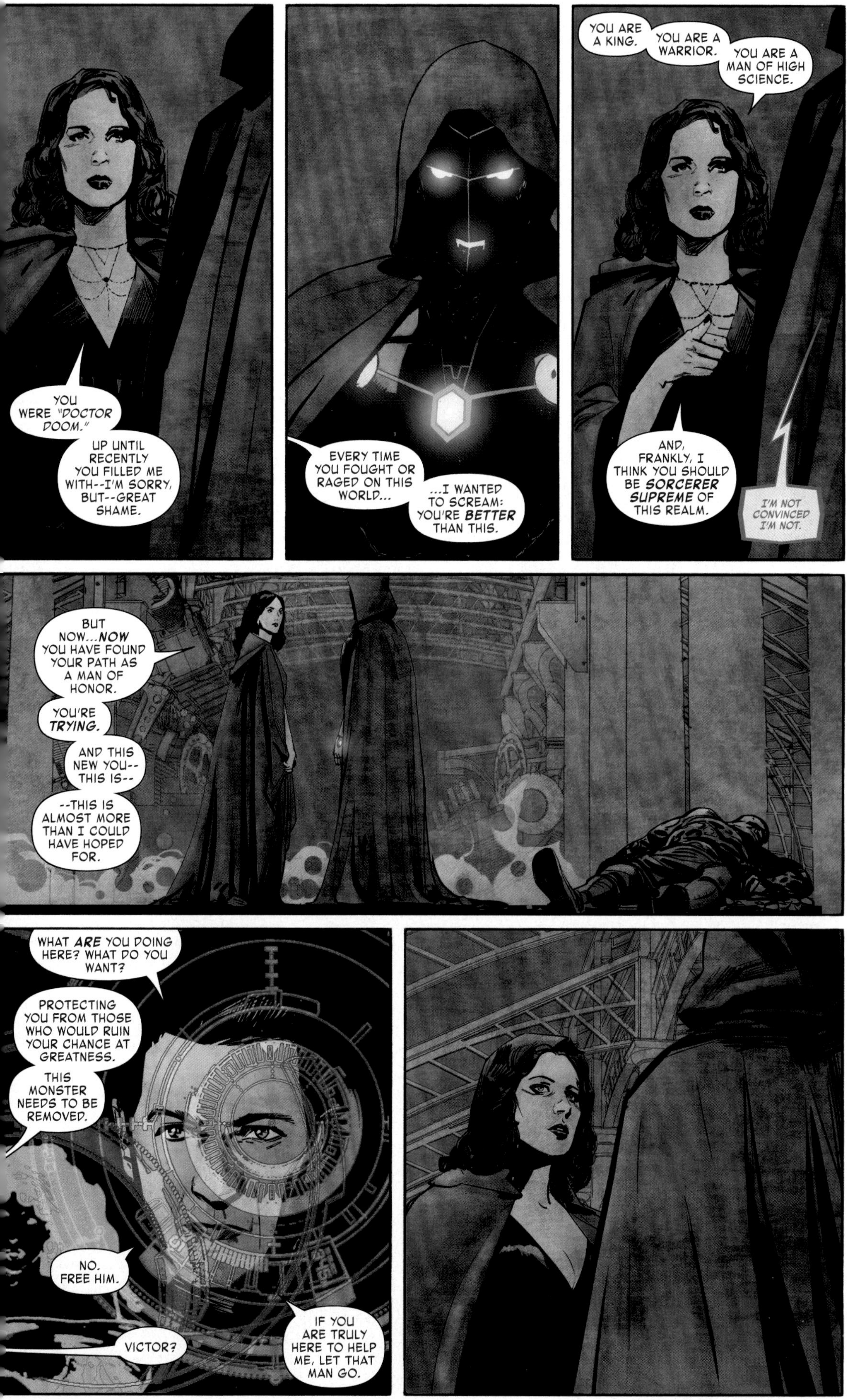

YOU WERE "DOCTOR DOOM."
UP UNTIL RECENTLY YOU FILLED ME WITH--I'M SORRY, BUT--GREAT SHAME.
EVERY TIME YOU FOUGHT OR RAGED ON THIS WORLD...
...I WANTED TO SCREAM: YOU'RE BETTER THAN THIS.
YOU ARE A KING.
YOU ARE A WARRIOR.
YOU ARE A MAN OF HIGH SCIENCE.
AND, FRANKLY, I THINK YOU SHOULD BE SORCERER SUPREME OF THIS REALM.
I'M NOT CONVINCED I'M NOT.
BUT NOW...NOW YOU HAVE FOUND YOUR PATH AS A MAN OF HONOR.
YOU'RE TRYING.
AND THIS NEW YOU--THIS IS--
--THIS IS ALMOST MORE THAN I COULD HAVE HOPED FOR.
WHAT ARE YOU DOING HERE? WHAT DO YOU WANT?
PROTECTING YOU FROM THOSE WHO WOULD RUIN YOUR CHANCE AT GREATNESS.
THIS MONSTER NEEDS TO BE REMOVED.
NO. FREE HIM.
VICTOR?
IF YOU ARE TRULY HERE TO HELP ME, LET THAT MAN GO.

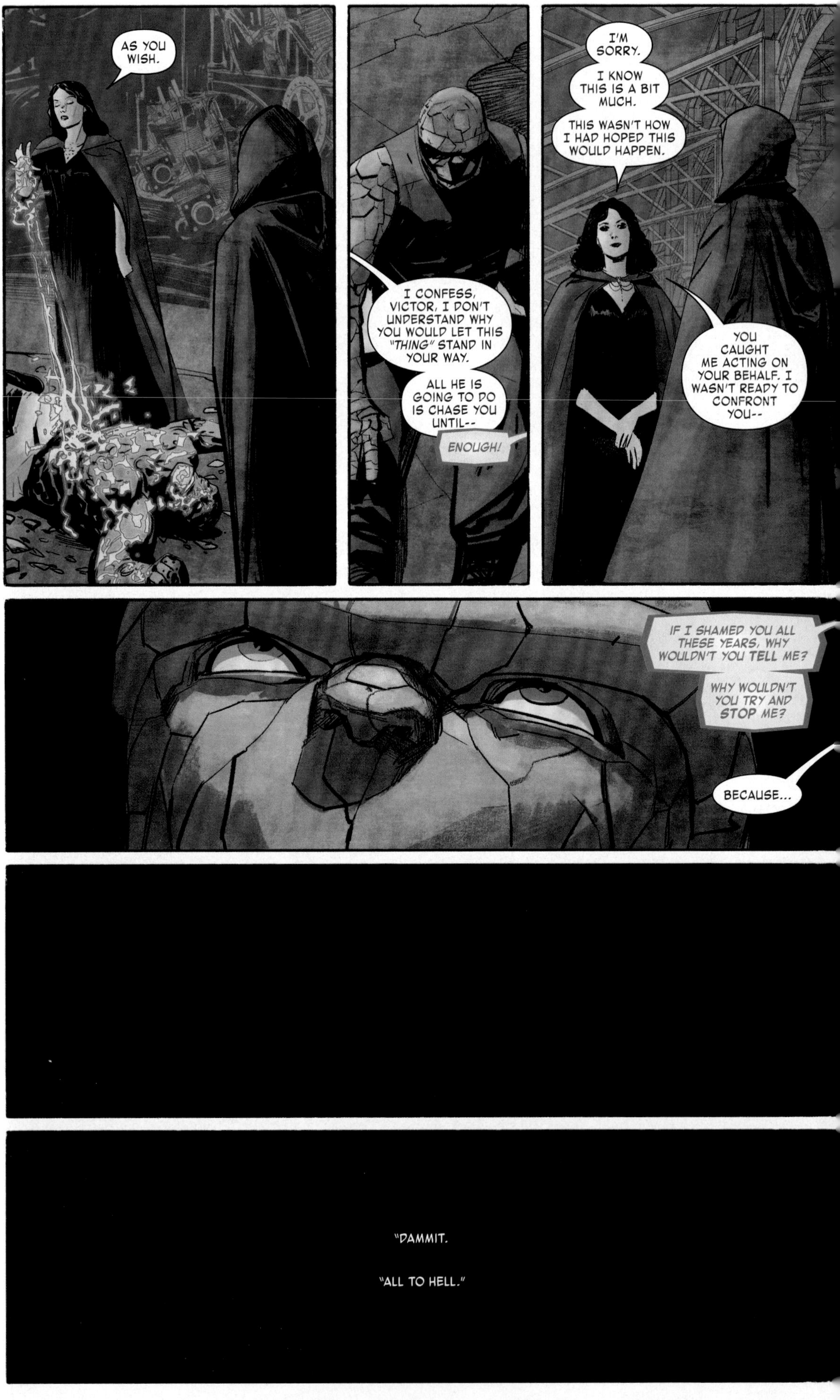
AS YOU WISH.
I CONFESS, VICTOR, I DON'T UNDERSTAND WHY YOU WOULD LET THIS "THING" STAND IN YOUR WAY.
ALL HE IS GOING TO DO IS CHASE YOU UNTIL--
ENOUGH!
I'M SORRY.
I KNOW THIS IS A BIT MUCH.
THIS WASN'T HOW I HAD HOPED THIS WOULD HAPPEN.
YOU CAUGHT ME ACTING ON YOUR BEHALF. I WASN'T READY TO CONFRONT YOU--
IF I SHAMED YOU ALL THESE YEARS, WHY WOULDN'T YOU TELL ME?
WHY WOULDN'T YOU TRY AND STOP ME?
BECAUSE...
"DAMMIT.
"ALL TO HELL."

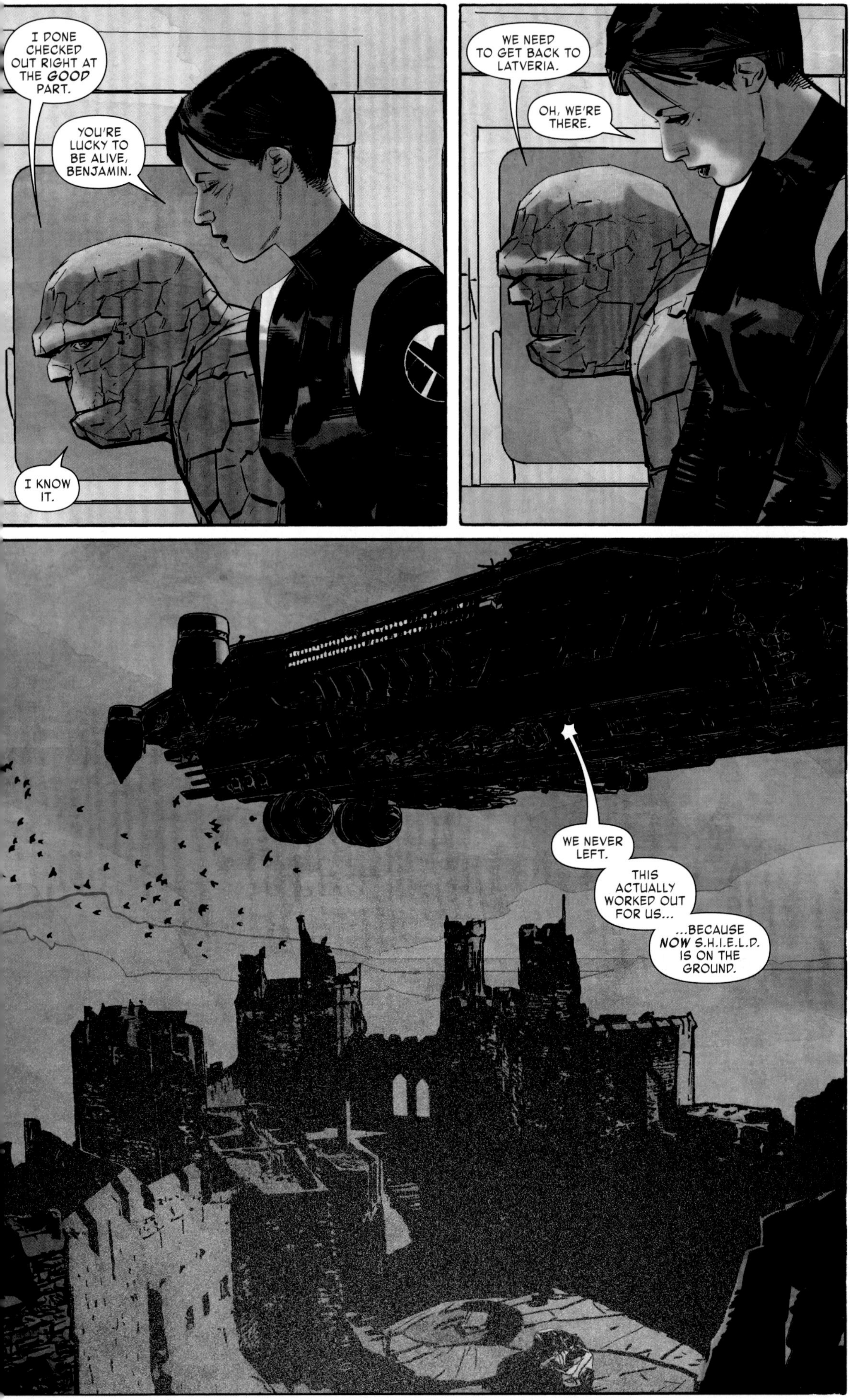
I DONE CHECKED OUT RIGHT AT THE GOOD PART.
YOU'RE LUCKY TO BE ALIVE, BENJAMIN.
I KNOW IT.
WE NEED TO GET BACK TO LATVERIA.
OH, WE'RE THERE.
WE NEVER LEFT.
THIS ACTUALLY WORKED OUT FOR US...
...BECAUSE NOW S.H.I.E.L.D. IS ON THE GROUND.

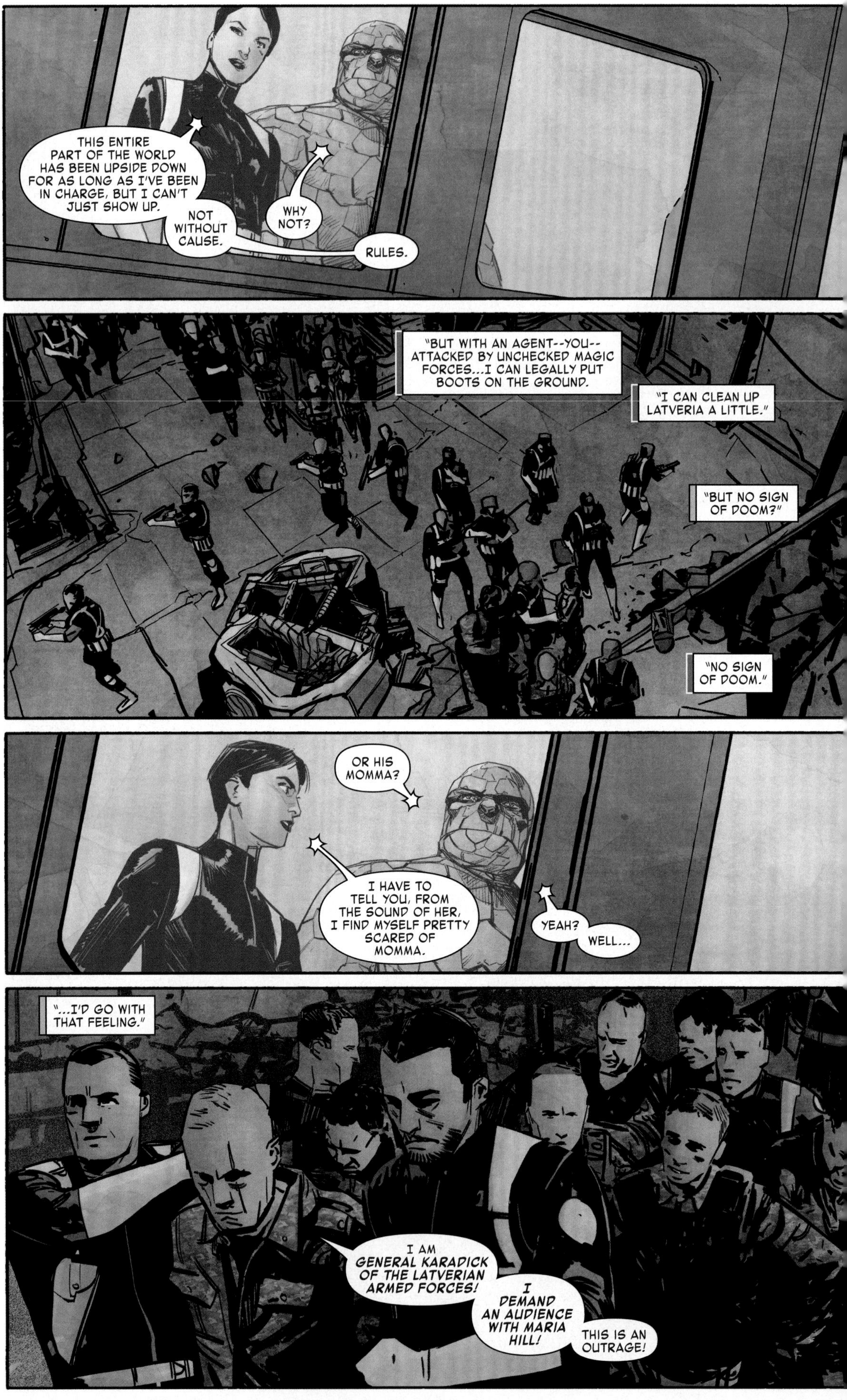
THIS ENTIRE PART OF THE WORLD HAS BEEN UPSIDE DOWN FOR AS LONG AS I'VE BEEN IN CHARGE, BUT I CAN'T JUST SHOW UP.
WHY NOT?
NOT WITHOUT CAUSE.
RULES.
"BUT WITH AN AGENT--YOU--ATTACKED BY UNCHECKED MAGIC FORCES...I CAN LEGALLY PUT BOOTS ON THE GROUND.
"I CAN CLEAN UP LATVERIA A LITTLE."
"BUT NO SIGN OF DOOM?"
"NO SIGN OF DOOM."
OR HIS MOMMA?
I HAVE TO TELL YOU, FROM THE SOUND OF HER, I FIND MYSELF PRETTY SCARED OF MOMMA.
YEAH?
WELL...
"...I'D GO WITH THAT FEELING."
I AM *GENERAL KARADICK OF THE LATVERIAN ARMED FORCES!*
I DEMAND AN AUDIENCE WITH MARIA HILL!
THIS IS AN OUTRAGE!

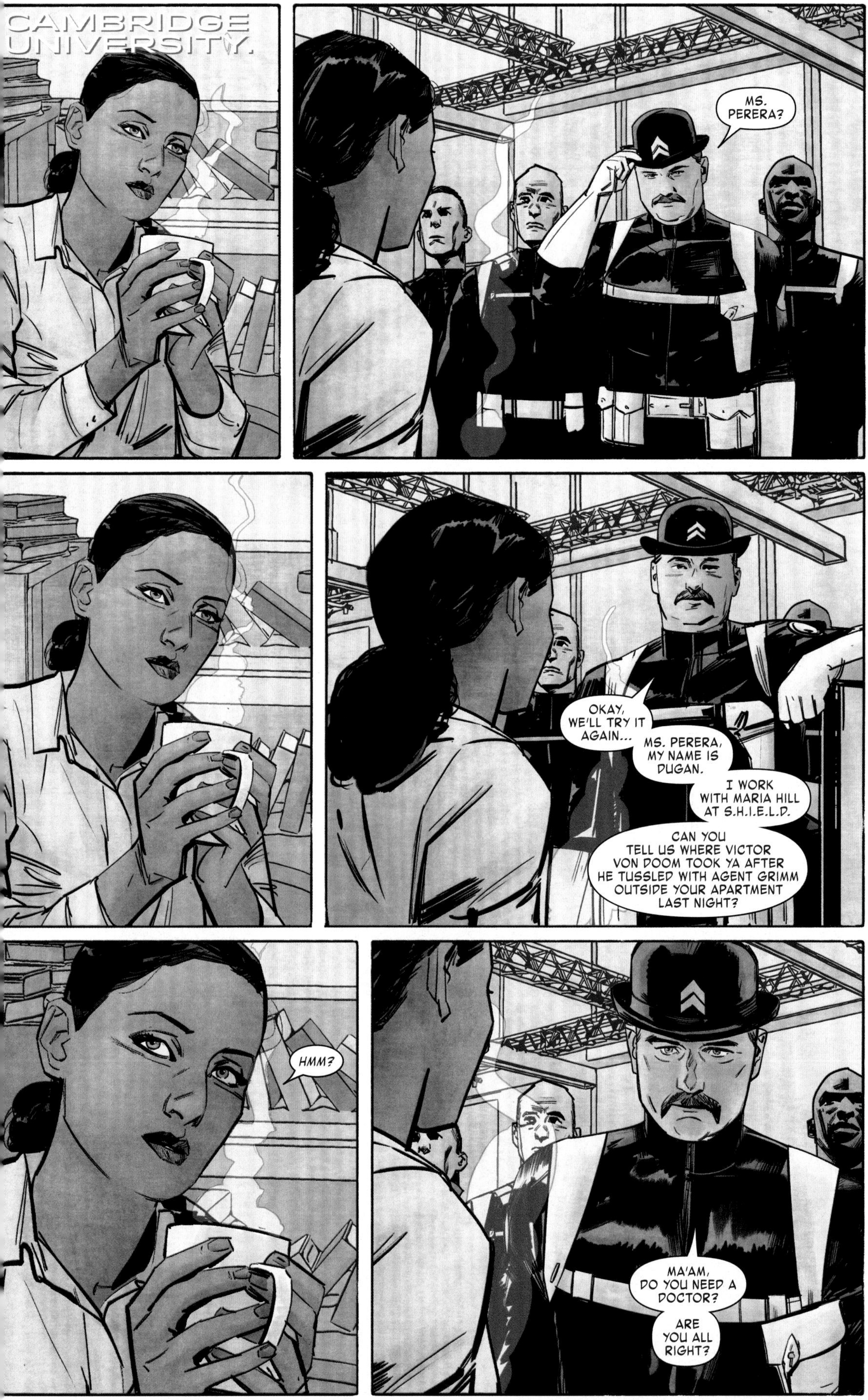
CAMBRIDGE UNIVERSITY.
MS. PERERA?
OKAY, WE'LL TRY IT AGAIN...
MS. PERERA, MY NAME IS DUGAN.
I WORK WITH MARIA HILL AT S.H.I.E.L.D.
CAN YOU TELL US WHERE VICTOR VON DOOM TOOK YA AFTER HE TUSSLED WITH AGENT GRIMM OUTSIDE YOUR APARTMENT LAST NIGHT?
HMM?
MA'AM, DO YOU NEED A DOCTOR?
ARE YOU ALL RIGHT?

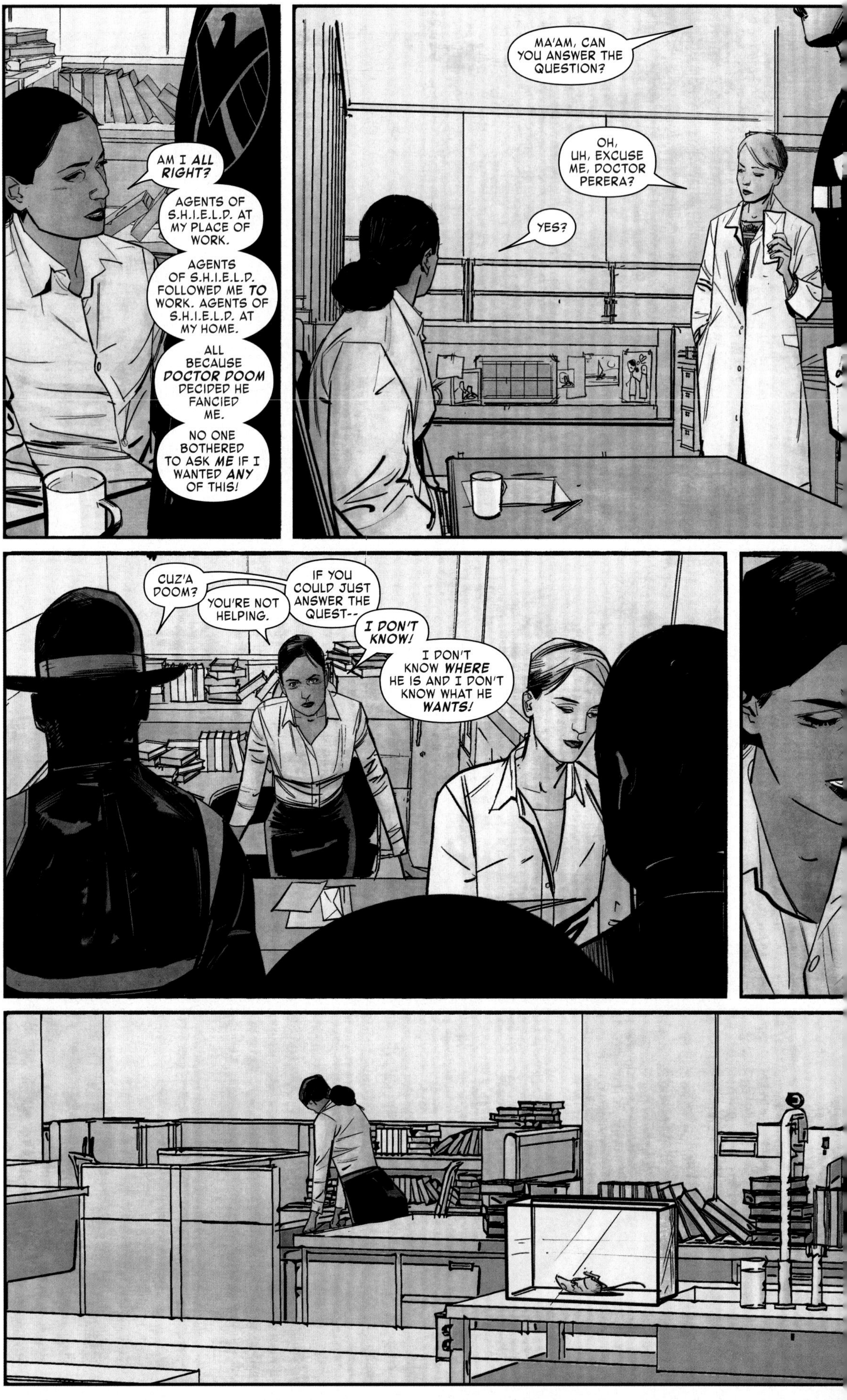
AM I ALL RIGHT?
AGENTS OF S.H.I.E.L.D. AT MY PLACE OF WORK.
AGENTS OF S.H.I.E.L.D. FOLLOWED ME TO WORK. AGENTS OF S.H.I.E.L.D. AT MY HOME.
ALL BECAUSE DOCTOR DOOM DECIDED HE FANCIED ME.
NO ONE BOTHERED TO ASK ME IF I WANTED ANY OF THIS!
MA'AM, CAN YOU ANSWER THE QUESTION?
OH, UH, EXCUSE ME, DOCTOR PERERA?
YES?
CUZ'A DOOM?
YOU'RE NOT HELPING.
IF YOU COULD JUST ANSWER THE QUEST--
I DON'T KNOW!
I DON'T KNOW WHERE HE IS AND I DON'T KNOW WHAT HE WANTS!

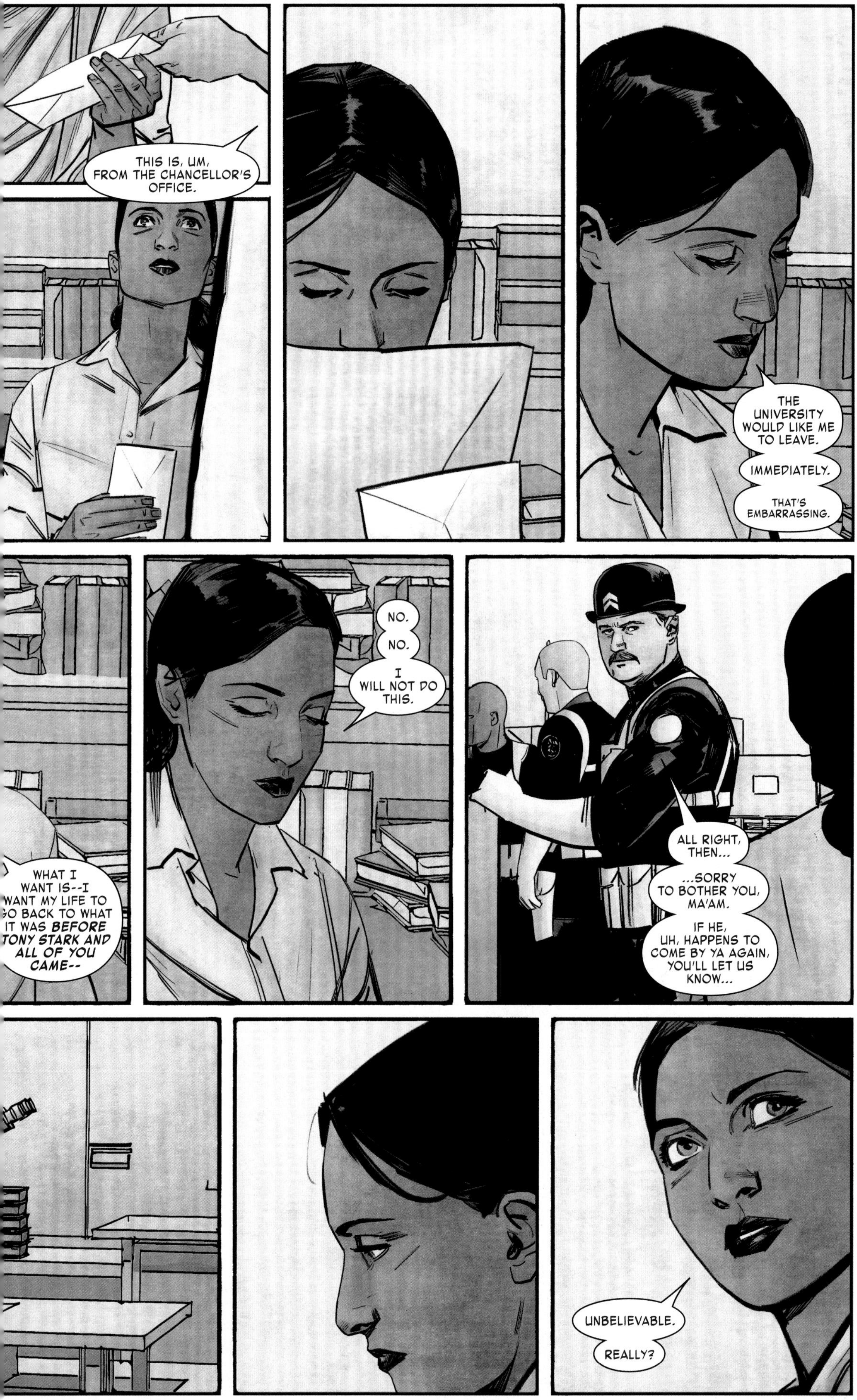
THIS IS, UM, FROM THE CHANCELLOR'S OFFICE.
THE UNIVERSITY WOULD LIKE ME TO LEAVE.
IMMEDIATELY.
THAT'S EMBARRASSING.
NO.
NO.
I WILL NOT DO THIS.
WHAT I WANT IS--I WANT MY LIFE TO GO BACK TO WHAT IT WAS *BEFORE TONY STARK AND ALL OF YOU CAME--*
ALL RIGHT, THEN...
...SORRY TO BOTHER YOU, MA'AM.
IF HE, UH, HAPPENS TO COME BY YA AGAIN, YOU'LL LET US KNOW...
UNBELIEVABLE.
REALLY?

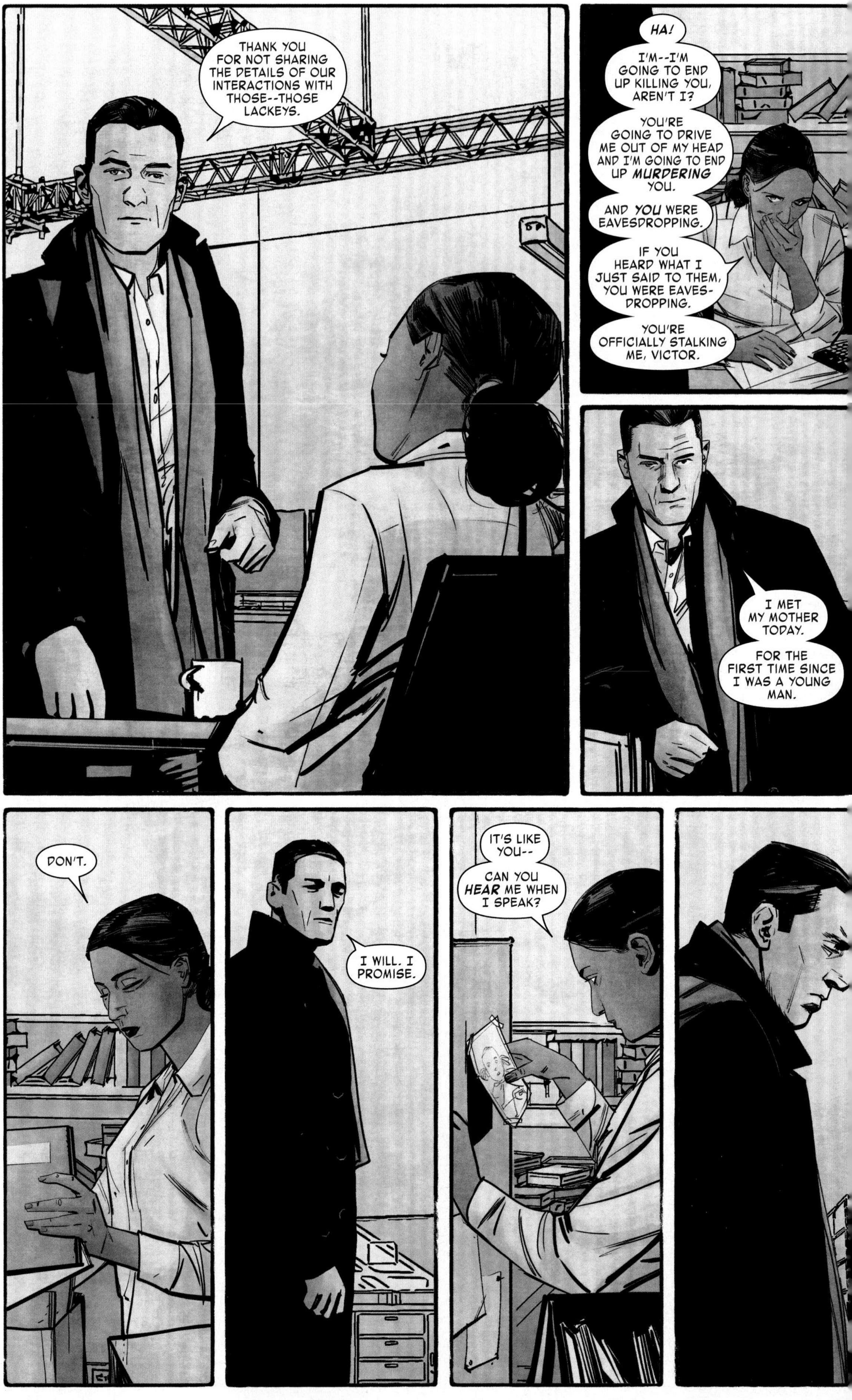
THANK YOU FOR NOT SHARING THE DETAILS OF OUR INTERACTIONS WITH THOSE--THOSE LACKEYS.
HA!
I'M--I'M GOING TO END UP KILLING YOU, AREN'T I?
YOU'RE GOING TO DRIVE ME OUT OF MY HEAD AND I'M GOING TO END UP MURDERING YOU.
AND YOU WERE EAVESDROPPING.
IF YOU HEARD WHAT I JUST SAID TO THEM, YOU WERE EAVES-DROPPING.
YOU'RE OFFICIALLY STALKING ME, VICTOR.
I MET MY MOTHER TODAY.
FOR THE FIRST TIME SINCE I WAS A YOUNG MAN.
DON'T.
I WILL. I PROMISE.
IT'S LIKE YOU--
CAN YOU HEAR ME WHEN I SPEAK?

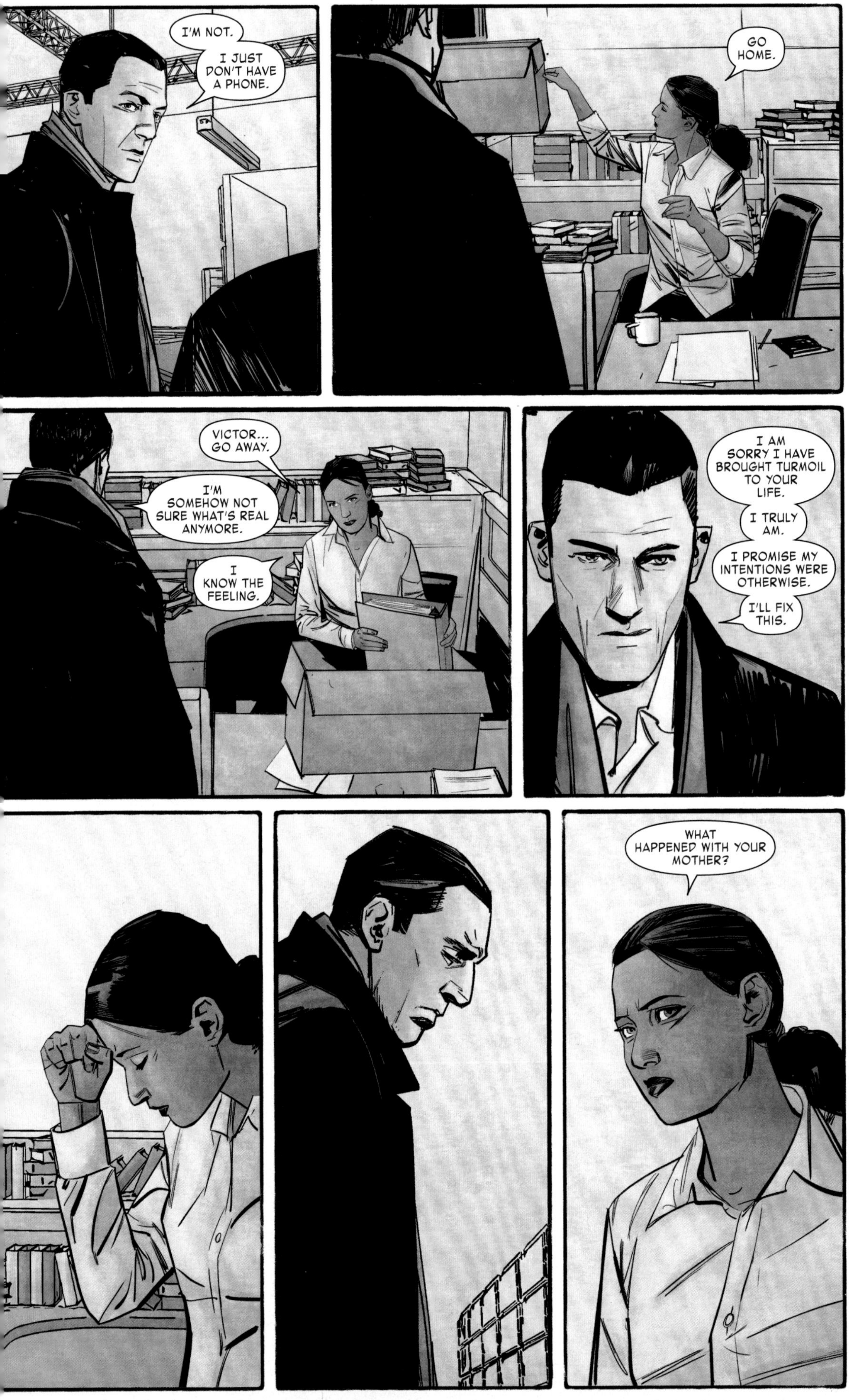
I'M NOT.
I JUST DON'T HAVE A PHONE.
GO HOME.
VICTOR... GO AWAY.
I'M SOMEHOW NOT SURE WHAT'S REAL ANYMORE.
I KNOW THE FEELING.
I AM SORRY I HAVE BROUGHT TURMOIL TO YOUR LIFE.
I TRULY AM.
I PROMISE MY INTENTIONS WERE OTHERWISE.
I'LL FIX THIS.
WHAT HAPPENED WITH YOUR MOTHER?

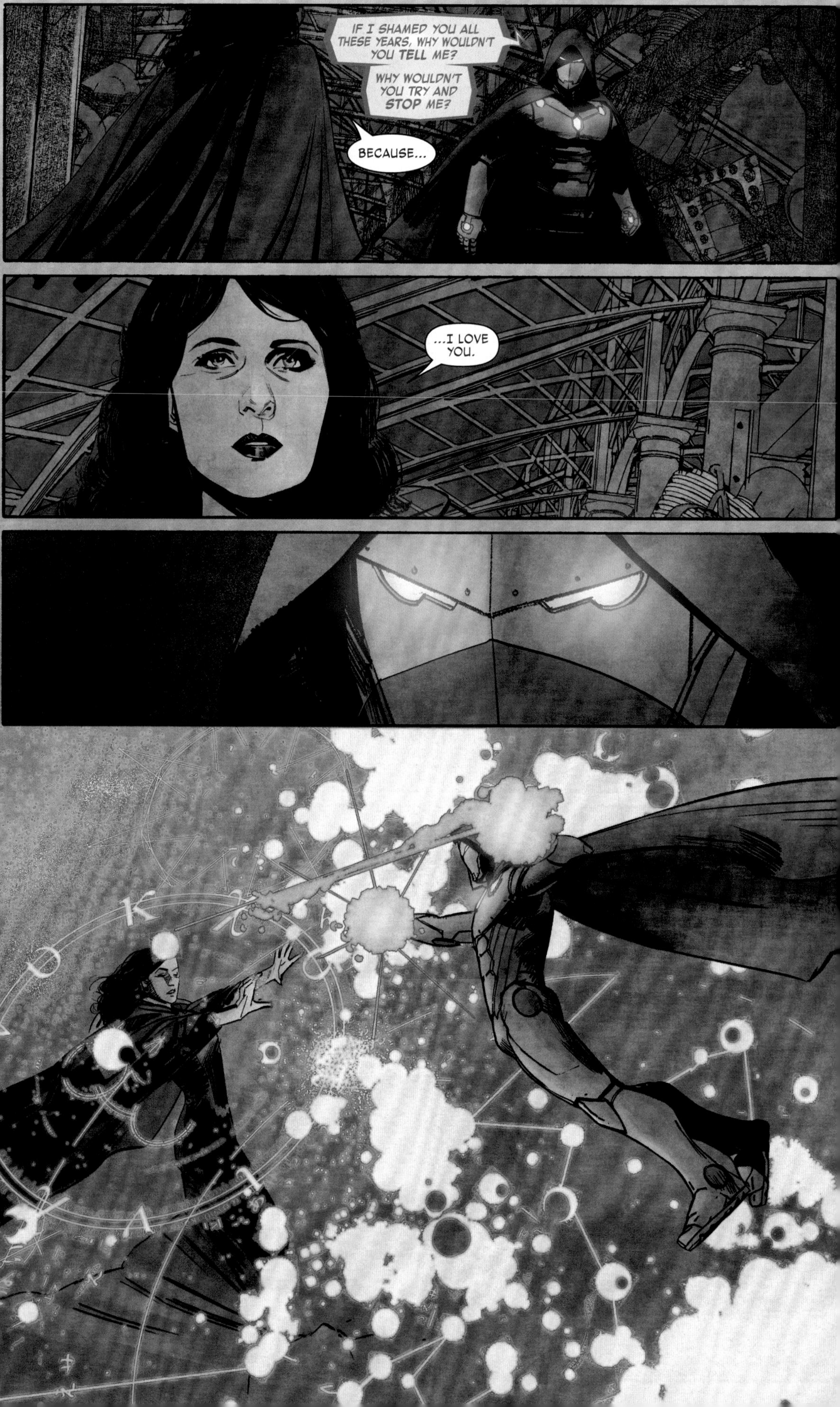
IF I SHAMED YOU ALL THESE YEARS, WHY WOULDN'T YOU TELL ME?
WHY WOULDN'T YOU TRY AND STOP ME?
BECAUSE...
...I LOVE YOU.

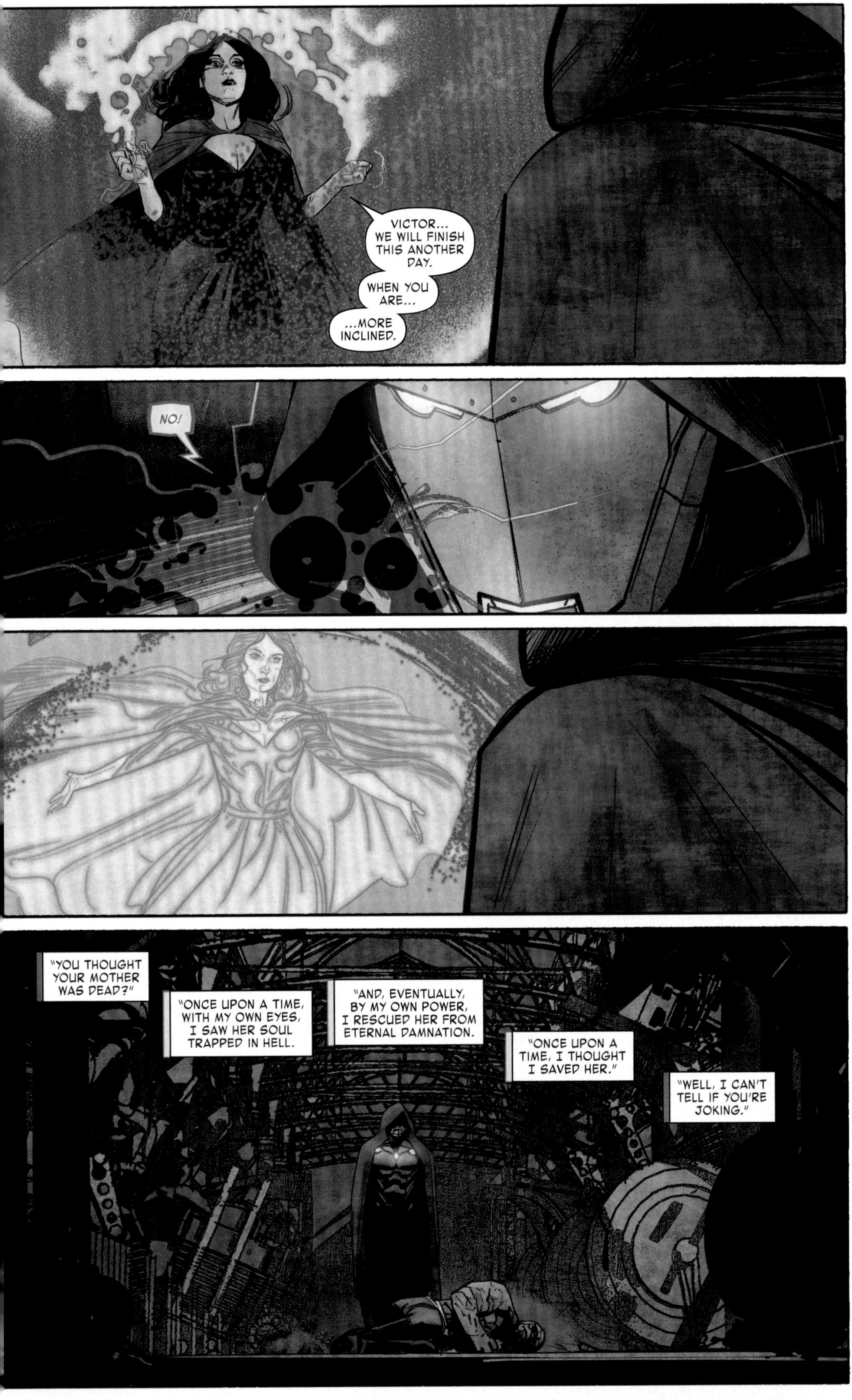
VICTOR... WE WILL FINISH THIS ANOTHER DAY.
WHEN YOU ARE...
...MORE INCLINED.
NO!
"YOU THOUGHT YOUR MOTHER WAS DEAD?"
"ONCE UPON A TIME, WITH MY OWN EYES, I SAW HER SOUL TRAPPED IN HELL.
"AND, EVENTUALLY, BY MY OWN POWER, I RESCUED HER FROM ETERNAL DAMNATION.
"ONCE UPON A TIME, I THOUGHT I SAVED HER."
"WELL, I CAN'T TELL IF YOU'RE JOKING."

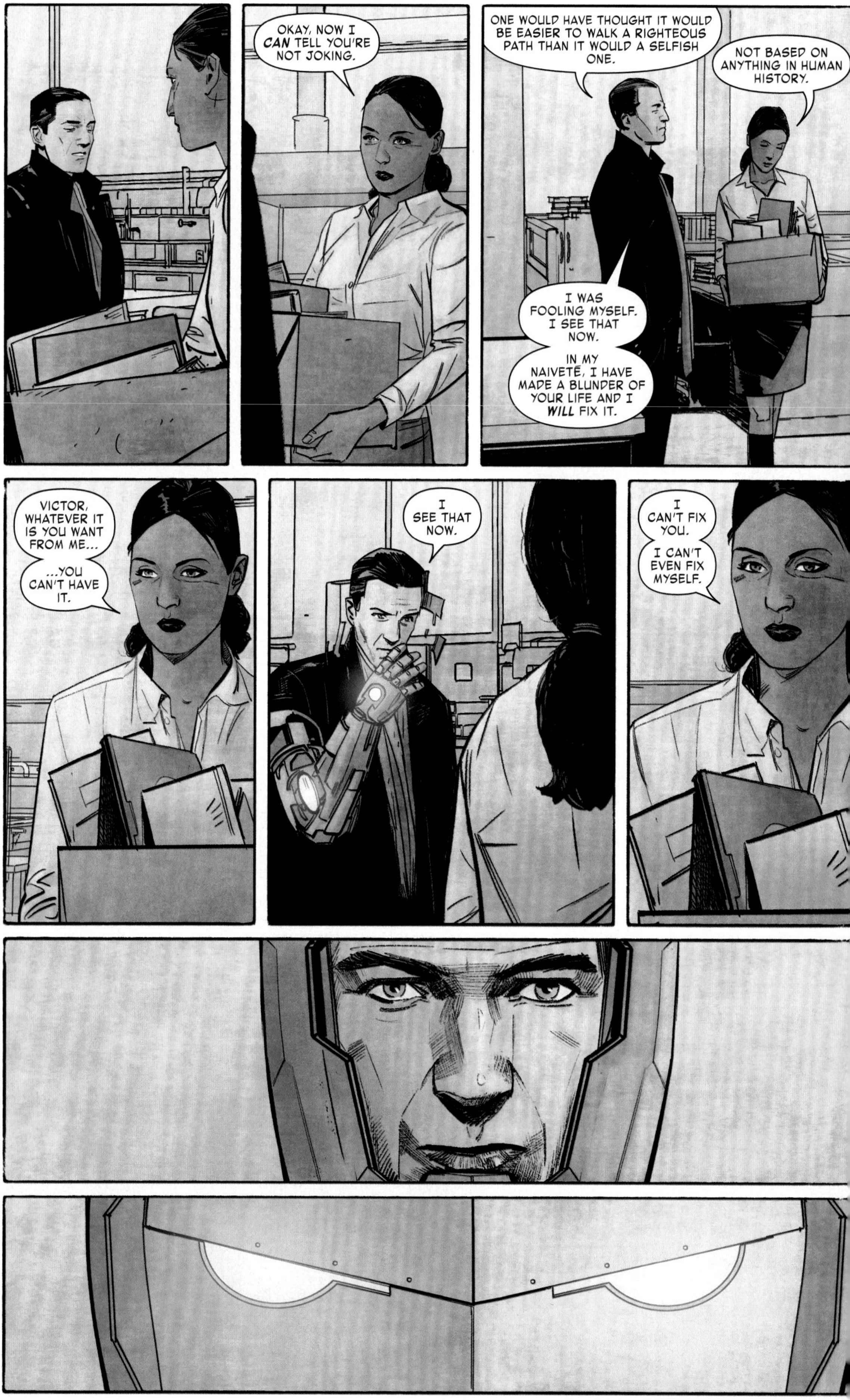
OKAY, NOW I *CAN* TELL YOU'RE NOT JOKING.
ONE WOULD HAVE THOUGHT IT WOULD BE EASIER TO WALK A RIGHTEOUS PATH THAN IT WOULD A SELFISH ONE.
NOT BASED ON ANYTHING IN HUMAN HISTORY.
I WAS FOOLING MYSELF. I SEE THAT NOW.
IN MY NAIVETÉ, I HAVE MADE A BLUNDER OF YOUR LIFE AND I *WILL* FIX IT.
VICTOR, WHATEVER IT IS YOU WANT FROM ME...
...YOU CAN'T HAVE IT.
I SEE THAT NOW.
I CAN'T FIX YOU.
I CAN'T EVEN FIX MYSELF.

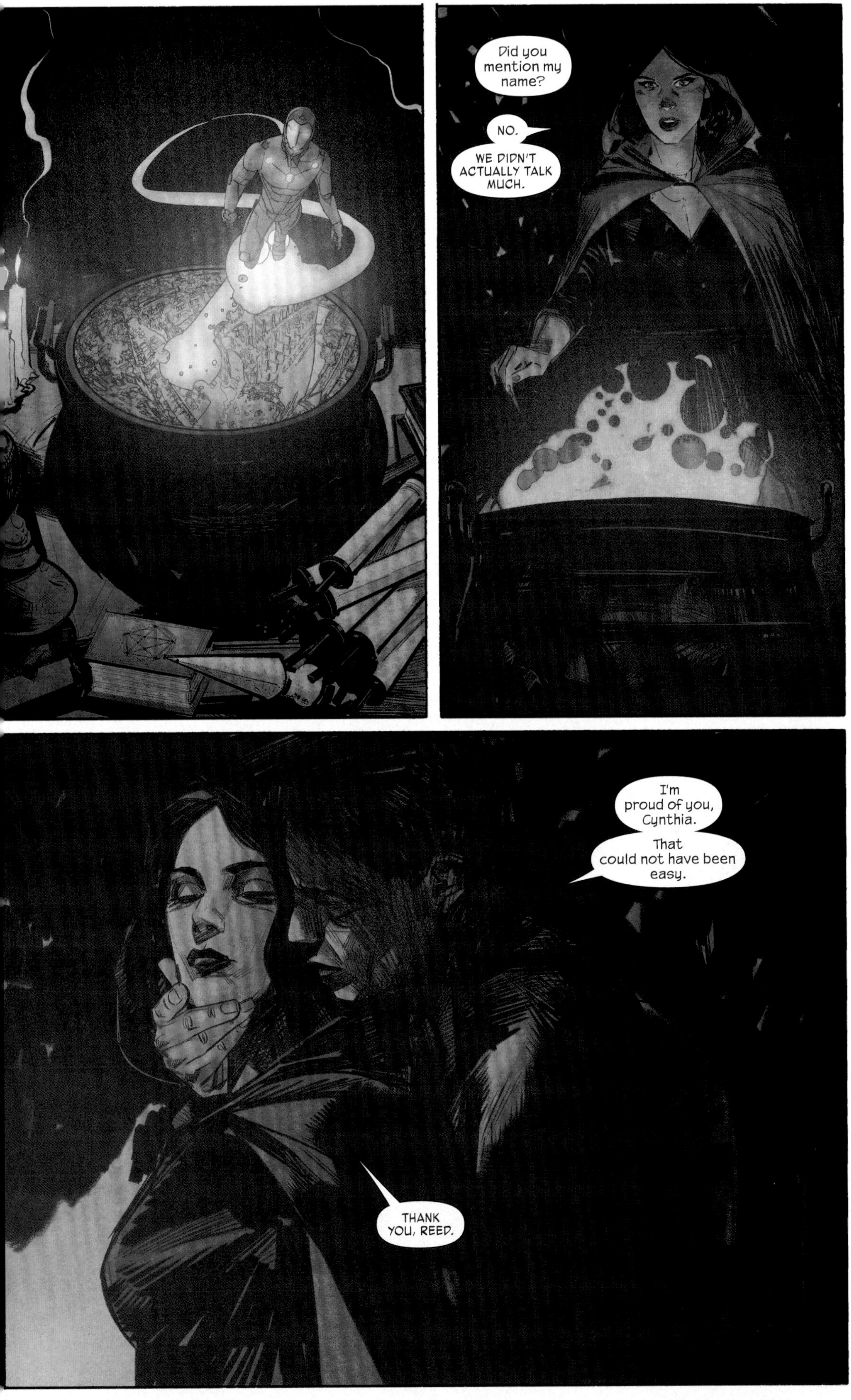
Did you mention my name?
NO.
WE DIDN'T ACTUALLY TALK MUCH.
I'm proud of you, Cynthia.
That could not have been easy.
THANK YOU, REED.

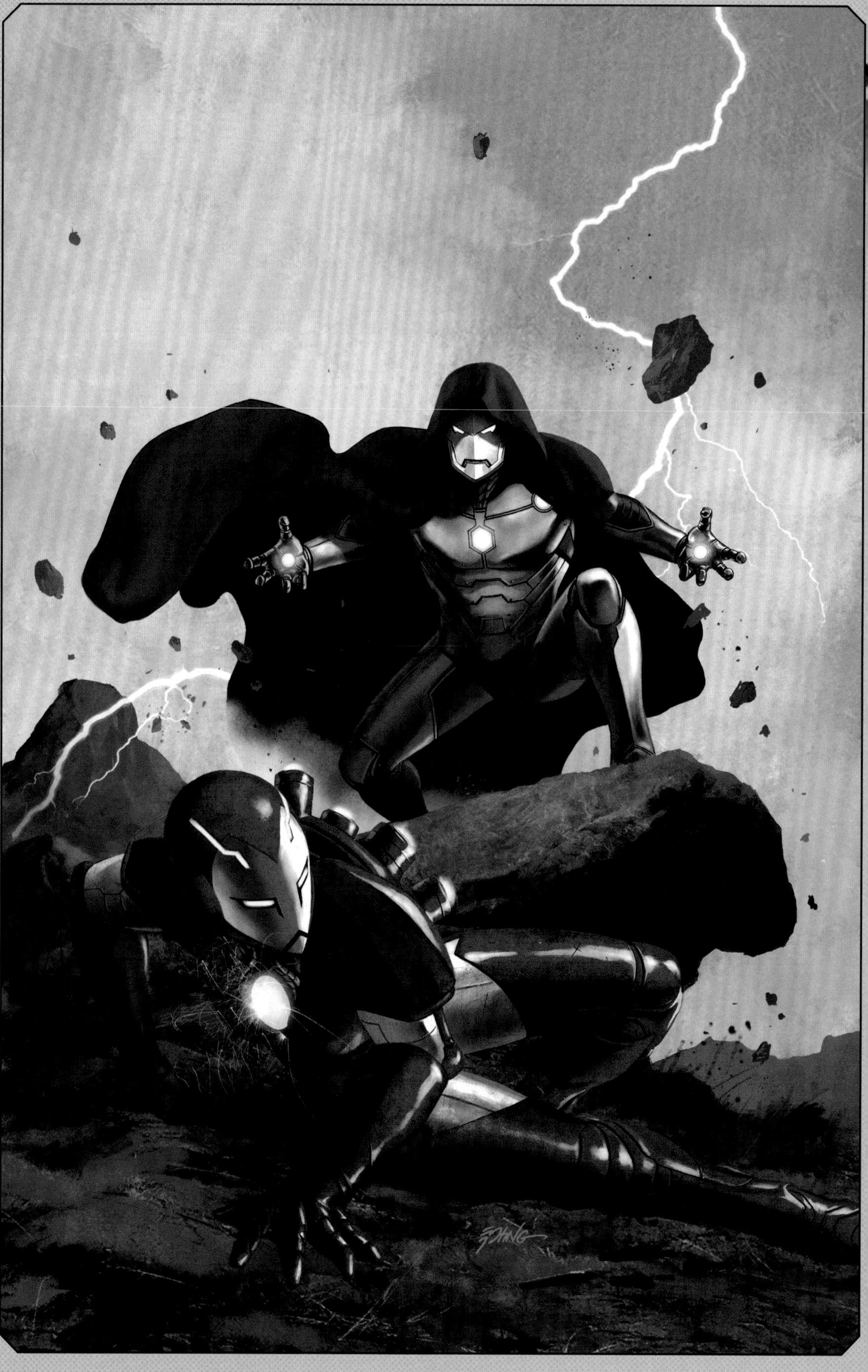

STEVE EPTING
3 VARIANT

6

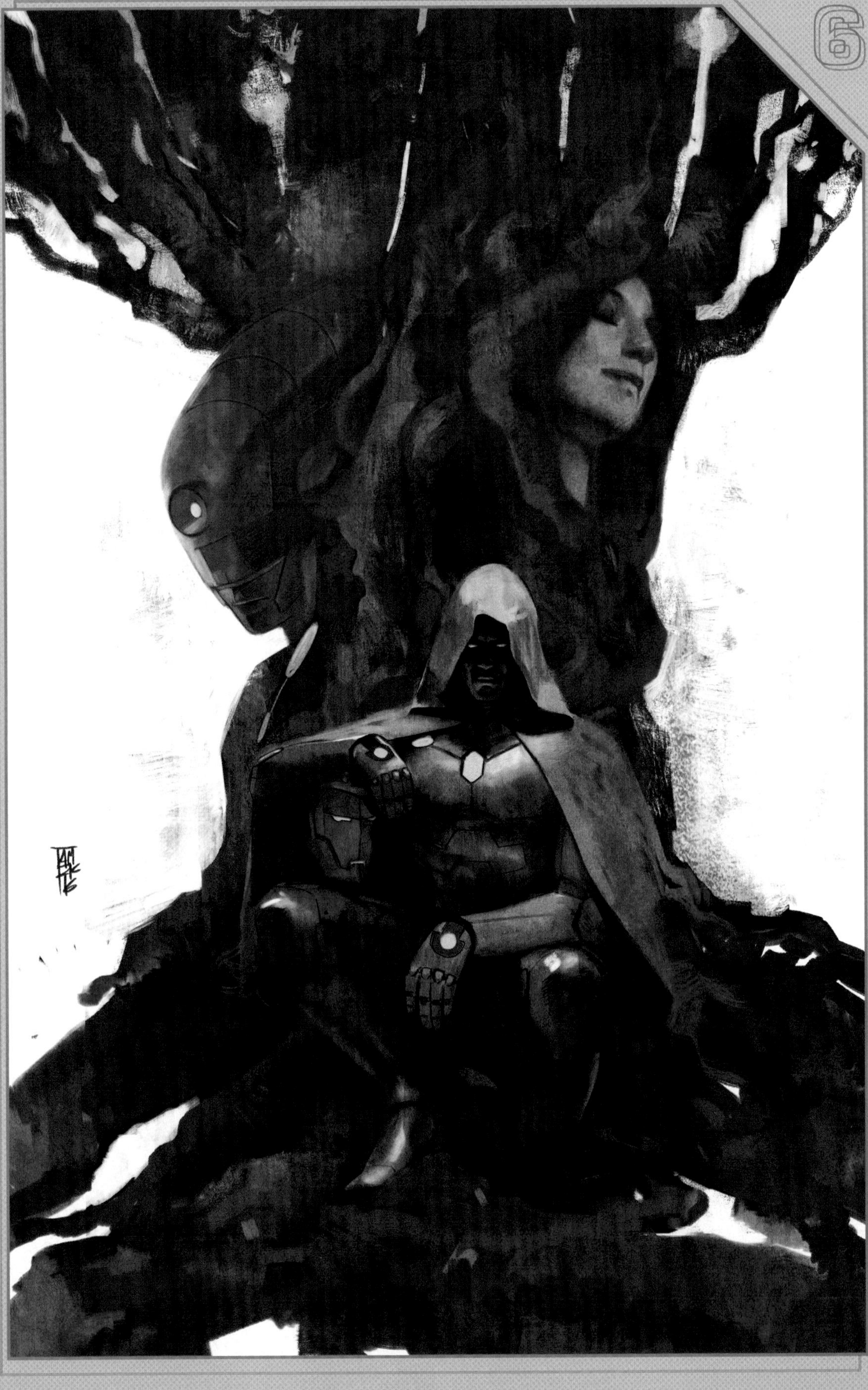

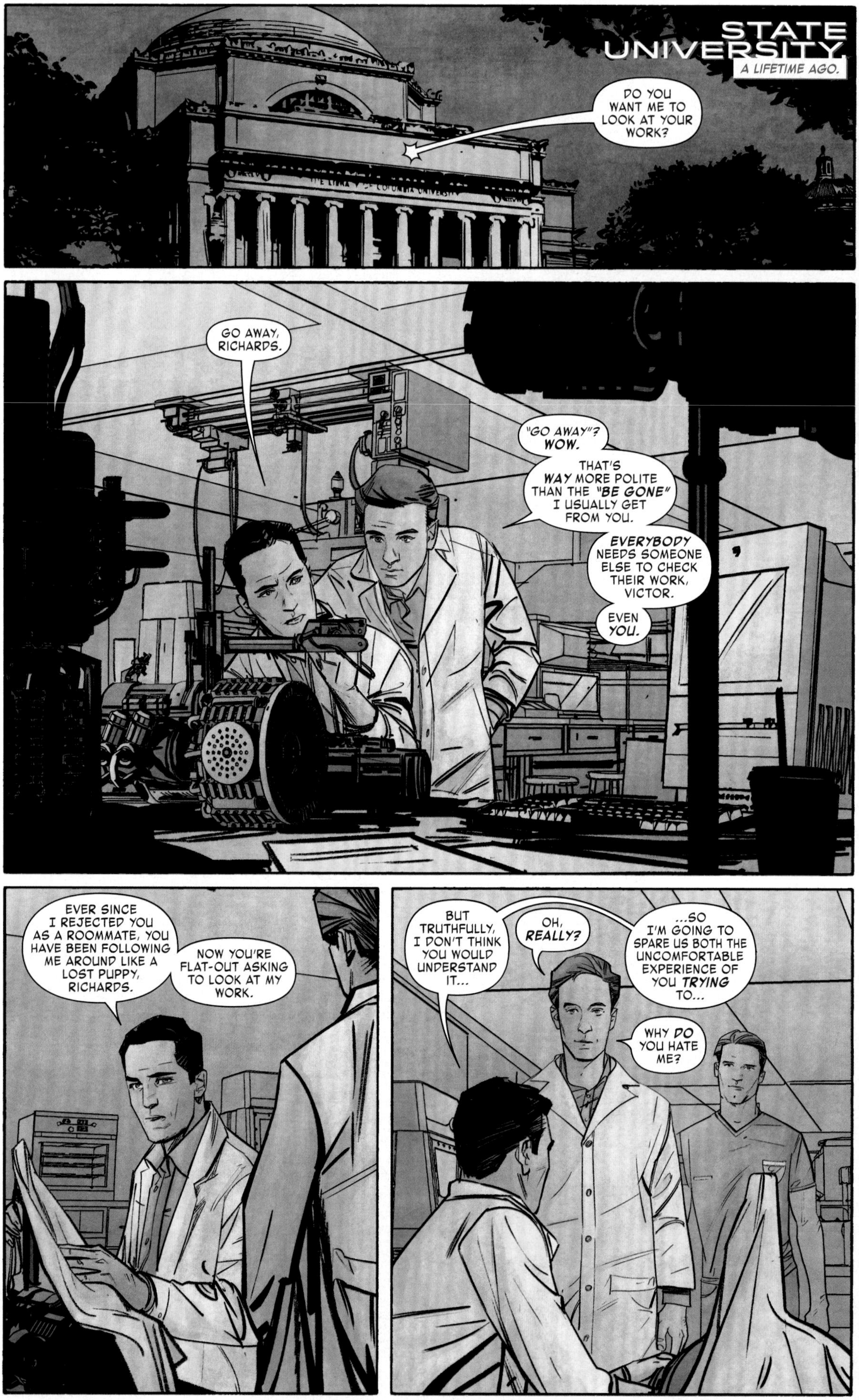
STATE UNIVERSITY
A LIFETIME AGO.
DO YOU WANT ME TO LOOK AT YOUR WORK?
GO AWAY, RICHARDS.
"GO AWAY"? WOW.
THAT'S WAY MORE POLITE THAN THE "BE GONE" I USUALLY GET FROM YOU.
EVERYBODY NEEDS SOMEONE ELSE TO CHECK THEIR WORK, VICTOR.
EVEN YOU.
EVER SINCE I REJECTED YOU AS A ROOMMATE, YOU HAVE BEEN FOLLOWING ME AROUND LIKE A LOST PUPPY, RICHARDS.
NOW YOU'RE FLAT-OUT ASKING TO LOOK AT MY WORK.
BUT TRUTHFULLY, I DON'T THINK YOU WOULD UNDERSTAND IT...
OH, REALLY?
...SO I'M GOING TO SPARE US BOTH THE UNCOMFORTABLE EXPERIENCE OF YOU TRYING TO...
WHY DO YOU HATE ME?

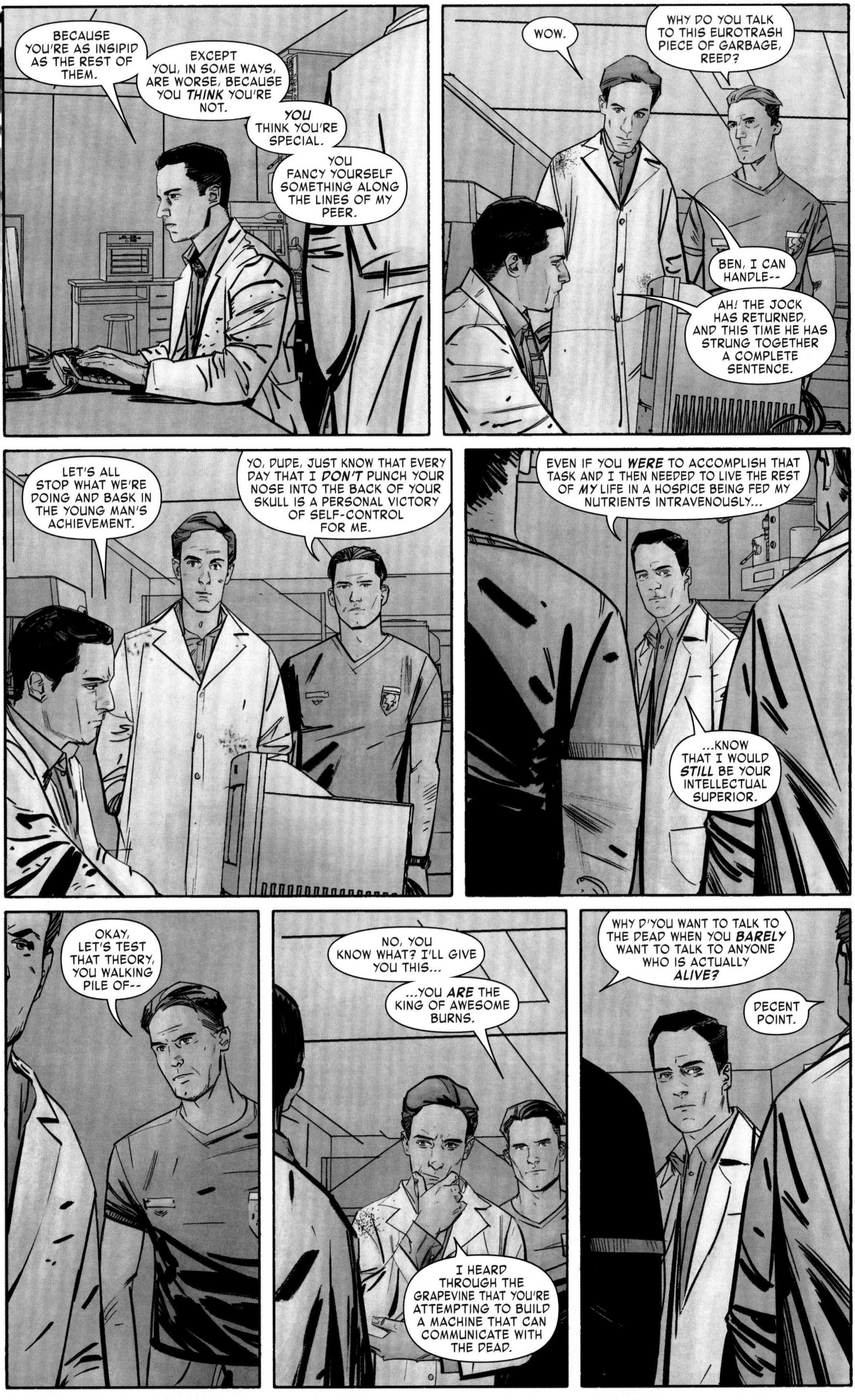
BECAUSE YOU'RE AS INSIPID AS THE REST OF THEM.
EXCEPT YOU, IN SOME WAYS, ARE WORSE, BECAUSE YOU THINK YOU'RE NOT.
YOU THINK YOU'RE SPECIAL.
YOU FANCY YOURSELF SOMETHING ALONG THE LINES OF MY PEER.
WOW.
WHY DO YOU TALK TO THIS EUROTRASH PIECE OF GARBAGE, REED?
BEN, I CAN HANDLE--
AH! THE JOCK HAS RETURNED, AND THIS TIME HE HAS STRUNG TOGETHER A COMPLETE SENTENCE.
LET'S ALL STOP WHAT WE'RE DOING AND BASK IN THE YOUNG MAN'S ACHIEVEMENT.
YO, DUDE, JUST KNOW THAT EVERY DAY THAT I DON'T PUNCH YOUR NOSE INTO THE BACK OF YOUR SKULL IS A PERSONAL VICTORY OF SELF-CONTROL FOR ME.
EVEN IF YOU WERE TO ACCOMPLISH THAT TASK AND I THEN NEEDED TO LIVE THE REST OF MY LIFE IN A HOSPICE BEING FED MY NUTRIENTS INTRAVENOUSLY...
...KNOW THAT I WOULD STILL BE YOUR INTELLECTUAL SUPERIOR.
OKAY, LET'S TEST THAT THEORY, YOU WALKING PILE OF--
NO, YOU KNOW WHAT? I'LL GIVE YOU THIS...
...YOU ARE THE KING OF AWESOME BURNS.
I HEARD THROUGH THE GRAPEVINE THAT YOU'RE ATTEMPTING TO BUILD A MACHINE THAT CAN COMMUNICATE WITH THE DEAD.
WHY D'YOU WANT TO TALK TO THE DEAD WHEN YOU BARELY WANT TO TALK TO ANYONE WHO IS ACTUALLY ALIVE?
DECENT POINT.

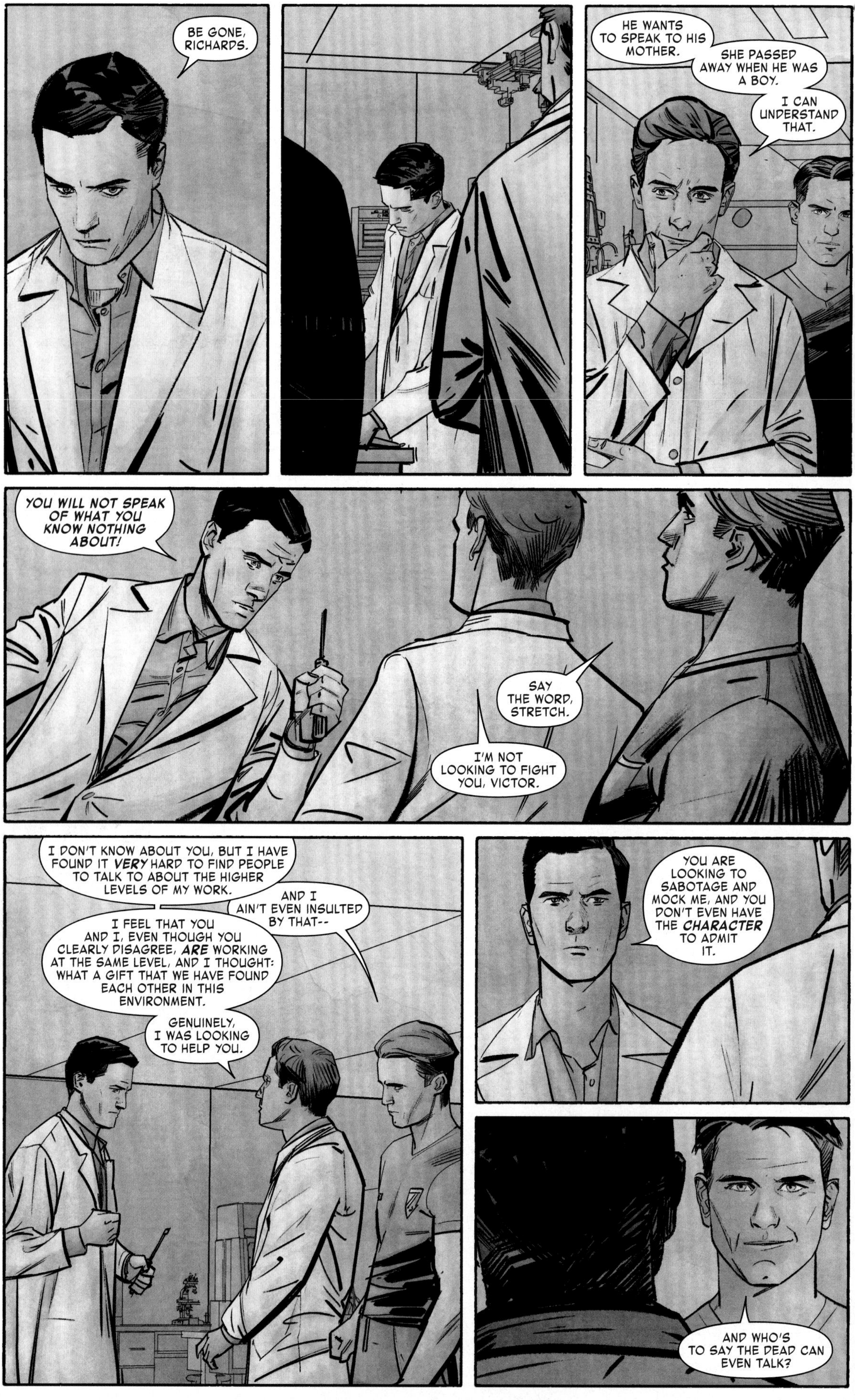
BE GONE, RICHARDS.
HE WANTS TO SPEAK TO HIS MOTHER.
SHE PASSED AWAY WHEN HE WAS A BOY.
I CAN UNDERSTAND THAT.
YOU WILL NOT SPEAK OF WHAT YOU KNOW NOTHING ABOUT!
SAY THE WORD, STRETCH.
I'M NOT LOOKING TO FIGHT YOU, VICTOR.
I DON'T KNOW ABOUT YOU, BUT I HAVE FOUND IT VERY HARD TO FIND PEOPLE TO TALK TO ABOUT THE HIGHER LEVELS OF MY WORK.
AND I AIN'T EVEN INSULTED BY THAT--
I FEEL THAT YOU AND I, EVEN THOUGH YOU CLEARLY DISAGREE, ARE WORKING AT THE SAME LEVEL, AND I THOUGHT: WHAT A GIFT THAT WE HAVE FOUND EACH OTHER IN THIS ENVIRONMENT.
GENUINELY, I WAS LOOKING TO HELP YOU.
YOU ARE LOOKING TO SABOTAGE AND MOCK ME, AND YOU DON'T EVEN HAVE THE CHARACTER TO ADMIT IT.
AND WHO'S TO SAY THE DEAD CAN EVEN TALK?

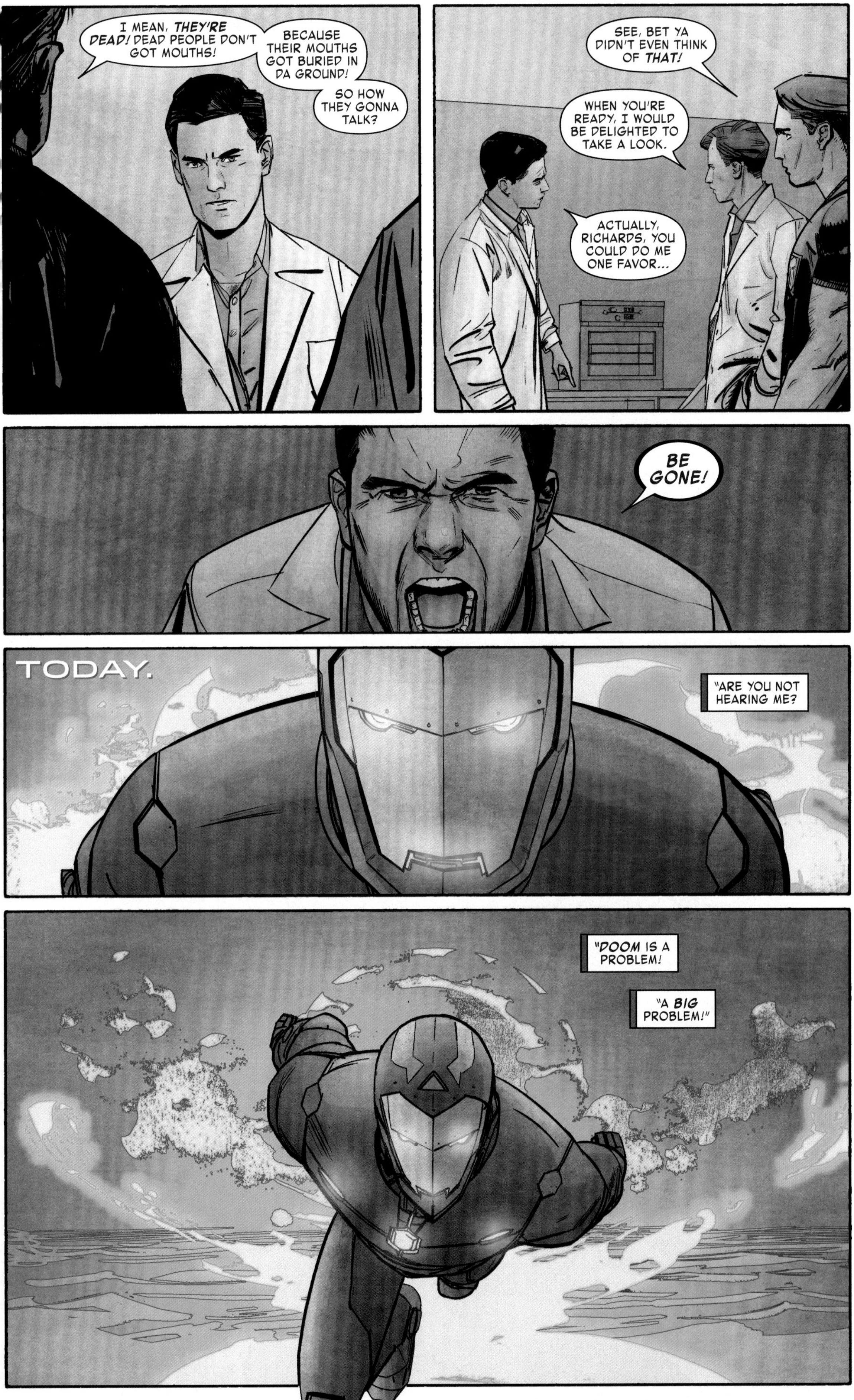
I MEAN, *THEY'RE DEAD!* DEAD PEOPLE DON'T GOT MOUTHS!
BECAUSE THEIR MOUTHS GOT BURIED IN DA GROUND!
SO HOW THEY GONNA TALK?
SEE, BET YA DIDN'T EVEN THINK OF *THAT!*
WHEN YOU'RE READY, I WOULD BE DELIGHTED TO TAKE A LOOK.
ACTUALLY, RICHARDS, YOU COULD DO ME ONE FAVOR...
BE GONE!
TODAY.
"ARE YOU NOT HEARING ME?
"*DOOM* IS A PROBLEM!
"A *BIG* PROBLEM!"

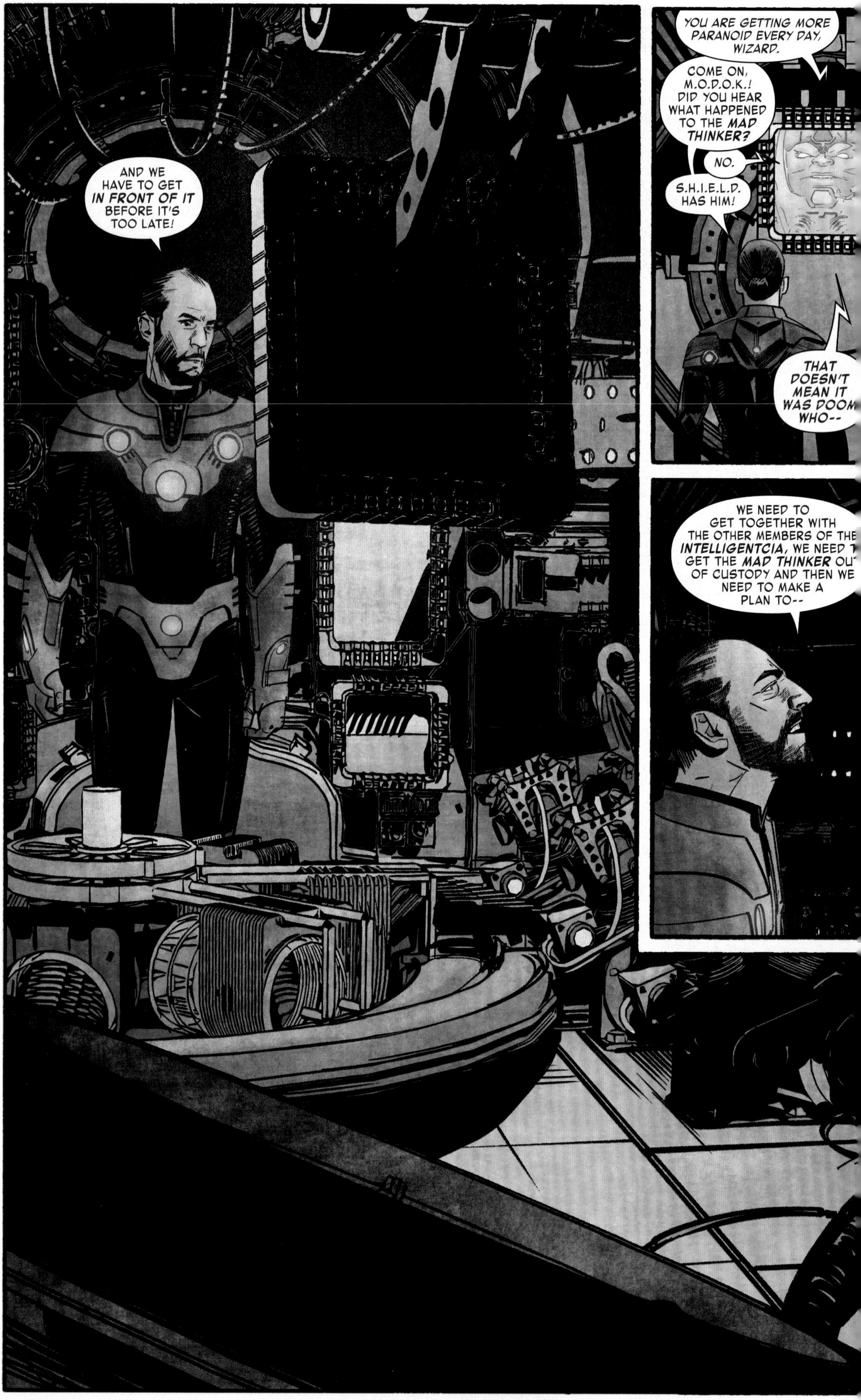
AND WE HAVE TO GET IN FRONT OF IT BEFORE IT'S TOO LATE!
YOU ARE GETTING MORE PARANOID EVERY DAY, WIZARD.
COME ON, M.O.D.O.K.! DID YOU HEAR WHAT HAPPENED TO THE MAD THINKER?
NO.
S.H.I.E.L.D. HAS HIM!
THAT DOESN'T MEAN IT WAS DOOM WHO--
WE NEED TO GET TOGETHER WITH THE OTHER MEMBERS OF THE INTELLIGENTCIA, WE NEED TO GET THE MAD THINKER OUT OF CUSTODY AND THEN WE NEED TO MAKE A PLAN TO--

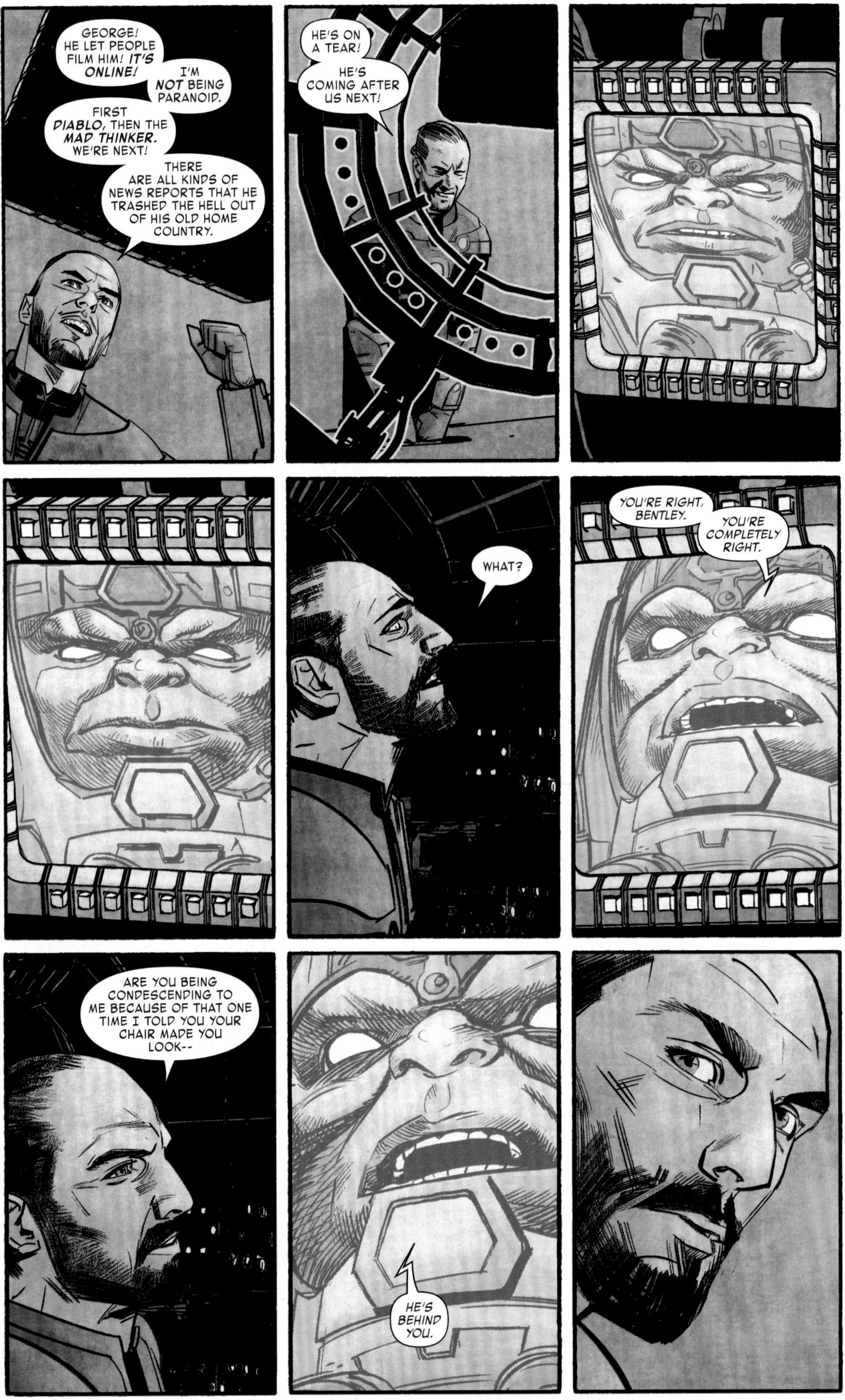
GEORGE! HE LET PEOPLE FILM HIM! IT'S ONLINE!
I'M NOT BEING PARANOID.
FIRST DIABLO, THEN THE MAD THINKER. WE'RE NEXT!
THERE ARE ALL KINDS OF NEWS REPORTS THAT HE TRASHED THE HELL OUT OF HIS OLD HOME COUNTRY.
HE'S ON A TEAR!
HE'S COMING AFTER US NEXT!
WHAT?
YOU'RE RIGHT, BENTLEY.
YOU'RE COMPLETELY RIGHT.
ARE YOU BEING CONDESCENDING TO ME BECAUSE OF THAT ONE TIME I TOLD YOU YOUR CHAIR MADE YOU LOOK--
HE'S BEHIND YOU.

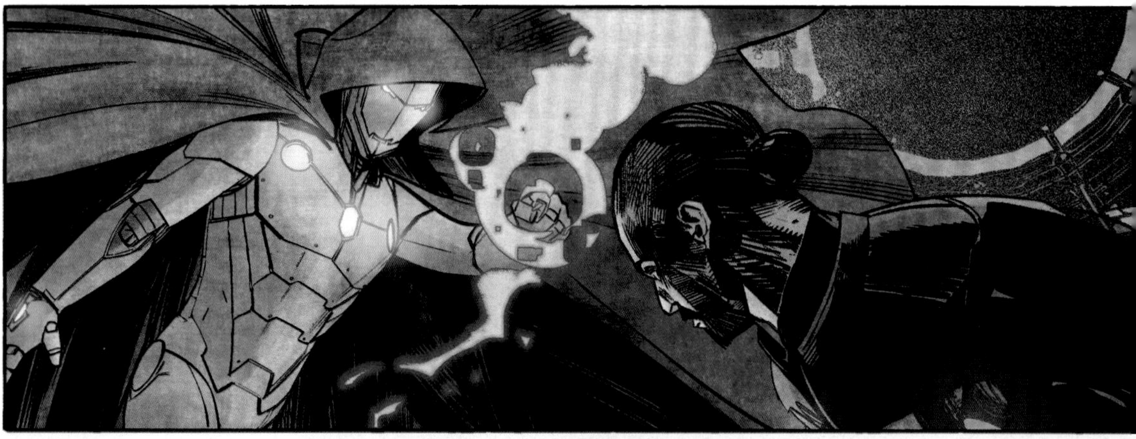

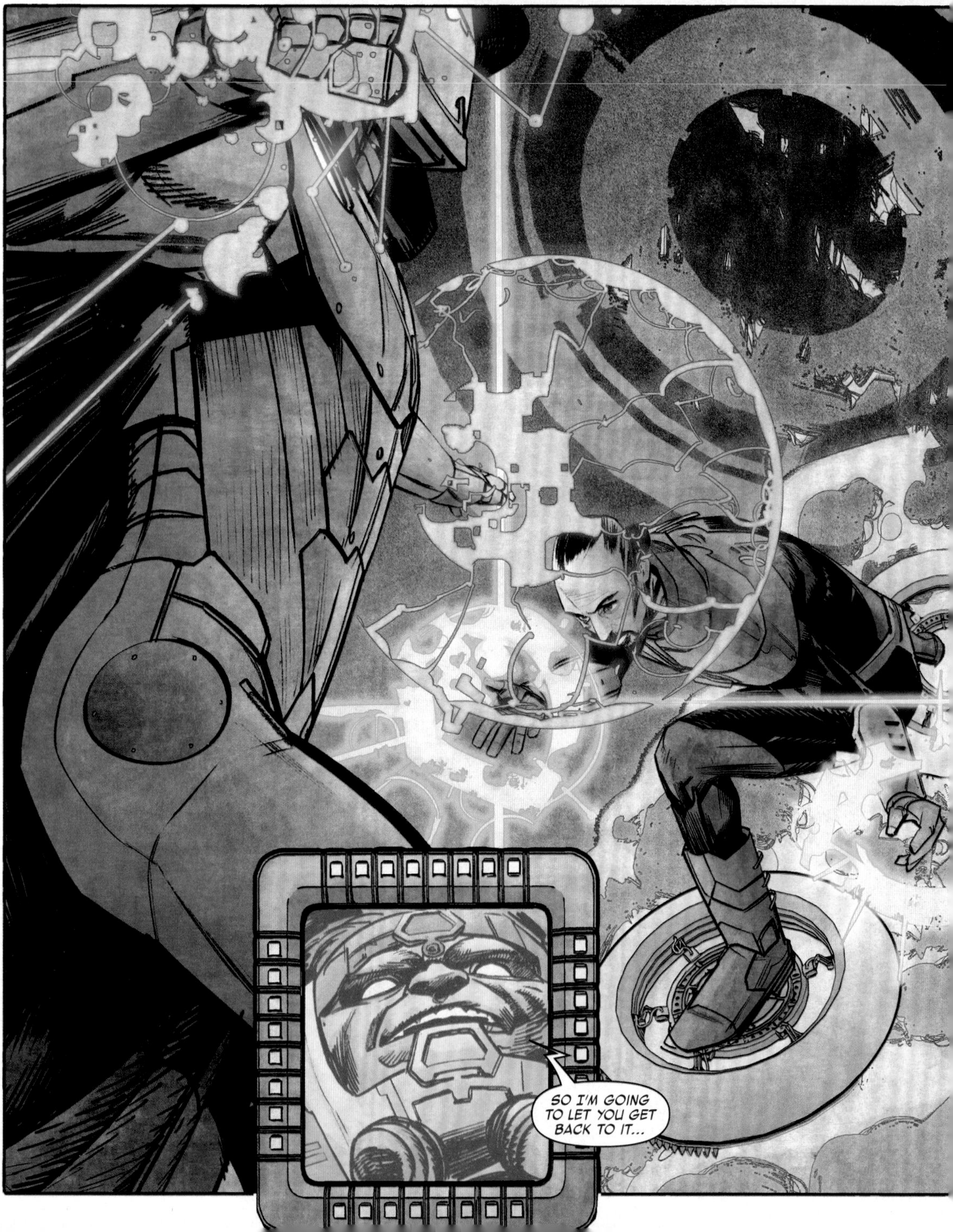

SO I'M GOING TO LET YOU GET BACK TO IT...

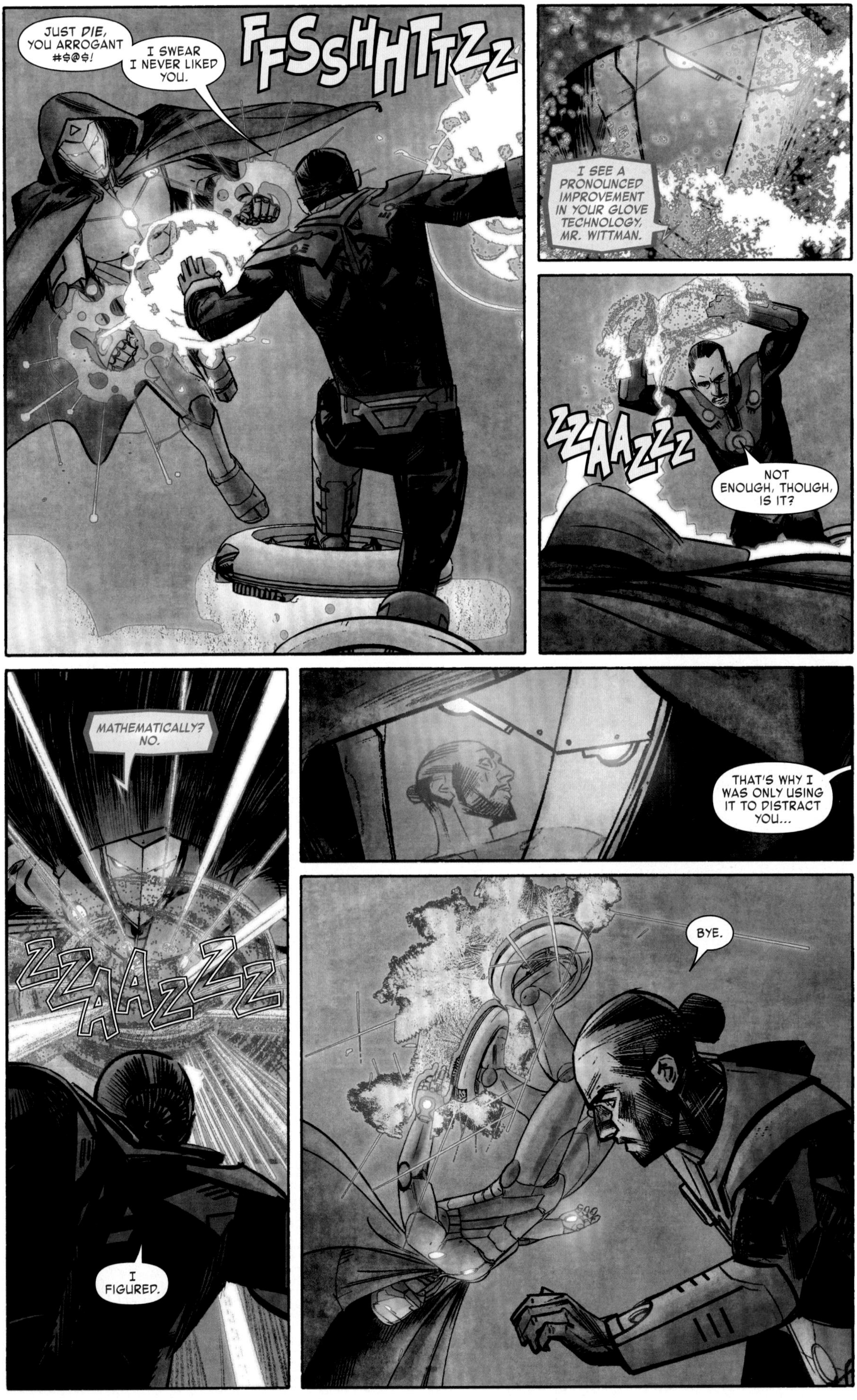
JUST DIE, YOU ARROGANT #$@$!
I SWEAR I NEVER LIKED YOU.
FFSSHHTTZZ
I SEE A PRONOUNCED IMPROVEMENT IN YOUR GLOVE TECHNOLOGY, MR. WITTMAN.
ZZAAZZZ
NOT ENOUGH, THOUGH, IS IT?
MATHEMATICALLY? NO.
ZZZAAZZZ
I FIGURED.
THAT'S WHY I WAS ONLY USING IT TO DISTRACT YOU...
BYE.

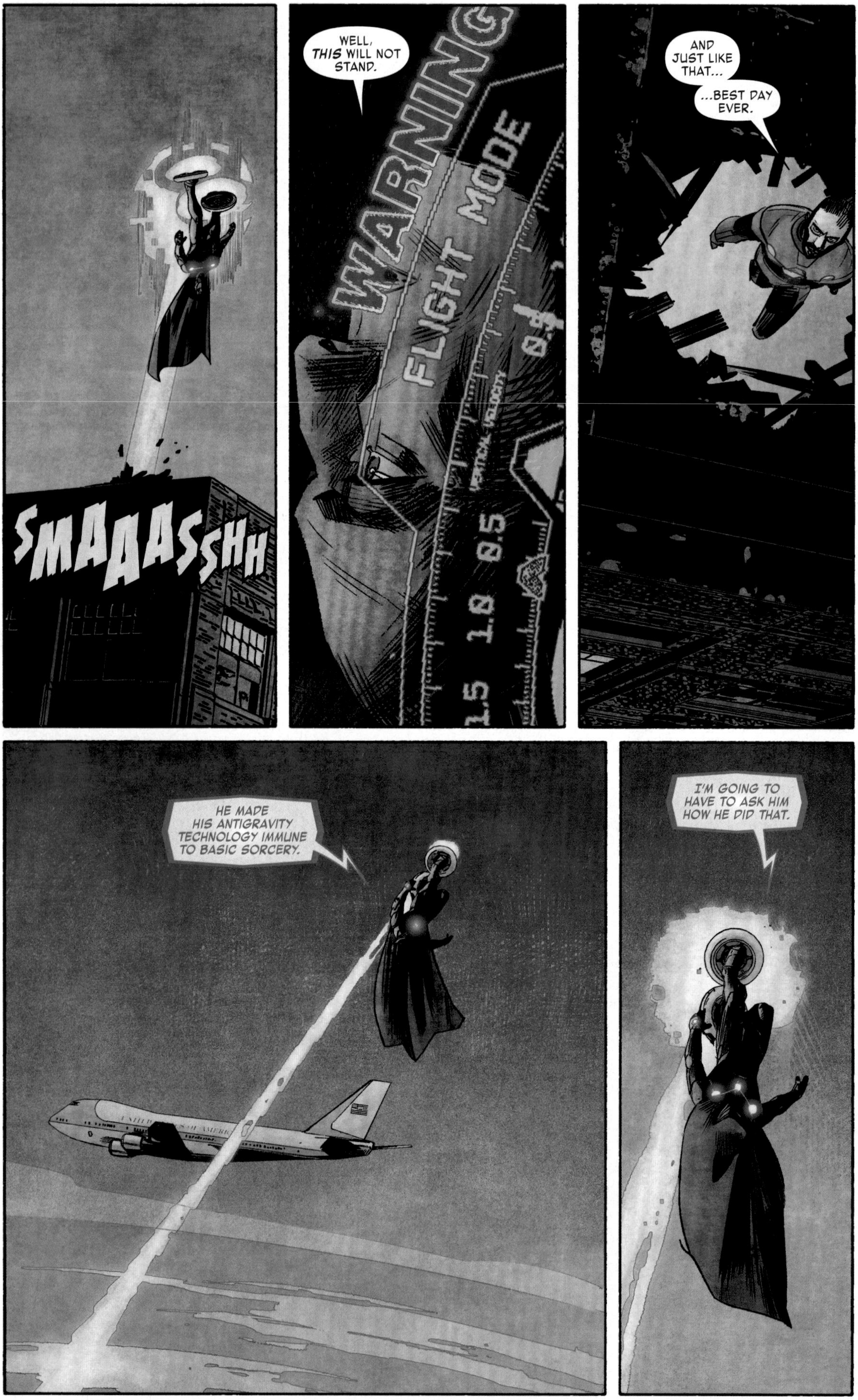
SMAAASSHH
WARNING
FLIGHT MODE
1.5 1.0 0.5
WELL, THIS WILL NOT STAND.
AND JUST LIKE THAT...
...BEST DAY EVER.
HE MADE HIS ANTIGRAVITY TECHNOLOGY IMMUNE TO BASIC SORCERY.
I'M GOING TO HAVE TO ASK HIM HOW HE DID THAT.

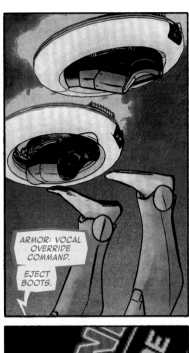

ARMOR: VOCAL OVERRIDE COMMAND.

EJECT BOOTS.

WARN[ING]

FLIGHT MODE

UH, WHAT IS *THAT?*

HEY, IT LOOKS LIKE *IRON MAN.*

IT LOOKS LIKE IRON MAN *CRASHING.*

UH...

IT'S HEADED RIGHT FOR US.

GO!

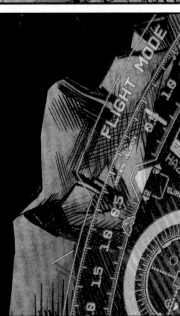

FLIGHT MODE

CRASH IMMINENT

THRUSTER L

THRUSTER R

HAZARD

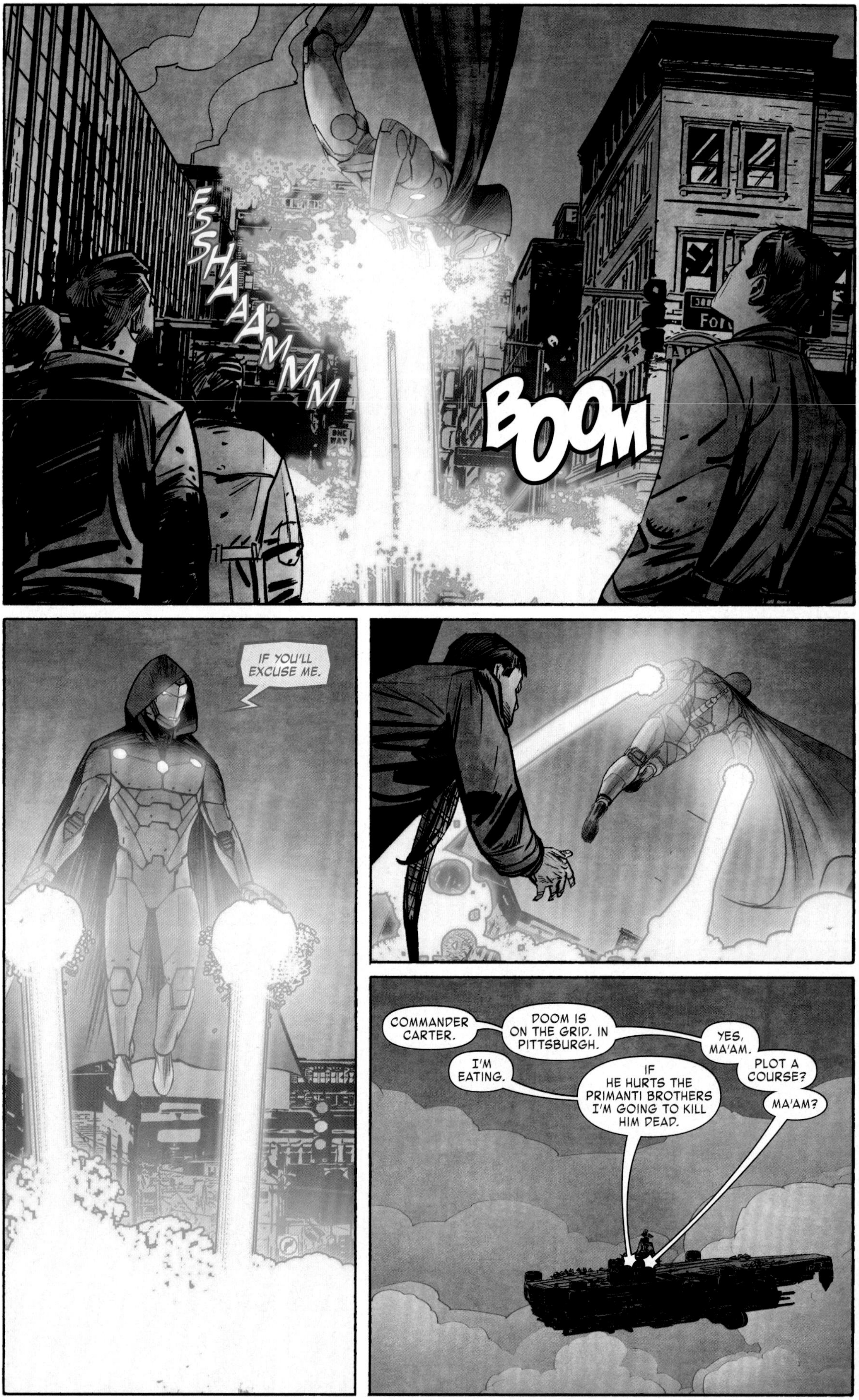
FSHAAAMMM
BOOM
IF YOU'LL EXCUSE ME.
COMMANDER CARTER.
DOOM IS ON THE GRID. IN PITTSBURGH.
YES, MA'AM.
I'M EATING.
IF HE HURTS THE PRIMANTI BROTHERS I'M GOING TO KILL HIM DEAD.
PLOT A COURSE?
MA'AM?

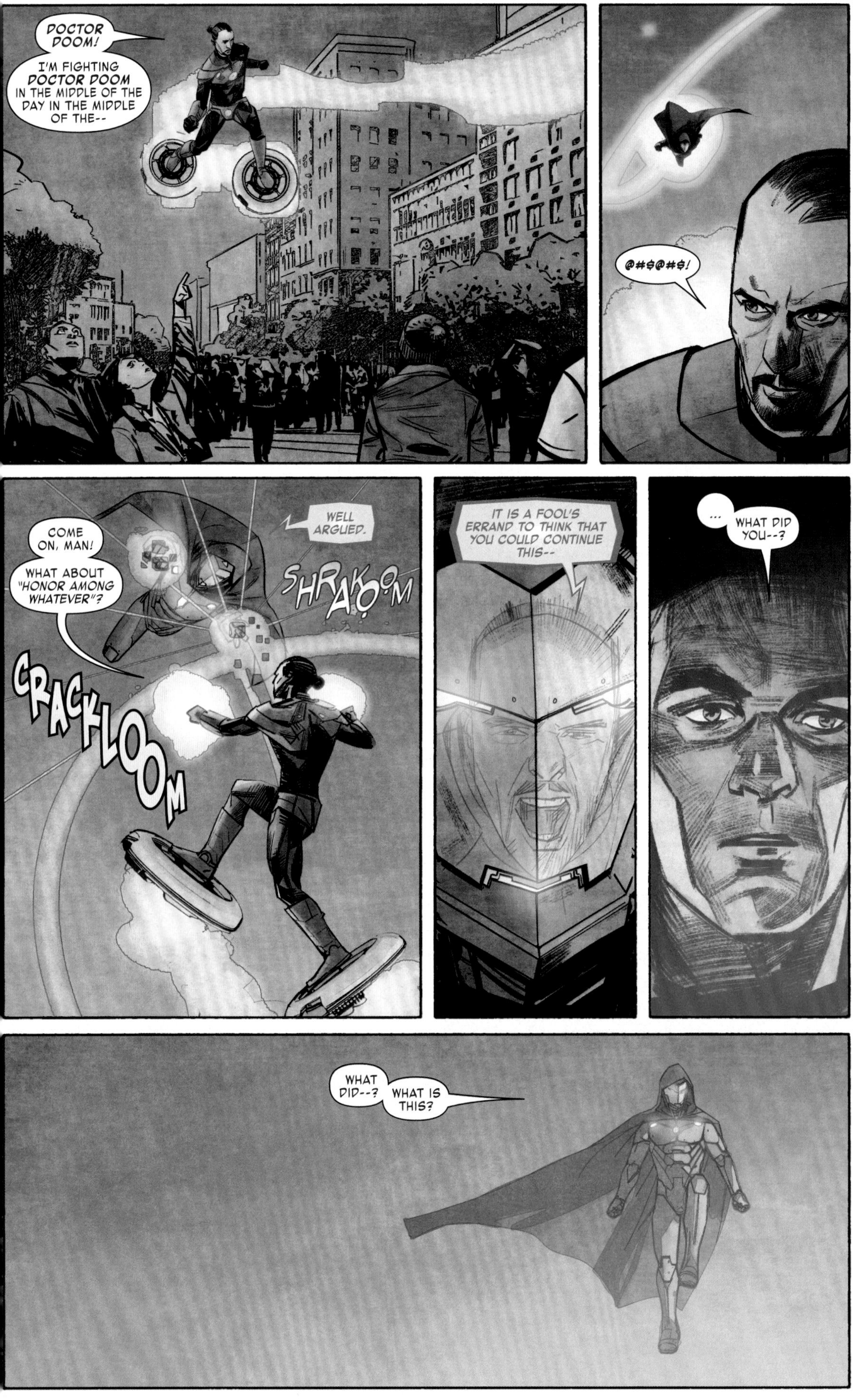
DOCTOR DOOM!
I'M FIGHTING DOCTOR DOOM IN THE MIDDLE OF THE DAY IN THE MIDDLE OF THE--
@#$@#$!
COME ON, MAN!
WHAT ABOUT "HONOR AMONG WHATEVER"?
WELL ARGUED.
SHRAKOOM
CRACKLOOM
IT IS A FOOL'S ERRAND TO THINK THAT YOU COULD CONTINUE THIS--
... WHAT DID YOU--?
WHAT DID--? WHAT IS THIS?

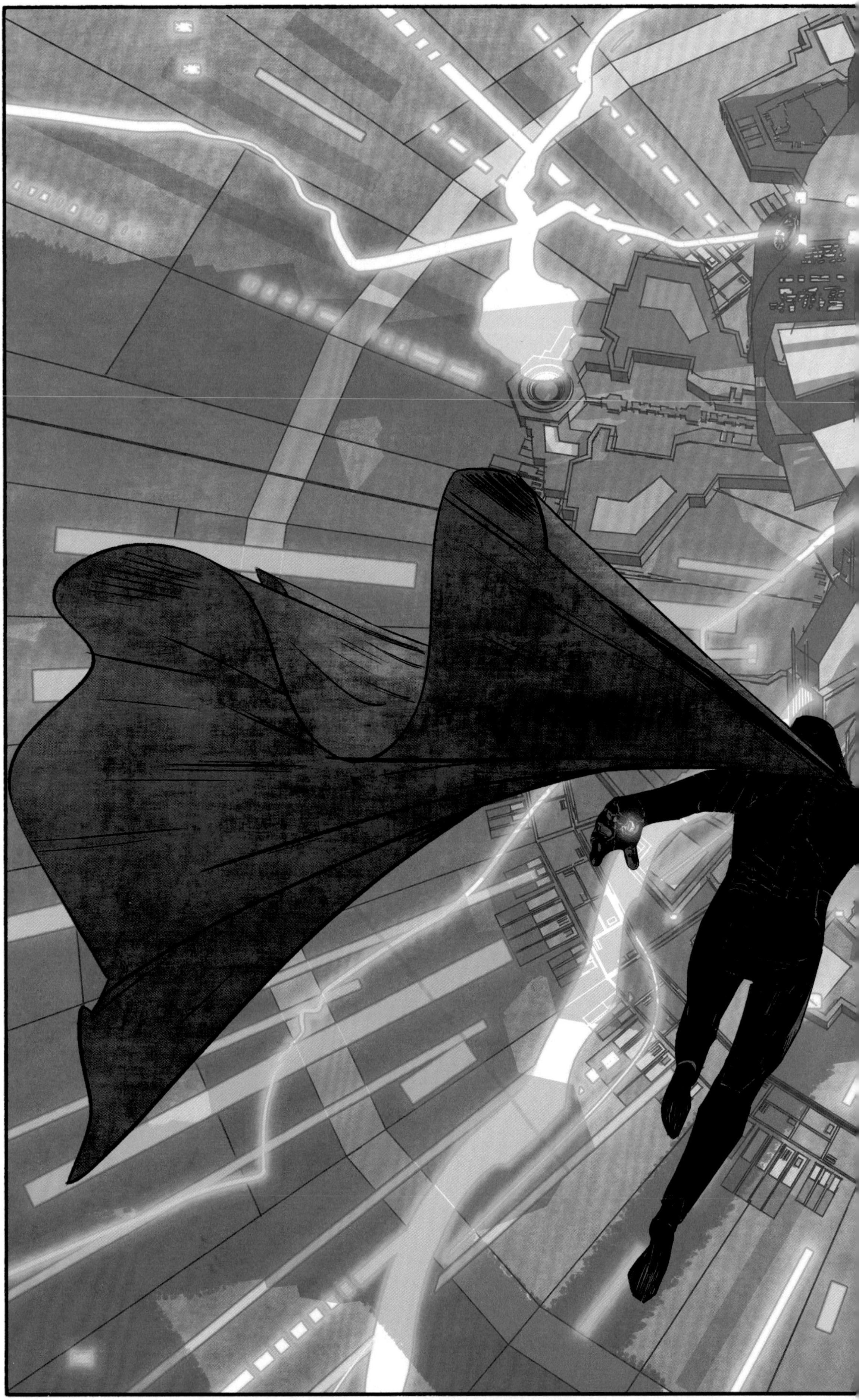

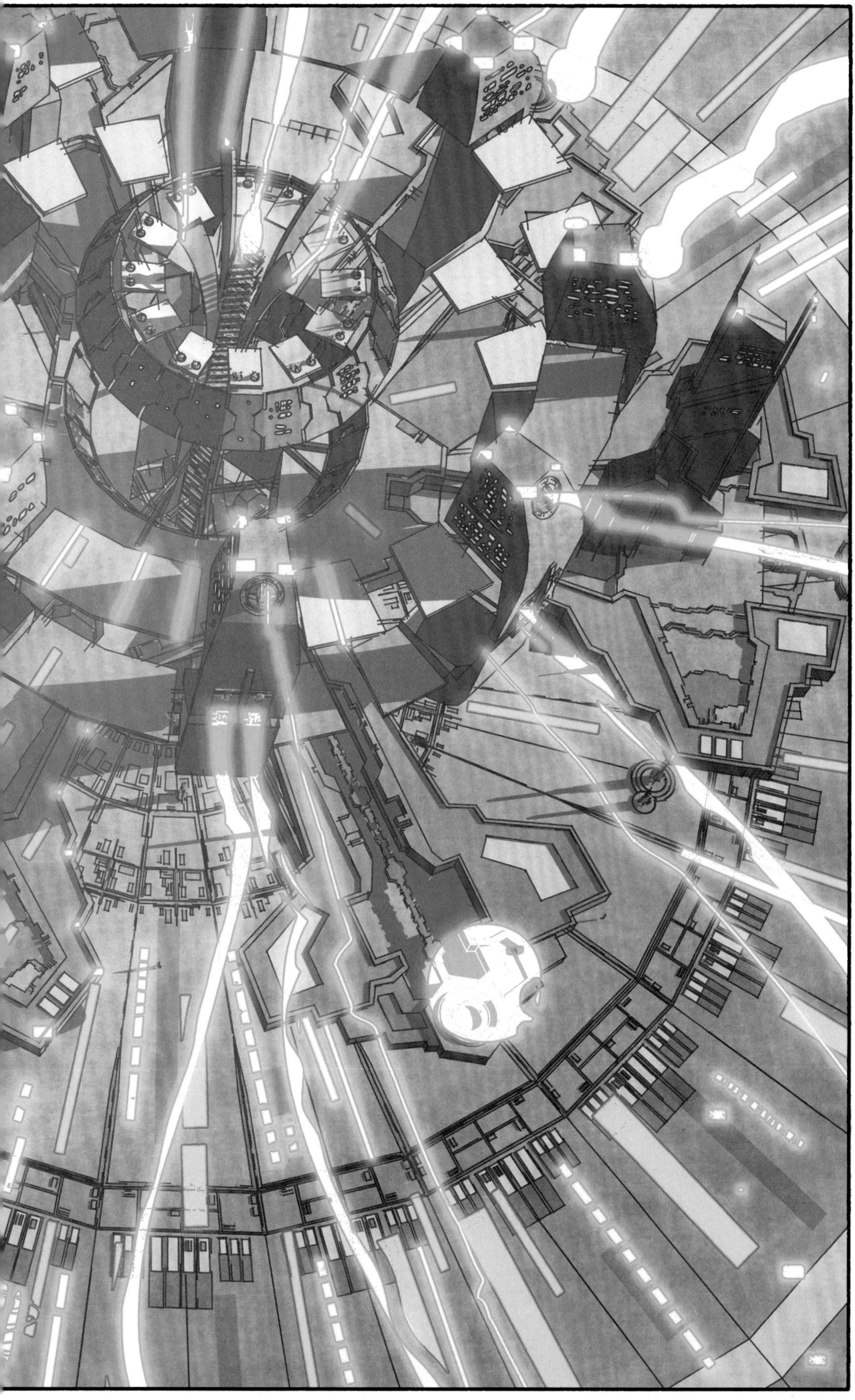

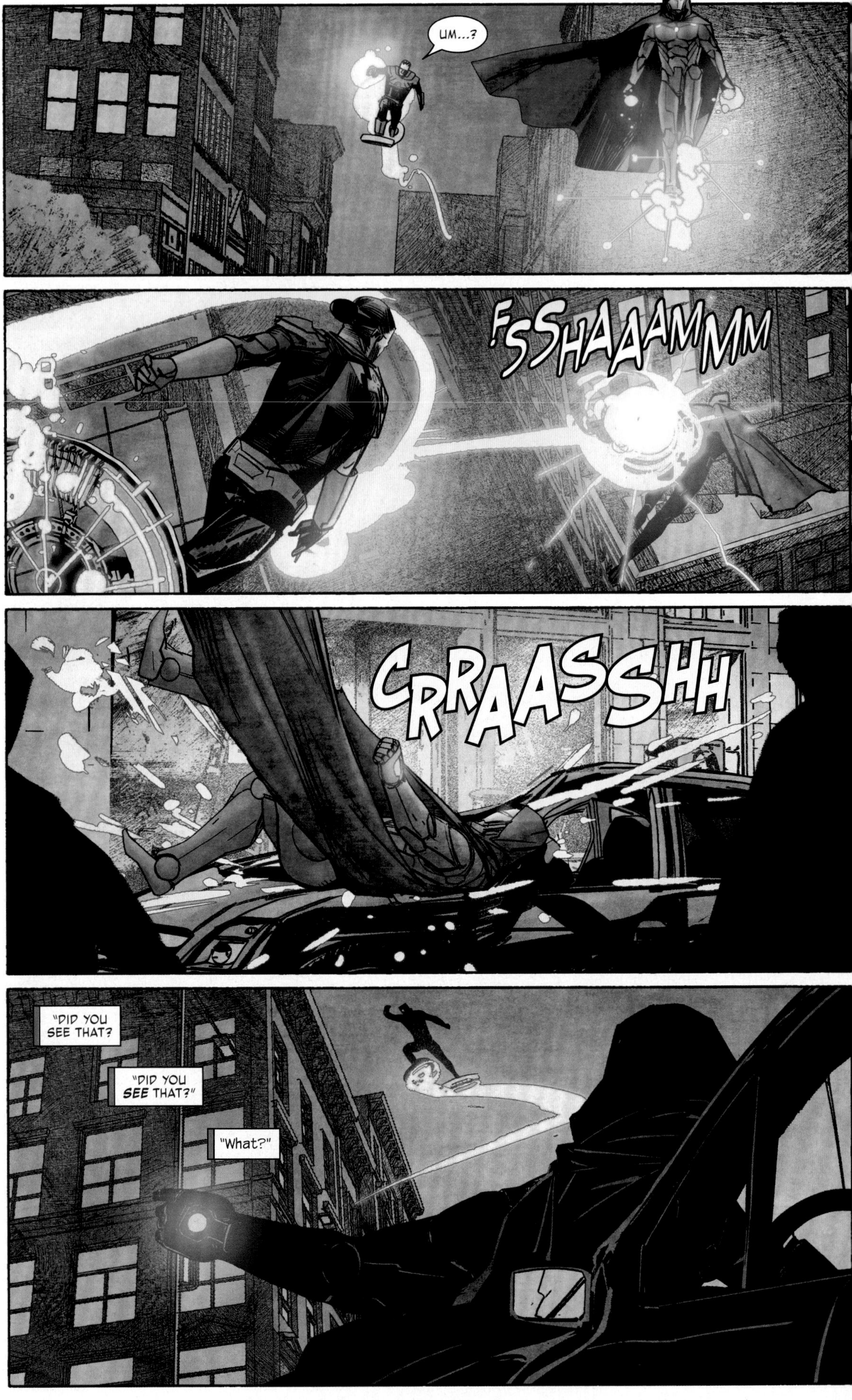
UM...?
FSSHAAAMMMM
CRRAASSHH
"DID YOU SEE THAT?
"DID YOU SEE THAT?"
"What?"

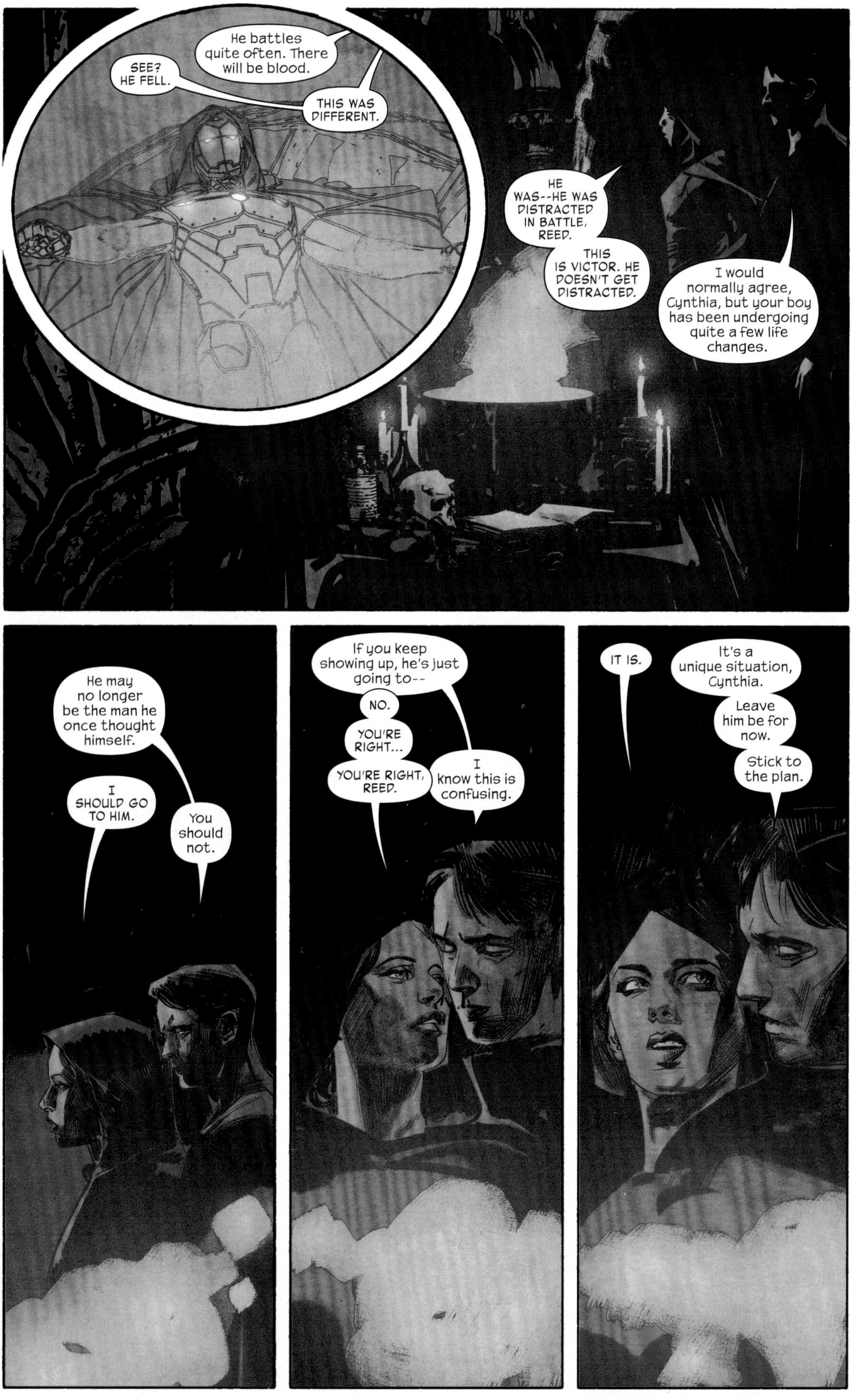
He battles quite often. There will be blood.
SEE? HE FELL.
THIS WAS DIFFERENT.
HE WAS--HE WAS DISTRACTED IN BATTLE, REED.
THIS IS VICTOR. HE DOESN'T GET DISTRACTED.
I would normally agree, Cynthia, but your boy has been undergoing quite a few life changes.
He may no longer be the man he once thought himself.
I SHOULD GO TO HIM.
You should not.
If you keep showing up, he's just going to--
NO.
YOU'RE RIGHT...
YOU'RE RIGHT, REED.
I know this is confusing.
IT IS.
It's a unique situation, Cynthia.
Leave him be for now.
Stick to the plan.

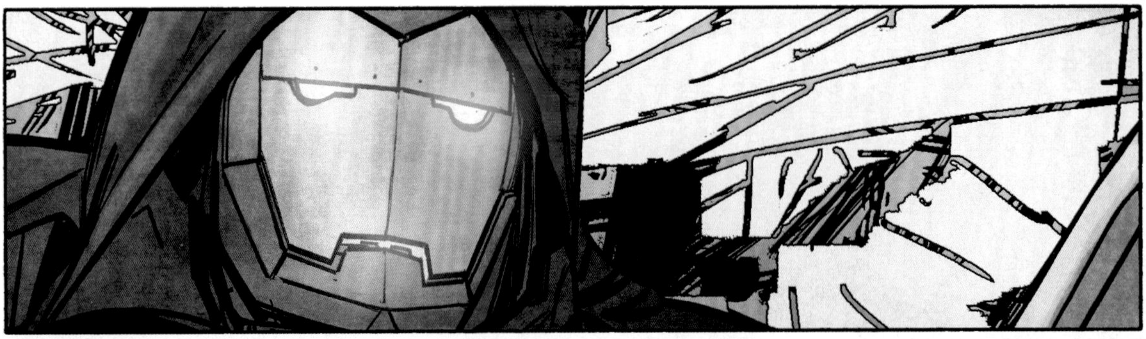

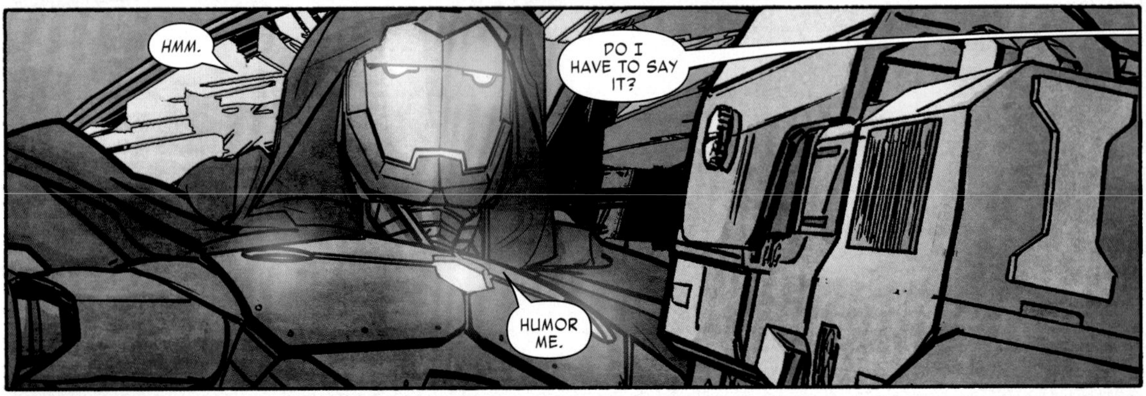
HMM.
DO I HAVE TO SAY IT?
HUMOR ME.

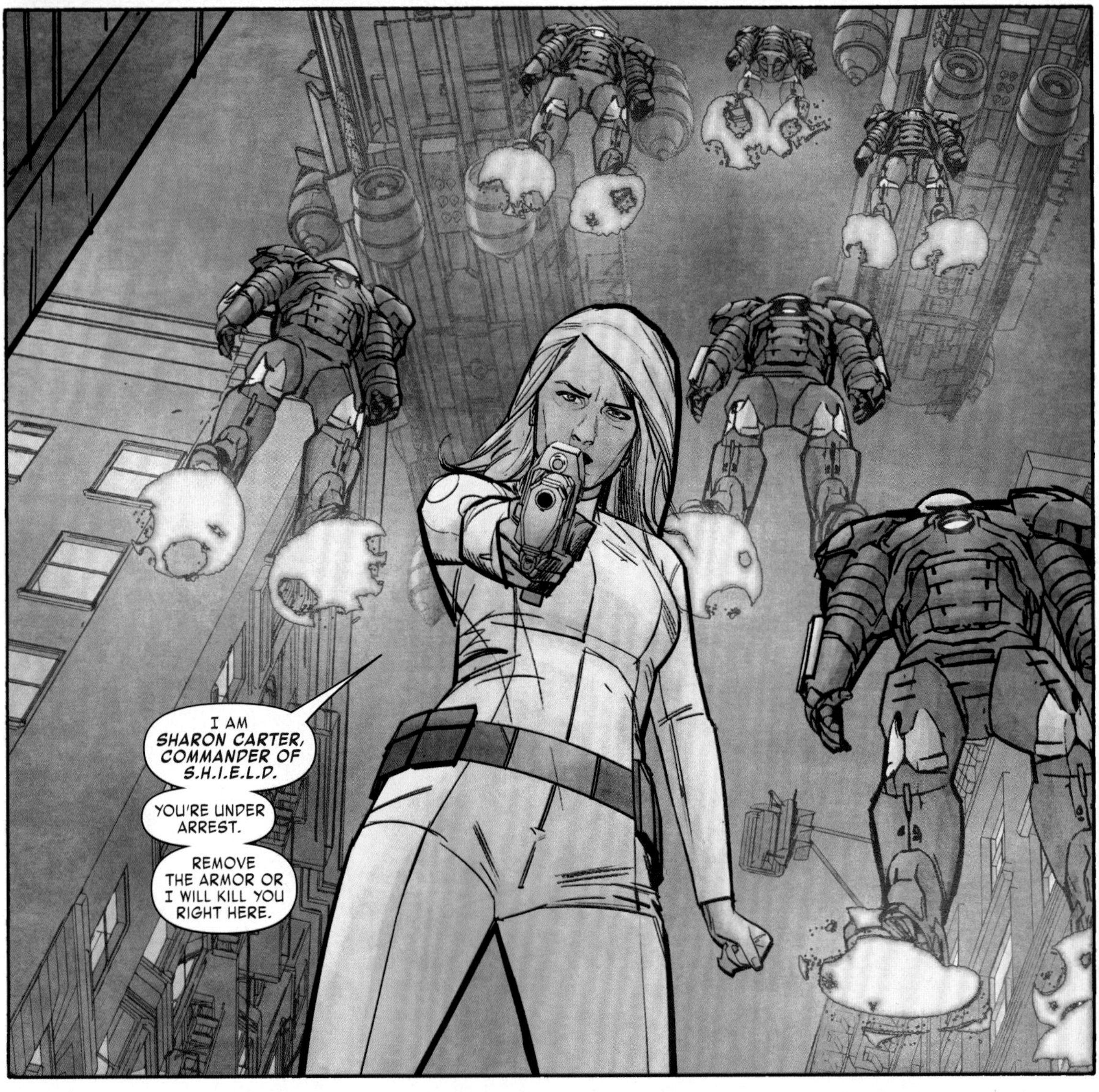
I AM SHARON CARTER, COMMANDER OF S.H.I.E.L.D.
YOU'RE UNDER ARREST.
REMOVE THE ARMOR OR I WILL KILL YOU RIGHT HERE.

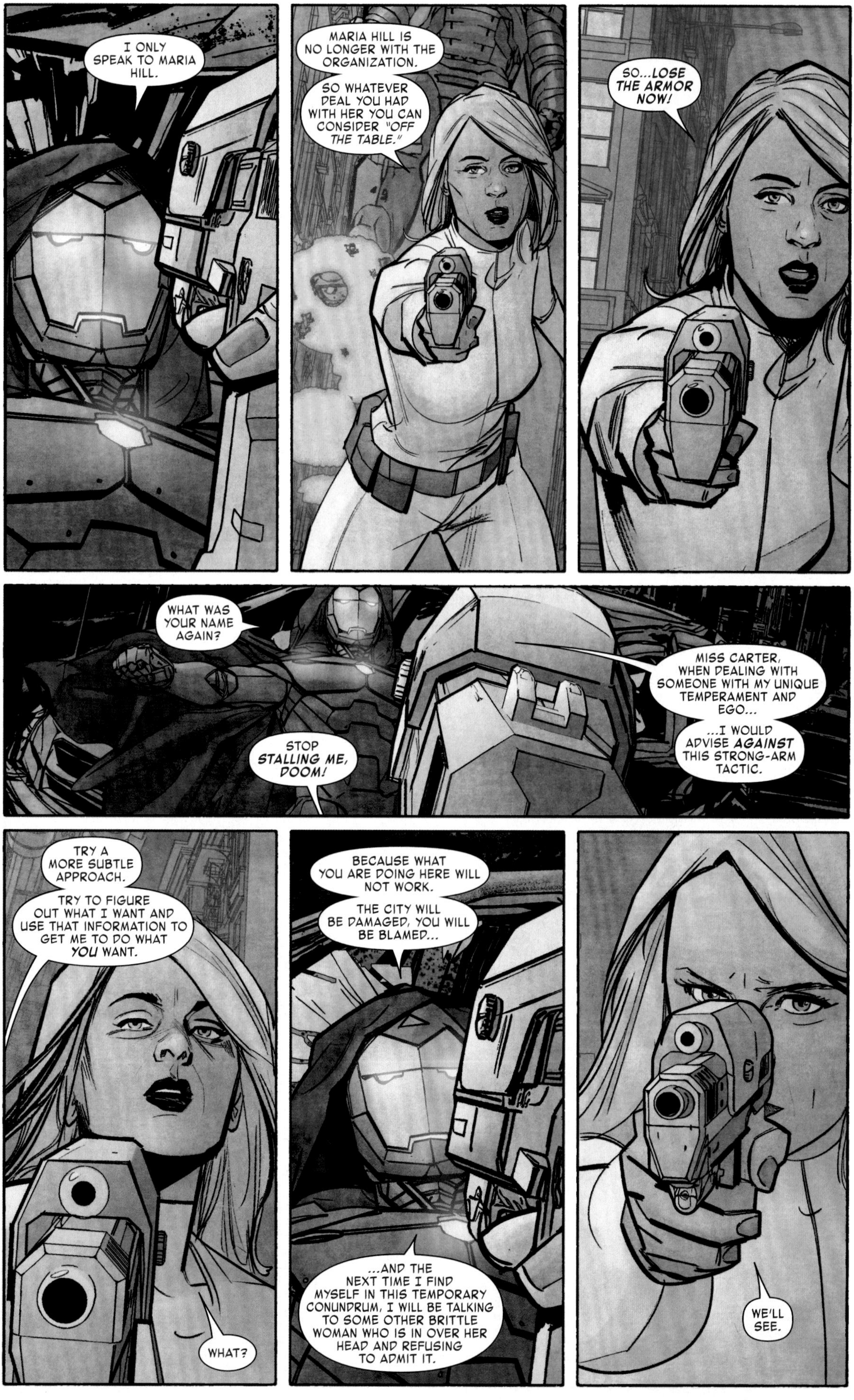
I ONLY SPEAK TO MARIA HILL.
MARIA HILL IS NO LONGER WITH THE ORGANIZATION.
SO WHATEVER DEAL YOU HAD WITH HER YOU CAN CONSIDER "OFF THE TABLE."
SO...LOSE THE ARMOR NOW!
WHAT WAS YOUR NAME AGAIN?
STOP STALLING ME, DOOM!
MISS CARTER, WHEN DEALING WITH SOMEONE WITH MY UNIQUE TEMPERAMENT AND EGO...
...I WOULD ADVISE AGAINST THIS STRONG-ARM TACTIC.
TRY A MORE SUBTLE APPROACH.
TRY TO FIGURE OUT WHAT I WANT AND USE THAT INFORMATION TO GET ME TO DO WHAT YOU WANT.
WHAT?
BECAUSE WHAT YOU ARE DOING HERE WILL NOT WORK.
THE CITY WILL BE DAMAGED, YOU WILL BE BLAMED...
...AND THE NEXT TIME I FIND MYSELF IN THIS TEMPORARY CONUNDRUM, I WILL BE TALKING TO SOME OTHER BRITTLE WOMAN WHO IS IN OVER HER HEAD AND REFUSING TO ADMIT IT.
WE'LL SEE.

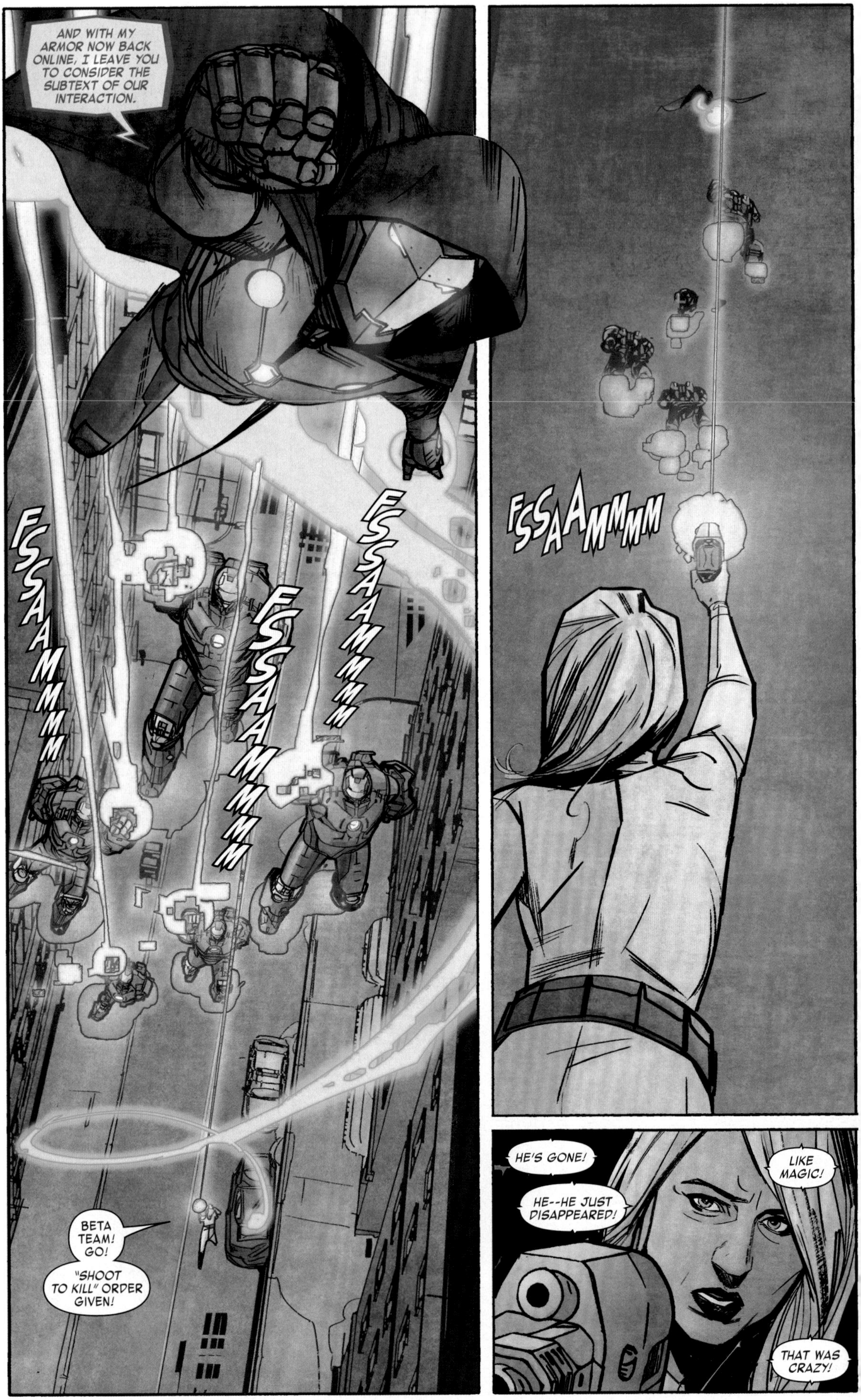
AND WITH MY ARMOR NOW BACK ONLINE, I LEAVE YOU TO CONSIDER THE SUBTEXT OF OUR INTERACTION.
FSSAAMMMM
FSSAAMMMM
FSSAAMMMM
BETA TEAM! GO!
"SHOOT TO KILL" ORDER GIVEN!
FSSAAMMMM
HE'S GONE!
HE--HE JUST DISAPPEARED!
LIKE MAGIC!
THAT WAS CRAZY!

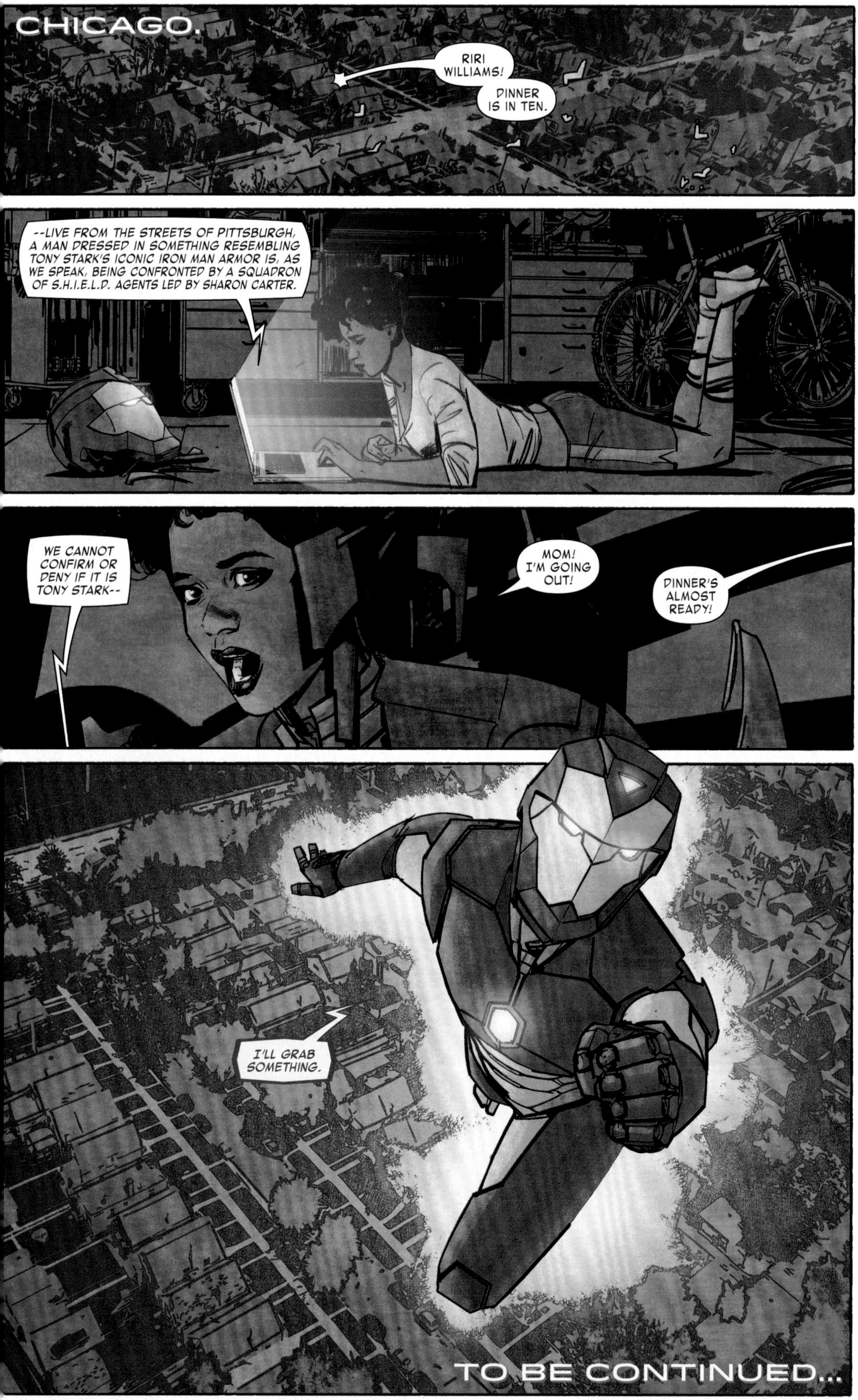
CHICAGO.
RIRI WILLIAMS!
DINNER IS IN TEN.
--LIVE FROM THE STREETS OF PITTSBURGH, A MAN DRESSED IN SOMETHING RESEMBLING TONY STARK'S ICONIC IRON MAN ARMOR IS, AS WE SPEAK, BEING CONFRONTED BY A SQUADRON OF S.H.I.E.L.D. AGENTS LED BY SHARON CARTER.
WE CANNOT CONFIRM OR DENY IF IT IS TONY STARK--
MOM! I'M GOING OUT!
DINNER'S ALMOST READY!
I'LL GRAB SOMETHING.
TO BE CONTINUED...

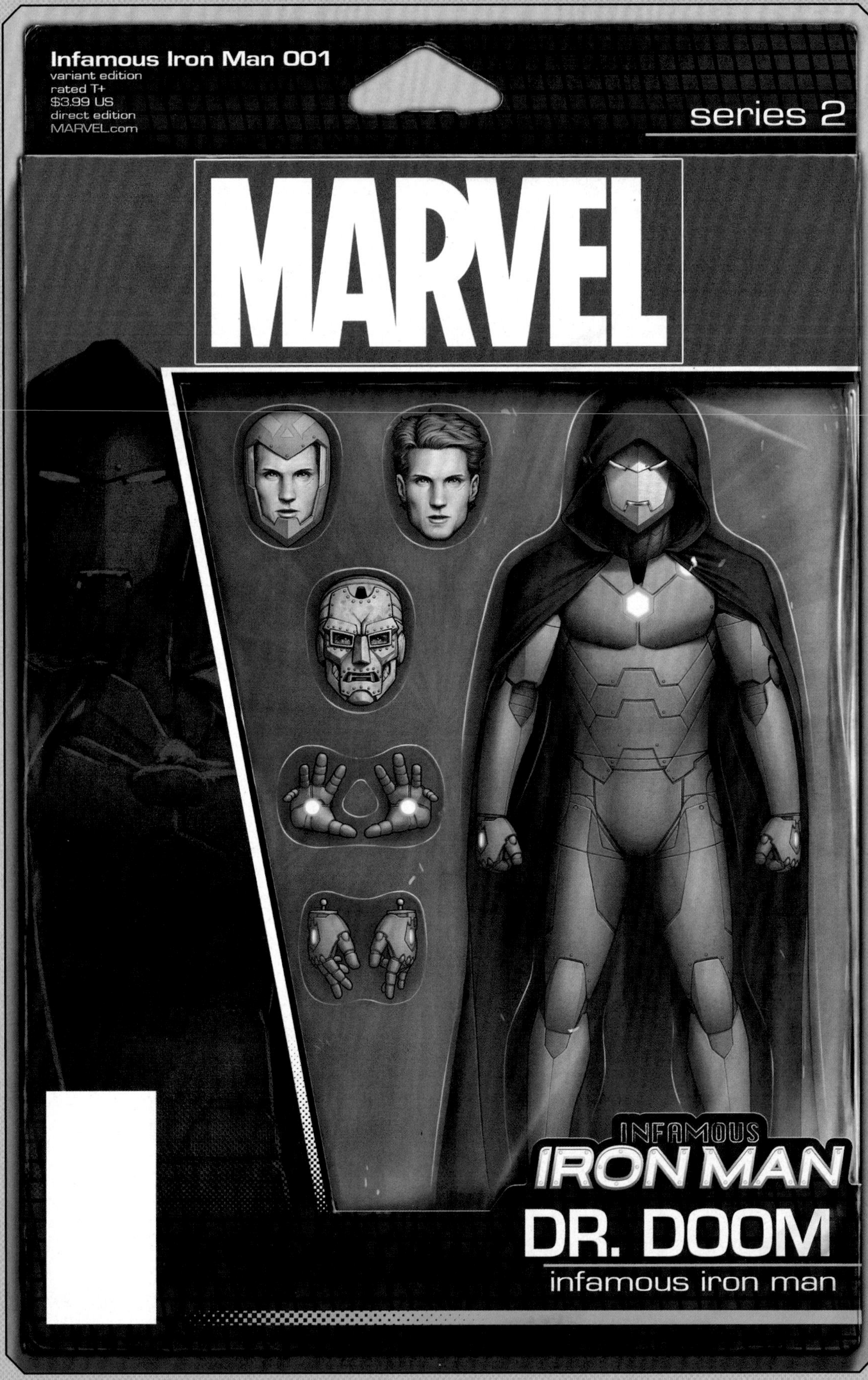
Infamous Iron Man 001
variant edition
rated T+
$3.99 US
direct edition
MARVEL.com
series 2
MARVEL
INFAMOUS
IRON MAN
DR. DOOM
infamous iron man

JOHN TYLER CHRISTOPHER
1 ACTION FIGURE VARIANT

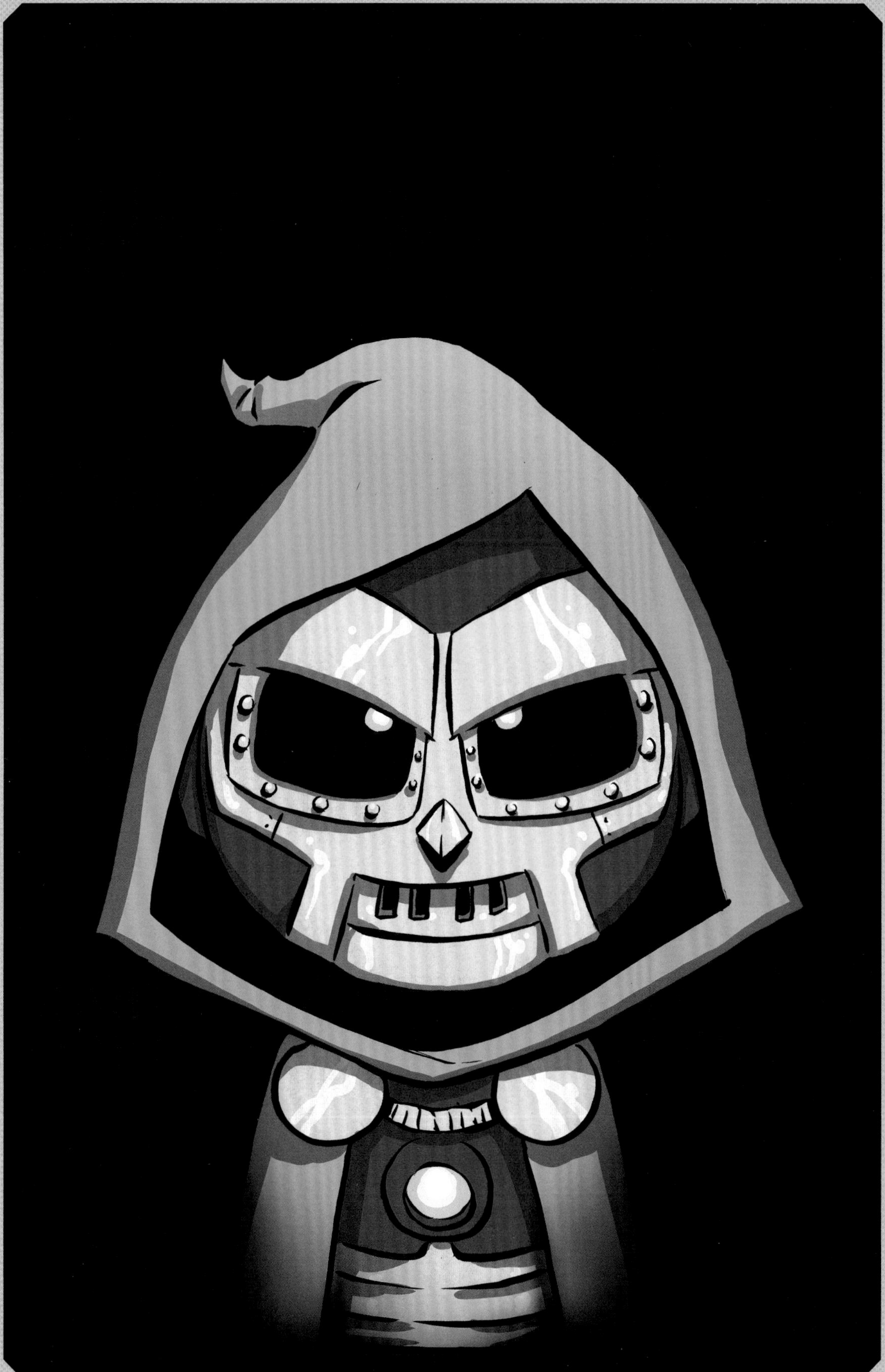

SKOTTIE YOUNG
1 VARIANT

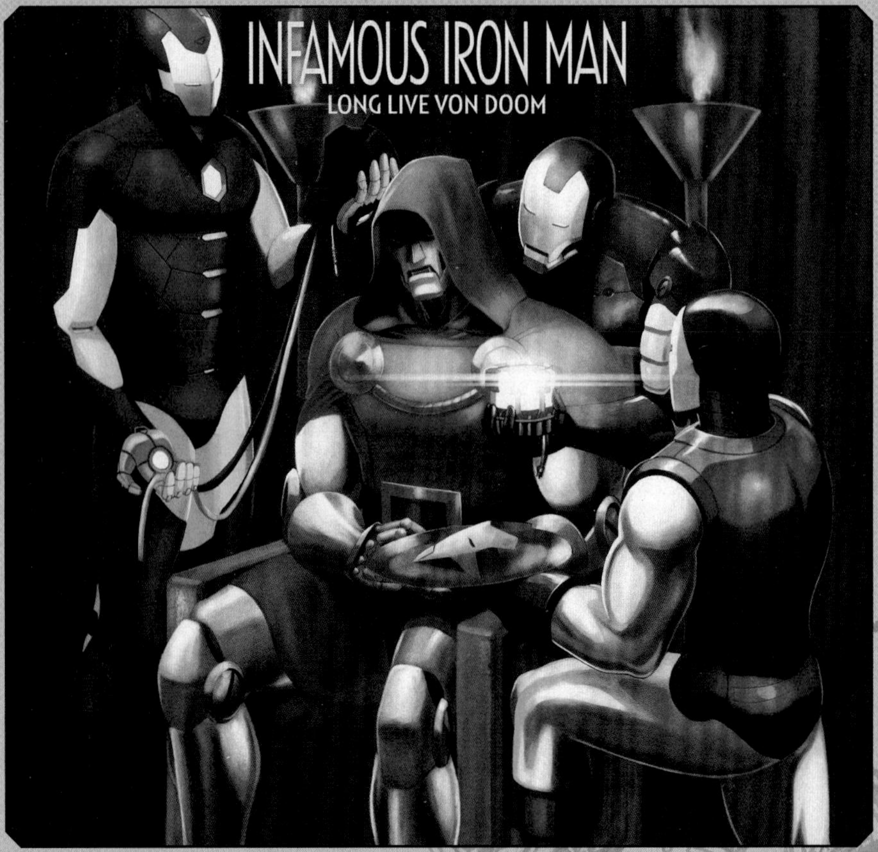
INFAMOUS IRON MAN
LONG LIVE VON DOOM

ANTHONY PIPER
1 HIP-HOP VARIANT

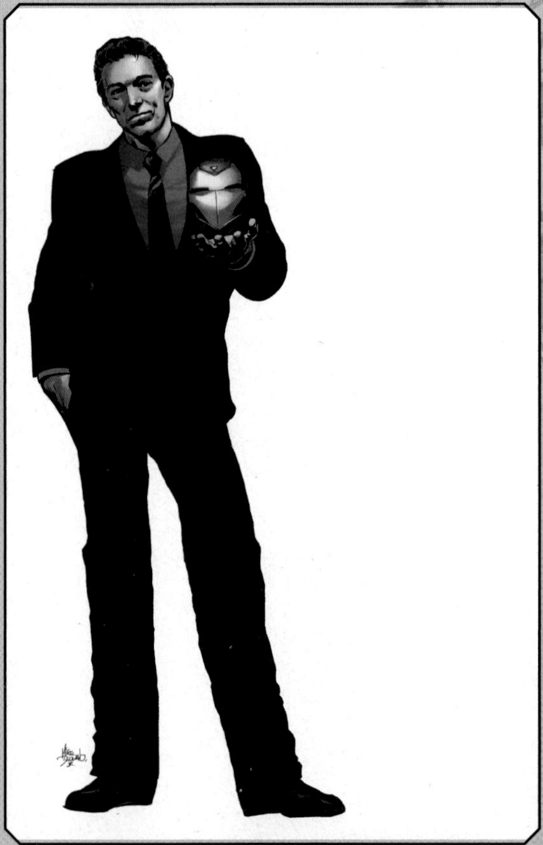

MIKE DEODATO JR. & FRANK MARTIN
1 TEASER VARIANT

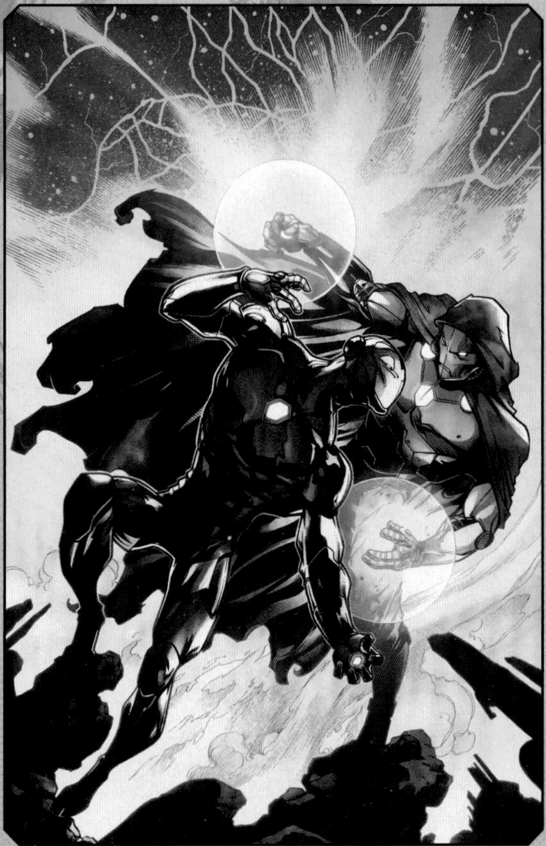

LARRY STROMAN, MARK MORALES & JASON KEITH
2 VARIANT